Cooking South
of the **Clouds**

Rick—
Wishing you many
delicious adventures.

Cooking South
of the Clouds

**Recipes and Stories from China's
Yunnan Province**

Georgia Freedman

photographs by Josh Wand

Kyle Books

Contents

Introduction

MY LOVE AFFAIR WITH YUNNAN began with a bowl of noodle soup. It was a sunny day in the summer of 2000, and I was sitting in a restaurant in Kunming, the capital of Yunnan Province. A young waitress approached. *"Guoqiao mixian?"* she asked, knowing already what I had come for. I nodded, and in just a couple of minutes she returned carrying a huge bowl of steaming broth and a tray covered with tiny white saucers, each filled with one of the soup's ingredients.

The waitress set the bowl on the table, handed me a pair of chopsticks, mimed stirring, and began adding the soup's ingredients. First came a little saucer of quail eggs that slid into the bowl and quickly turned into silky strands. Next came rich, salty Yunnan ham, sliced so thin that the pieces were translucent. Then an assortment of vegetables and herbs, from cabbage to fresh porcini mushrooms to delicate scallions. And lastly, a tangle of thick, freshly made rice noodles, which became soft and toothsome in the broth. When everything had cooked through, I took a sip. The flavor was rich and complex, with hints of earthiness from the ham and mushrooms and bright vegetal flavors from the herbs.

This soup, called Crossing the Bridge Rice Noodles (*guoqiao mixian*), was the whole reason I was in Kunming, a tiny city on the southwestern edge of China. I was a college student and had been studying Mandarin in Beijing when I came across a story about this soup's history in one of my textbooks. According to legend, there was once a scholar who was studying for his exams on an island in the center of a lake near the town of Mengzi, in southern Yunnan. His wife (whose name is lost to antiquity) brought the scholar lunch every day, but it was always cold by the time she arrived. One day, when the wife had not had time to prepare a full meal, she grabbed a pot of rich broth and all the raw ingredients that she could find in her kitchen and made her way to the island. When she arrived, she realized that the fat in the broth had risen to the top of the pot, keeping the soup underneath piping hot. She quickly added all the other ingredients to the bowl, where the heat of the soup cooked them perfectly. The scholar loved the soup, and just like that, a delicious classic was born.

opposite: ingredients for Crossing the Bridge Rice Noodles at a restaurant in southern Yunnan

clockwise from top left:
an afternoon snack in a Mosuo
family home; Shibao Shan (Stone
Treasure Mountain); a building
in the Zhu Family Garden in
Jianshui

For some reason this story stuck with me. Perhaps it was the idea of
the eggs and the noodles and the ham, which sounded like an ideal
combination of flavors. Or perhaps it was the descriptions of Yunnan—a
province of forests filled with native rhododendrons and azaleas, towns
full of mud brick houses with sloping tiled roofs, jungles teeming with
monkeys and elephants, and a population that includes dozens of different
Chinese minority groups, each with its own unique traditions and
customs. Yunnan had captured my imagination, so when I had a break
from classes, I went in search of that soup.

After the heat and frenzy of Beijing in July, Kunming seemed like heaven.
The weather was beautiful and spring-like, with warm days and cool,
clear nights. The city itself was beautiful, full of peaceful temples and old
wooden buildings. Even the pace of daily life seemed calmer and quieter
than in other parts of China; one afternoon I sat out a rain shower in the
city's central park reading and drinking tea without seeing another soul
walk by. It was idyllic.

As soon as I got my bearings, I started looking for somewhere to try
Crossing the Bridge Rice Noodles. At the city's famous bird and flower
market—a narrow street shaded by sycamore trees and lined with stalls
selling parakeets, lovebirds, baby rabbits, tiny turtles, and even flying
squirrels—an elderly man in a Mao suit and a cloth cap pointed me to a
building on the corner. In a couple of minutes, I found myself in an airy,
sunny room overlooking the market, sipping that wondrous bowl of soup.

I left Yunnan very reluctantly that summer, and for years I dreamed
about going back. I visited China for work and vacation a few times in the
following years, exploring Beijing, Shanghai, Hong Kong, and the scenic
towns of Suzhou and Yangshuo, but Kunming, the city of perpetual spring,
was always on my mind, and every winter I found myself craving that
magical soup.

Finally, in the spring of 2011, my husband, Josh, and I quit our jobs, packed up our lives (and our two cats), and moved everything to Yunnan with a vague idea about exploring the province's many food traditions. Kunming had changed dramatically since my first visit. Like the rest of China, it was in the midst of a massive economic boom. The population had doubled, new suburbs full of high-rise apartment buildings were springing up, and the roads were choked with cars. Much of the city's center, however, retained its unique character, with its winding tree-lined streets, small family-run shops, and flower-filled parks. Josh and I found a lovely apartment on the sixth floor of a building on a narrow street just two blocks from a park (the same one where I had sipped tea during that rainstorm), and from there we set out to explore everything Yunnan had to offer.

Yunnan is the other China, the place where the culture of the Han majority gives way to the traditions and histories of the country's minorities. The province is the most diverse part of China culturally, biologically, and meteorologically. Stretching from the southern edge of the Tibetan plateau down to Laos and Vietnam, Yunnan has glacier-topped mountains, vast alpine meadows, and enormous swaths of tropical rain forest in an area so small you could drive from one extreme to the other in just two days. Even its name—made up of the characters for *clouds* and *south*—evoke the province's unique profile as a warm, sunny land tucked just below one of the highest and coldest places on earth.

The great rivers of Asia—the Lancang (also called the Mekong), the Jinsha (or Yangtze), the Pearl River, the Red River, and the Salween (or Nu)—all flow through Yunnan, carving deep valleys and trenches into the mountainous landscape. The province's many mountain ranges have given gardeners everything from ornamental bamboos to rhododendrons, and hundreds of varieties of mushrooms grow here, from truffles to matsutakes. Biologists from around the world travel to Yunnan to study the region's thousands of still-mysterious plant, animal, and insect species.

Twenty-four of China's official minority groups, or "nationalities," call Yunnan home. These include the Tibetans in the north; the Bai, who have lived in central Yunnan for thousands of years; the Dai, who are related to the Tai people of Thailand and Laos; the Miao, who live near the Vietnamese border; the Jingpo, along the Burmese border to the west; and dozens of others, each with its own culture, religion, and foodways.

below, from top: Miao minority shoppers in Babao; terraced rice paddies outside of Jinping, near the Vietnamese border

Yunnan is also China's Wild West, a place defined by rugged terrain that has attracted explorers and naturalists while sometimes giving cover to bandits, dissidents, and others who have fallen out of favor. The region may have been the first part of China to be inhabited by *homo sapiens*, but China's emperors were unable to conquer the area until Genghis Khan's army arrived in the thirteenth century, and even after it was incorporated into the rest of the country it continued to be ruled by local elites on behalf of the imperial government. For centuries retreating armies and persecuted ethnic groups have climbed up into Yunnan's mountainous country, and for centuries conquering armies have been happy to leave them there. And, like the American West, Yunnan is known as a laid-back place, the region with the best weather, a comfortable lifestyle, and beautiful vacation destinations.

Most important (to me, anyway), Yunnan is a region of delicious foods. The area's biodiversity and the many cultures thriving in this tiny bit of the world have come together to create a wide variety of food traditions. In addition to its amazing wealth of mushrooms, the region is famous for its hams, which rival those of Italy; its pickled vegetables, which are especially popular in the province's central regions; its many kinds of edible flowers, which are cooked in soups and stir-fries; and its spicy chiles and Sichuan peppercorns. The province offers a seemingly endless array of things to eat, and people from all over China travel there to enjoy its marvelous foods. In a food-obsessed country, Yunnan is the food destination everyone wants to visit.

To be honest, however, there is really no such thing as "Yunnan food." The province is so diverse that it contains a number of distinct styles, each a reflection of a particular area's natural resources and the cultural practices of the people who live there. In the tropical areas in the south, grilled foods are common, and most dishes are flavored with fresh herbs and searingly spicy chiles. Grilled foods and raw vegetable salads are also popular to the west, along Yunnan's border with Myanmar, but the dishes there also reflect the influences of cross-border trade, and many foods resemble Burmese dishes. In the east, where Yunnan borders the provinces of Guizhou and Guangxi, the food is milder and includes ingredients more commonly found in southern China, while up north, on the edge of the Tibetan plateau, you'll find hearty cold-weather foods as well as traditional

above, from top: Songzanlin Monastery in Shangri-la; porcini mushrooms picked by foragers in the mountains of northern Yunnan

above, left to right:
Clay Pot Noodle Soup in Qujing;
Lige Island juts into Lugu Lake

Tibetan dishes like yak-filled *momos*. And in central Yunnan, cooks combine these styles with flavors popular in nearby Sichuan, adding lots of pickled vegetables, dried chiles, and Sichuan peppercorns to the mix.

Some characteristics of Yunnan food are nearly universal. Spicy chiles, whether fresh or dried, are practically ubiquitous. Pickles of some sort make their way into dishes in most parts of the province, as do the area's renowned mushrooms. Rice noodles, called *mixian*, are eaten for breakfast and lunch almost everywhere. And Yunnan is particularly famous for the fact that, unlike most Chinese, many of the local minorities eat raw vegetables in various forms, as well as dairy products, including stir-fried goat cheese in Kunming, grilled cow's-milk cheese in Dali, British-style canned milk in Mangshi, and butter and sweet-sour aged cheeses in Shangri-la.

To accommodate all of Yunnan's different styles of food, I've arranged this book in five sections, each focused on a particular part of the province. These regions are not geographically defined areas—instead I have defined them by their predominant flavors and cooking influences. Each section includes a variety of dishes that showcase the cooking styles found in that area. There are, of course, thousands of dishes made in Yunnan that are not represented here. And a few of the dishes I've included can also be found in one variation or another in other parts of China (or, in some cases, other parts of Asia). But these are all dishes that are made regularly by cooks there. Taken together, this collection offers a window on the flavors and cooking techniques of the province.

I have been privileged to learn about the region and its foods from dozens of cooks who have welcomed me into their homes and restaurants, and I have translated their recipes here as faithfully as possible, substituting ingredients available in the United States and other Western countries where needed and adapting cooking techniques to the tools found in Western kitchens. Along with their recipes, I have included some of these cooks' stories, as well as just a bit of what I've learned over the years about Yunnan and the many minorities who live there. I hope that this culinary tour of China's most diverse region serves as a delicious introduction to this extraordinary corner of the world.

A Note About Chinese Minority Designations

Though the Chinese government recognizes twenty-four official minorities in Yunnan, those groups are actually made up of hundreds of smaller self-identified ethnic groups. The official *minzu*, or "nationalities," were mostly determined in 1954, just after the People's Republic of China was founded, by a team of linguists who traveled around the country interviewing locals and looking for connections among their various languages. As a result, some official *minzu* groups are composed of a few (or even dozens of) smaller ethnic groups that still maintain their own traditions and cultures. For the purposes of this book, I refer mostly to the officially designated groups as a matter of expediency. I also use Chinese names for all the people and foods highlighted in the book; each local group has its own language and its own names for these foods (and many groups have their own alphabets), but Mandarin is Yunnan's lingua franca.

How to Build a Yunnan-Style Meal

Cooks in Yunnan, like those in other parts of China, serve a variety of dishes at each meal. With a few exceptions (such as the noodle soups), the dishes in this book are meant to be shared as part of a spread that includes, at a minimum, one meat dish and one vegetable dish, plus enough jasmine rice (or sticky rice, if you're making dishes from southern or western Yunnan) to go around. A good rule of thumb is to have as many dishes on the table as there are people sitting around it, and if you want to be a bit generous, add one extra dish—so a meal for four would include five dishes, plus rice. Most meals of three or more dishes include a soup of some kind.

below: a meal of grilled meat and vegetables at a restaurant on the banks of Lugu Lake

Ingredients

Pantry Staples

Dried Thai chiles 干辣椒/乾辣椒 Small dried red Thai chiles are perhaps the most frequently used ingredient in Yunnan kitchens, employed to flavor everything from stir-fried meat to soups. In Chinese markets they are usually just labeled as "dried chiles"; look for small red chiles roughly 2 to 3 inches long.

Dried chile flakes 辣椒面 The chile flakes called for in these recipes are the standard red chile flakes that are available in Chinese markets, often labeled "dried red chile powder"; while some brands look powdery, you should also see some whole chile flakes in the mix. You can also use Italian-style chile (red pepper) flakes from the supermarket spice aisle, which have a similar flavor.

Dried ground chile 辣椒粉 Yunnan cooks use a variety of ground chile powders that are not available in the United States. To make these recipes, I usually use Korean Red Pepper Powder, sometimes labeled Tower Red Pepper Powder. Occasionally some paprika is added to the pepper to more accurately approximate the flavor of Yunnan's chiles.

Sichuan peppercorns 花椒 Small, round Sichuan peppercorns have a citrusy flavor and leave a delightful tingling, numbing sensation in your mouth. Most of these recipes call for red Sichuan peppercorns, which can be used whole or ground. To make a recipe that calls for ground peppercorns, you can buy Sichuan peppercorn powder, but you'll get a superior flavor if you toast and grind whole peppercorns yourself (see page 274 for a method).

Black cardamom 草果 This spice is readily available in Asian markets, but is not well-known in the United States. The pods are brown, fibrous, and about an inch long. Both whole black cardamom pods and ground black cardamom seeds are used in Yunnan cooking. If a recipe calls for ground black cardamom, see the instructions on grinding the spice on page 274.

Salt 盐巴 Cooks in Yunnan use various salts, depending on where they live and what's readily available, but all the recipes in this book have been

below: red Sichuan peppercorns, dried Thai chiles, and black cardamom pods

tested using standard Diamond Crystal brand kosher salt. If you use other salts, make sure to taste as you go; other brands of kosher salt can be twice as salty as Diamond Crystal (and don't dissolve as quickly), and both table salt and sea salt also add different amounts of saltiness.

Soy sauces 酱油 Recipes in this book mostly call for **Chinese light soy sauce,** which has a delicate, fragrant flavor. Some recipes specify **dark soy sauce,** a thicker soy sauce that has a syrupy consistency and is usually used sparingly to add a bit of color and a little punch of umami to dishes. Note that these soy sauces are *not* the same as Japanese soy sauce or tamari, which have a completely different flavor profile.

Vegetable oil 植物油 You can use any standard vegetable oil you like in these recipes, but the one commonly used in Yunnan is rapeseed oil (sold as canola in many places). In fact, farmers in Yunnan grow a lot of rapeseed, so much of the rapeseed oil used by rural cooks is produced locally.

Sesame oil 芝麻油 The sesame oil used in these recipes is Chinese-style toasted sesame oil, which has a warm-brown hue and a rich, nutty flavor.

Vinegars 醋 Cooks in Yunnan use a variety of vinegars, each of which has a distinct flavor: **Zhenjiang vinegar** 镇江香醋 is a dark rice vinegar (sometimes labeled "Chinkiang vinegar") that is made in Zhenjiang City and is one of the most popular in China. **Shanxi vinegar** 山西老陈醋 is another aged vinegar, from Shaanxi Province. It has a slightly richer, deeper fragrance and a woody flavor. **Chinese rice vinegar** 米醋 is a light, yellow-hued vinegar that is bright and acidic, like white wine vinegar. Kong Yen brand from Taiwan is readily available in the United States.

Hot chile oil 辣椒油 A clear, orange-red oil that has been filtered to completely remove any pieces of chile, this condiment is often used to dress cold noodle or vegetable dishes.

Chile-bean paste (*douban jiang***)** 豆瓣酱 This spicy, savory ingredient is made by fermenting chiles and beans together. Yunnan's versions of *douban jiang* have their own particular flavors. Most are similar to **southern Chinese chile-bean paste**, often labeled *"toban djan"* in the United States, and are a bit sweet and contain sugar and garlic. (Lee Kum Kee brand is readily available in the U.S.) In some cases, adding some **ground bean sauce**—thick and salty, made from fermented soybeans—to a dish along with the chile-bean sauce brings it closer to the local flavor. (Koon Chun brand is available in Asian markets and online.)

above: the oils, vinegars, sauces, and other flavorings needed to make Yunnan dishes are available in most Chinese markets

Some of Yunnan's chile-bean pastes are closer to Sichuan's versions, which are made with only beans, chiles, salt, and a little flour. In the United States, look for a brand called **Sichuan Pixian Douban Co.**, which comes in foil packets. If you can't get *pixian douban jiang*, you can substitute the southern-style paste, above, in any recipe, but the flavor of the finished dish will change a bit.

Fragrant chile sauce (*xiangla jiang*) 香辣酱 Made with broad beans, chiles, and fermented flour paste, this sauce is sometimes labeled "spicy bean paste" and is sweeter and less funky than *douban jiang* (above). In the United States and Europe, you can find an excellent version made by Lao Gan Ma, a popular Guizhou-based company that produces a number of chile-based sauces (including southern-style *douban jiang*).

Chile sauce (*lajiao jiang*) 辣椒酱 Chile sauce (as distinct from hot chile oil or chile-bean paste) is a bright-red sauce made from mashed fresh chiles, salt, sugar, and sometimes some sesame oil and citric acid. It has a texture somewhat akin to a jarred salsa and a bright, slightly sour taste. Look for sauce that is sold in jars and is a bright, brick-red, such as Lee Kum Kee brand's version.

Sour bamboo 酸笋 Shredded sour pickled bamboo is a staple of Dai cooking in western Yunnan. The bamboo, which has a sour, astringent, and slightly funky flavor, is not available in the United States, but Thai versions, which have a similar flavor, are available packed in jars in Thai markets and online.

opposite, from top:
sawtooth herb; banana blossoms; banana leaves

Rice 饭 Farmers in Yunnan grow thousands of rice varieties—more than in any other part of the world—and Yunnan cooks use them all. For the recipes in this book, however, you'll only need a few that are available in most Asian markets (and online). **Jasmine rice** and similar long-grain types are the most commonly served rice in China; most meals served in northern, central, and eastern Yunnan include a helping of steamed jasmine rice (or a similar variety), as a complement to stir-fried dishes, cold salads, and simple soups, and this is also the type of rice used for making fried rice. **Sticky rice** is popular in place of regular steamed rice in many parts of southern and western Yunnan. When buying sticky rice, look for varieties from Thailand, which are sometimes labeled "sweet rice" or "glutinous rice." **Purple sticky rice** (also called "black sticky rice") is also used in western Yunnan. If you want to make Yunnan's famous *er kuai* rice cakes, you'll need to find **Nishiki rice**, a Japanese-style rice grown in the United States.

Herbs and Vegetables

Chrysanthemum greens 茼蒿 These tender lacy greens have a unique, delicious flavor, similar to the fragrance of chrysanthemum flowers or chrysanthemum tea. The greens are often sold under their Cantonese name, *Tong Ho*, or their Japanese name, *Shinguku*. Make sure you get lacy greens that look like a wider version of carrot greens or like a delicate arugula leaf, as other, wide-leaf greens can sometimes be mislabeled with these names.

Celtuce 莴笋 Also known as "stem lettuce," this mild vegetable has a silky texture. Be sure to discard the leaves and peel off the fibrous skin before using.

Banana flowers 芭蕉花 Only the yellow inner petals of banana flowers are tender enough to eat, so look for large, heavy blossoms. If you cannot find fresh ones, frozen or canned banana flowers can be used as a substitute.

Lotus root 莲藕 When buying sweet, crunchy lotus root, choose the freshest-looking roots you can find, and be sure to trim the ends and peel the roots before using (a regular vegetable peeler works well). Unlike lotus roots sold in most places in China, those found in U.S. markets often have a bit of gray decay inside. If it doesn't rinse out easily, use a small bottle brush to clean the insides of the roots, or clean them gently after you've sliced them.

Banana leaves 芭蕉叶 Banana leaves are an important cooking tool in southern and western Yunnan, used to wrap up ingredients that will be grilled or steamed. Many local cooks use fresh, young banana leaves, but frozen versions are available at many Asian and Latin markets. While young leaves are very pliable, more mature leaves may split when folded. If they do, add a second layer of leaves with the grain of the inner layer running perpendicular to the outer layer so that they won't split in the same direction. (Like any vegetable, the leaves should be rinsed before use.)

Cilantro 香菜 Cilantro leaves and stems are used liberally in many dishes across southern and western Yunnan, often alongside *yan xin*, a lacy herb that tastes like cilantro but has a milder, less soapy flavor. While *yan xin* is generally not found in the United States, flowering cilantro that has reached the stage where it produces tiny leaves (and is sometimes marketed as coriander) is similar. Seeds for *yan xin* (usually labeled by its Vietnamese name, *bac lieu*) are available from specialty seed companies.

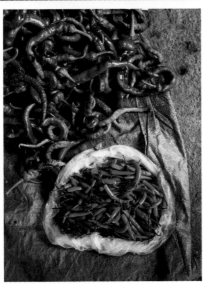

Sawtooth herb 刺芫荽 This long-leafed herb with sharp-ridged edges, often called culantro, has a flavor similar to cilantro but stronger and earthier.

Vietnamese coriander 越南香菜 Often labeled with its Vietnamese name, *rau ram*, this herb with small spade-shaped leaves is peppery and aromatic.

Fennel 茴香 Chinese cooks use a type of herb fennel that grows without a bulb and is prized just for its fronds. The leaves of the bulb fennels found in markets in the United States are a bit stronger tasting, but the flavor is similar, making them a fine substitute.

Fish mint and fish mint roots 魚腥草, 折耳根 Strong, fragrant fish mint has wide spade-shaped leaves with a pungent flavor. The hollow white roots of the fish mint plant are also used in Yunnan foods; they have an even stronger flavor than the leaves and add an astringent note to some salads.

Asiatic pennywort (*mati cai*) 马蹄菜 Asiatic pennywort has a long, thin stem and a heart-shaped leaf with a rounded bottom and wavy edges. In flavor it is similar to parsley but much milder, which makes it an excellent base for some of the cold salads found in western Yunnan.

Thai chiles 小米辣 Cooks throughout Yunnan use fresh small red chiles called *xiaomila* ("millet chiles"). These chiles, however, are not all from the same cultivar, and those used in western and southern Yunnan are generally much spicier than those in other parts of the province, despite the fact that they're all known by the same name. In the United States these chiles are generally sold as Thai chiles, and while they too are not all uniform, they are nearly always very spicy, like those in southern Yunnan. The recipes in this book have been adjusted for the Thai chiles found in American markets. Look for bright red chiles that are 2 to 3 inches long, or adjust the amounts as necessary.

Korean long chiles Fleshy, flavorful, and relatively mild, these long green hybrid chiles are quite similar to the green chiles used in Yunnan and are excellent cooked with meat or mushrooms; some cooks simply fry them with a bit of salt, and serve them on their own. These are readily available in the United States, and may be labeled *"cheong-gochu"* or *"putgochu."*

Other chiles Cooks across Yunnan use a variety of other fresh chiles. Among the most popular are long, thick red Qiubei chiles (丘北辣椒). While there are no similar chiles in Western markets, red Anaheim chiles, which are much smaller but have a nice flavor and a medium spice, make a good stand-in.

Meats

Black-skinned chicken 乌骨鸡 Black-skinned chickens are also known as silkie chickens because of their soft, fluffy white feathers. Silkies are often raised as pets in the West, but they are prized in Chinese cooking for their gamy flavor and their black skin and bones. Silkie chickens are available in Chinese markets, often frozen. If you can't find this type of chicken, try to substitute a free-range bird to get similarly rich meat.

Beef 牛肉 Most of the beef prepared in Yunnan is aged before it is cooked. Restaurants buy whole carcasses or large sides of beef and hang them for a few days before using them, and home cooks can buy aged meat at wet markets. Because aged beef is less common (and more expensive) in the United States, these recipes have been adapted for regular beef and often call for a little extra soy sauce to boost the meat's umami flavor. If possible, use grass-fed beef, which has a rich, meaty flavor. If aged beef happens to be available and you want to use it in these recipes, reduce the amount of soy sauce by half to start, then taste the meat once it has browned and add more as needed. When buying ground beef of any kind, always get a blend with lots of fat so that it will stay moist and flavorful when cooked.

A NOTE ABOUT MEASUREMENTS AND SIZES:

In Yunnan, as in the rest of the world, no two cooks make a dish the same way. Some will add more of a seasoning or ingredient; some will add less. All the cooks I've ever cooked with in Yunnan eyeball all their ingredients (and intuit all their cooking times, testing the tenderness, crispness, or flavor of a dish to see if it's ready). So if you find yourself worrying that your garlic cloves may be too big or your scallions too thick, don't!

COOKING CHICKEN SOUPS:

Chinese chicken soups, such as the Steam Pot Chicken with Ginger and Goji Berries (page 45) and the Chicken and Chestnut Soup (page 107), are usually made by cutting a whole bird up, across the bone, into 1½- to 2-inch pieces. If you'd like to make these dishes with the meat removed from the bones so that it is easier to eat, substitute 1½ lb. chicken thighs with the bones in and skin on and 1 chicken back in place of a 2-lb chicken. Use a sharp knife to cut the bones out of the thighs, and cut the thigh meat into quarters or sixths (the pieces should be about 1 to 2 inches by 2 inches). Use the bones, the meat (and skin), and the chicken back to follow the original recipe, and when the soup is done, remove the bones and chicken back before serving.

opposite, from top: Vietnamese coriander; fish mint on bundles of fish mint root and cilantro; long green chiles and red Thai chiles

Tools

Traditional Tools

Burners, Stoves, and Other Heat Sources

Cooks in Yunnan use a variety of different heat sources to cook food. Some do most of their cooking over wood fires, some use stoves fired by large cakes of pressed coal, and many use stand-alone wok stoves that produce a strong, high flame. All the recipes in this book, however, have been tested on a conventional American stove, and the timing and instructions have been tailored to the levels of heat these stoves produce. If you have a stronger stove, or access to a wok stove, these dishes will cook more quickly than indicated in the recipes. Also, with a hotter stove you will not have to heat cooking oil as much because the temperature won't drop as drastically when you add the other ingredients.

Kitchen Fan/Hood

Nearly all Chinese kitchens have a fan built into the wall above the stove. It may be a fancy vent hood or just a plastic fan stuck into a hole in the wall. Whatever the type, the fan is just as important a part of the cooking setup as the stove or the wok. When preparing Yunnan dishes, be sure to use your kitchen fan, especially when you're cooking with fresh or dried chiles. If you don't have a built-in fan, place a box fan in front of an open window, and use it to blow air out of your kitchen.

Wok

For cooks with a conventional American-style stove, a flat-bottom wok is preferable to a round-bottom model because the design will allow the wok to sit closer to the flame than a round-bottom wok in a wok ring. Many cooks find that a wok with two handles (a long one on one side and a loop on the other) is easier to pick up than a wok with a single handle or two small round handles—especially when the wok is full of heavy ingredients. The only kind of wok that is not suitable for making these recipes is one with a nonstick finish, because nonstick woks don't have the same cooking properties as metal woks. But don't worry; if you season a wok properly when you buy it, and then wash it properly after you use it, the surface will develop its own nonstick properties and food will slide off easily. (Good

above: the most commonly used cooking tools in Yunnan kitchens

wok vendors, such as the Wok Shop in San Francisco, which has a great online store, will be able to provide instructions on how to season a wok.)

Wok Shovel

A wok shovel, designed to scoop up and flip ingredients in a wok, is significantly more useful for Chinese cooking than a wooden spoon.

Wok Cover

A simple wok cover is an indispensable aid in Chinese cooking. The easiest to use have large wooden handles. Get one that will fit just inside the rim of your wok.

Spider Strainer

This wire strainer, sometimes called a Chinese skimmer, is perfect for removing foods from oil and can also act as a strainer when you are cooking large pieces of food.

Perforated Scoop

A very large perforated scoop, which looks like a flat ladle with holes in it, is an ideal tool for deep-frying and particularly useful for lowering ingredients carefully into hot oil. It is also used by Chinese chefs to strain oil out of cooked foods because it won't let any food fall through.

Chinese Vegetable and Meat Cleavers

Chinese cooks rely on two knives: a very sharp, medium-weight cleaver for cutting vegetables, and a thicker, heavier cleaver designed for cutting meat (including cutting through bones). The vegetable cleavers, which have wide, flat blades with sharp tips, are much more versatile than a Western knife and can be used for everything from evenly slicing vegetables to crushing garlic and ginger. If you have access to a good butcher who will cut meat to your specifications, you may not need a meat cleaver, but it is ideal to have both knives at your disposal.

Steamer

Many of the recipes in this book require a steamer that can be set on top of a pot where boiling water won't touch it. Chinese steamers made of bamboo are inexpensive and lightweight. When using a steamer to cook dumplings, cover the bottom of the basket with paper liners (available at Asian markets) or large cabbage leaves to keep food from sticking.

Mandoline

Many Chinese restaurateurs and home cooks use mandolines with a julienne-blade insert to prepare ingredients that need to be cut into thin strips (called *si* or 丝 in Chinese cooking). This shape is traditionally achieved by using a cleaver to cut a vegetable into thin slices and then into slivers, but a mandoline makes the process much faster and keeps the pieces uniform.

Dumpling Rolling Pin

The easiest way to roll out wrappers for making dumplings or flatbreads is to use a short, narrow rolling pin. These small wooden dowels are usually 11 to 12 inches long and ¾ of an inch to 1 inch in diameter, but the most important quality is that they do not have handles or tapered ends. You can find these "Asian style" or "Chinese" rolling pins online and in Asian supermarkets, or you can make one with a ¾-inch-wide dowel.

Cast-Iron Pan

In northern Yunnan, cooks use a flat cast-iron pan to cook flatbreads like Lijiang's famous stuffed *baba* (page 110). Any well-seasoned cast-iron pan will do as long as it's at least 10 inches in diameter.

Metal Container and Sieve

Many Chinese recipes call for deep-frying ingredients in oil and then draining off the hot oil. To do this, you'll need a good heatproof container like a bain-marie or a medium-sized metal bowl. You'll also want to have a sturdy sieve (or a very large perforated scoop) to place on top of the bowl to catch any ingredients that fall out of the wok along with the oil.

Yunnan-Specific Tools

Pickle Jar

Yunnan food is full of pickles, from pickled greens to pickled chiles, pickled garlic, and even pickled chive blossoms. Most of these are traditionally made in a specially designed Chinese pickle jar that has a lip at the top to create a water seal. I prefer the clear-glass versions because they allow me to see how the pickles are progressing. You can find these online and at Asian markets (including Korean markets, as they can also be used for making kimchi), but you can also make Chinese pickles in a traditional Western pickle jar as long as it has a weight that fits inside it to keep the vegetables submerged in the pickling liquid.

Large Mortar and Pestle

Cooks in southern and western Yunnan rely on a very large wooden mortar (about 15 inches in diameter) and a long, hefty pestle for mashing all kinds of vegetables and meats. An 8-inch mortar with a

below: making spice paste with a large mortar and pestle

large pestle (or a very sturdy wooden mixing bowl and a large pestle) make a useful substitute.

Spice Grinder or Small Mortar and Pestle

Cooks all over Yunnan use smaller stone mortars and pestles to make Sichuan peppercorn powder or to grind up black cardamom seeds. A small electric spice grinder or dedicated coffee grinder is even more effective and a lot easier to use.

Grill Basket

A popular way of cooking food in southern and western Yunnan is to grill it over an open fire, using a wire grill basket to hold the ingredients together. A traditional Western grill basket is the same size as those used in many places and is indispensable when preparing dishes like Dai Grilled Chicken with Herbs (page 134), or any of the many Yunnan dishes that are cooked in banana leaves.

Sand Pots

Some of Yunnan's delicious noodle soups are made in special, individual-sized clay pots that can be brought from the stove directly to the table. These pots are not essential for making the Clay Pot Noodle Soup (page 70), but if you want to get some, look for those called Chinese Clay Pots that have a glaze inside, a long handle on one side, and a lid.

Yunnan Steam Pot

One of Yunnan's most famous dishes, Steam Pot Chicken (page 45), is prepared in a special kind of clay pot with a funnel in the center that allows steam to gently cook the soup. The dish can be made in a regular pot, but if you want to try it in a traditional steam pot (which can also be used to make other kinds of dishes), be sure to get one that will sit comfortably on top of your stockpot.

Sticky Rice Steamer

Sticky rice can be prepared in a variety of vessels, but the easiest way to make it is in a traditional Thai sticky rice setup, which includes a conical bamboo basket with a special pot to boil water below it.

Meat Grinder

You'll need a meat grinder if you want to try your hand at making Yunnan's famous *er kuai* rice cakes from scratch. In Yunnan, cooks use a specific kind of grinder to turn their steamed rice into smooth dough; outside China a regular meat grinder (a stand-alone or an attachment for an electric mixer) is the best substitute.

Central Yunnan

THE NARROW LANES of Luofeng Street curve through the center of Kunming, Yunnan's capital city. The street is lined with stately trees crowned with golden blooms, and below them a variety of small shops offer hand-tailored clothes and eclectic cooking supplies; vendors sell fruit out of the backs of vans; and noodle shops serve steaming bowls of soup topped with salty pickles, fragrant garlic chives, and spicy-numbing Sichuan peppercorn.

This neighborhood is one of the few vestiges of old Kunming, a once tranquil town that is now a modern city full of malls and high-rise apartment complexes. "Spring City," as Kunming is called, is still quieter than other Chinese metropolises, and the region's famously temperate weather and abundant flora attract both the grown children of rural farmers, who move to the city to build a modern life, and Chinese tourists, who come here to escape the heat and crowds of mega-cities like Shanghai and Guangzhou.

On weekends, locals gather in Cuihu Park, in the center of town, to enjoy the balmy weather. Orchestras of amateur musicians wielding *er hus* and *pipas* practice classic Chinese folk songs in one corner, while a dozen women set up a boom box just a few yards away for "public square dancing," a popular form of exercise that looks like a mash-up of traditional Chinese dance and jazzercise. Tourists use fancy cameras on tripods to capture the lake's enormous lotus blossoms, and local parents take their children out for a stroll and buy them wedges of pineapple to snack on.

A mile south, the narrow streets of the city's center give way to sunny plazas and busy malls where members of the city's newly minted middle class sip Starbucks coffee and shop for international luxury goods. In the evenings, teenagers come here on dates, the young women decked out in frilly camo mini skirts and rhinestone-studded high heels, their

clockwise, from top left: Old Town Dali; Green Lake Park in Kunming; ingredients displayed in a restaurant in Kunming; tai chi in Green Lake Park; old buildings in Kunming; Lao Fangzi restaurant in Kunming

boyfriends toting their purses and snacking on fried chicken or skewers of candy-coated crabapples. In the northern suburb of Beichen, a subway ride away, expats gather at a popular Irish pub to sip Belgian beer and watch soccer, while a few blocks away, local parents take their kids to hip-hop classes and then sit outside, watching through the window as they learn to imitate their J-pop heroes.

~

Beyond Kunming's growing sprawl, central Yunnan is farm country, its lush valleys perfect for growing nearly any kind of crop. Rapeseed is popular, as are tobacco, corn, and rice. One of the lushest areas is the Dali Valley, home to much of the Bai minority. The Bai people (who historically called themselves Minjia) are the second-largest minority group in Yunnan, and they have lived in this region since at least the third century, ruled by the kingdom of Nanzhao (740–973 AD) and the kingdom of Dali (973–1253 AD) until Kublai Khan conquered them and claimed the area as part of China.

The Bai community is centered around Old Town Dali, which sits between the Cangshan mountain range and Erhai, or "Ear Lake." The seventh-largest freshwater lake in China, Erhai contains more than forty kinds of fish, which the Bai traditionally caught using cormorants with snares around their necks that kept the birds from swallowing their catch. You can still see fishermen with cormorants on the lake, but these days they're more of a tourist attraction than a practical fishing method.

opposite, top and bottom: the Confucious Temple in Jianshui; the streets of Sideng Old Town in the Shaxi Valley

Despite centuries of self-rule, the Bai have a long history of cultural exchange with Imperial China, and Bai scholars claim that their culture influenced the Tang Dynasty, the period considered the golden age of Chinese culture. In particular, Bai music is said to be the music of the Tang Dynasty, and scholars point to records of musical instruments, songs, and even troupes of musicians exchanged between the Tang court and the Kingdom of Nanzhao. The Bai have borrowed from the Han as well, becoming largely Sinicized and practicing Confucianism and Buddhism alongside their traditional animist Benzhu religion. Travel around Erhai, and you'll find local temples devoted to a variety of Bai and Han gods and historical figures, from Guanyin to Kublai Khan to Duan Siping, the founder of the Dali Kingdom.

These days, Old Town Dali is a collection of beautiful white Bai-style houses with sloping tiled roofs and blue decorative patterns painted on the walls. Many of the Bai in the area are farmers, but the town itself

top to bottom: vintage alarm clocks in a second-hand market in Kunming; mushrooms for sale; a Hui minority cook makes cakes in Xizhou

has become a popular destination for artists and young Chinese who are looking for a slower, more comfortable way of life, as well as Western travelers in search of a quiet place to hike and relax and Chinese tourists who descend on the area by the thousands during national holidays.

~

While the Bai stick to the valleys, the high mountains of central Yunnan are home to communities of Yi, the largest minority group in the province. Though identified as a single group by the Chinese government, the Yi are actually 50 different self-identified minority groups who live throughout the province and in Sichuan, Guizhou, and Guangxi. Some of the groups have lived in this part of central Yunnan for centuries, but their origins have been hotly debated over the years. Many Yi see themselves as direct descendants of the Yuanmou Man—a 1.7-million-year-old fossil of a human ancestor found in Yuanmou County, in central Yunnan—and, therefore, as the area's indigenous people. Some scholars trace Yi writing back to Neolithic pottery found in Xi'an, 3,000 years before the earliest known forms of Chinese characters. Some even claim that the foundations of Chinese civilization emerged from primitive Yi philosophies.

Historically, the Yi in this area have kept to themselves, living in small communities high in the mountains where they practice swidden agriculture (also called "slash-and-burn" agriculture) and plant multiple crops together in one garden plot to maximize the diversity of their diet and enable them to harvest food year-round and remain self-sufficient. Though some Yi now live in small cities like Jingdong, the capital of the Yi Autonomous County, many continue to live in mountain villages, supplementing their subsistence farming by foraging for rare mushrooms, and native azalea and rhododendron shrubs, which they bring down to weekly markets in more populated areas.

~

Many of Yunnan's Muslim Hui minority also live in this area. The Hui are one of China's largest ethnic groups and are the seventh-largest minority group in the province. Their ancestors first came to China from the Middle East during the seventh century when Islamic, Persian, and Arab scholars and traders settled in central China; more arrived in the thirteenth century, when Genghis Khan established the Yuan Dynasty and conquered much of the Middle East. The Hui came to Yunnan as soldiers in 1253, during Kublai Khan's conquest of western China, then remained here as an occupying army. These soldiers eventually intermarried with locals and formed communities that blended native traditions with Islamic religious practices. Many became traders, running caravans along the Tea Horse Road from central Yunnan down into northern Thailand. Today, Hui restaurants, which specialize in halal beef dishes, are some of the most popular eateries in Yunnan.

Mongols also came to Yunnan with the Yuan Dynasty armies, and some remained in the area after the Mongolian Dynasty was defeated by the Ming. Like many armies in Chinese history, the Yuan had retreated to Yunnan before they were defeated in the mid-fourteenth century, and the Mongols who remained in the area mostly settled in Tonghai, a county in the mountains near the city of Yuxi, 50 miles south of Kunming. Like the Hui, the Mongols intermarried with other local groups and took on many of their neighbors' traditions. In recent years, however, the Mongols in Tonghai have started developing stronger relationships with communities in Mongolia and celebrating some traditional Mongolian festivals.

～

Though the Bai, the Yi, the Hui, the Mongols, and various other minority groups in the region all have their own food traditions, central Yunnan's dishes share many common ingredients and flavors. Strong pickles made with everything from mustard greens to garlic chive blossoms or fern tips are extremely popular, as are chiles, both fresh and dried, which can be used as flavorings or as ingredients on their own. Sichuan peppercorns grow readily here, and many dishes are enhanced by their signature citrusy, numbing flavor. Cooks in central Yunnan also use cheese in their cooking. And because this part of the province is particularly fertile, cooks have access to an extremely wide variety of foraged ingredients, from delicate daylily blossoms to young fern shoots to the sour leaves from *xiangchun* trees (Chinese toon), all of which find their way onto local tables.

top to bottom: ground chiles and Sichuan peppercorns; Chinese mustard greens; jasmine tea

Kunming-Style Cold Noodle Salad

This tangle of cold noodles and vegetables in a sweet, sour, and savory sauce is a staple at restaurants in Kunming. The combination is both hearty and refreshing—a perfect dish in a city known for its temperate climate. Some restaurants make this dish by arranging the vegetables on top of the noodles in a sunburst pattern to highlight the various colors, but this simpler version is served at Laotao Home Style Restaurant in Jiexiao Alley, one of the few old-fashioned walking alleys remaining in the city. The restaurant uses freshly made rice noodles the shape and size of spaghetti, which can be piled directly into a bowl of sauce because they are dense and springy enough that they don't absorb much of the liquid. Other types of rice noodles, which can be more absorbent, should be dressed just before they're eaten.

1 lb. fresh rice noodles or 6 oz. dried rice noodles, such as Vietnamese rice sticks

¼ cup light soy sauce

2½ tbsp. Shanxi vinegar

1 tbsp. granulated sugar

¼ tsp. Sichuan Peppercorn Oil (page 277)

¼ tsp. hot chile oil

1 garlic clove, minced and then crushed into paste with the side of a cleaver

1 medium carrot (about 7 inches long)

¼ Chinese or English cucumber (about 3 inches)

¼ tsp. sesame oil

¼ cup Mushrooms Preserved in Oil (page 34) or ¼ cup wood ear mushrooms, boiled for 1 minute, rinsed with cold water, and thinly sliced (optional)

½ tsp. Dried Chile Oil (page 276)

1 tsp. cilantro leaves

If using dried rice noodles, bring a large pot of water to a boil and cook the noodles until just toothsome and tender but still a bit al dente. Drain the noodles and set aside.

In a small bowl, combine the soy sauce, vinegar, sugar, Sichuan Peppercorn Oil, hot chile oil, and garlic, and mix until the sugar is dissolved. Add 2 tbsp. of water to the sauce to thin it a little, and set the dressing aside.

Peel the carrot and use a mandoline or a cleaver to cut it into long, thin strips. Cut the cucumber in half lengthwise, scoop out the soft seeds, and use a mandoline or cleaver to cut it into long, thin strips the same size as the carrot. Add the vegetables to the fresh noodles and mix.

If using fresh Kunming-style rice noodles that don't absorb liquid very quickly, pour the dressing into the bottom of a shallow serving bowl. Transfer the noodle mixture to the serving bowl. Drizzle the sesame oil on top of the noodles and crown with the mushrooms (if using), the Dried Chile Oil, and the cilantro. Or, if using noodles that will absorb liquid quickly, set the dressing aside, assemble the noodle mixture with the sesame oil and other toppings, and then pour the dressing over everything just before serving.

Mushrooms Preserved in Oil

1½ cups vegetable oil

¾ cup very thinly sliced flavorful mushrooms, such as porcini or hen of the woods

In a wok, heat the oil over a high flame until very hot. Add the mushrooms and fry, stirring occasionally with a wok shovel, until the mushrooms have lost much of their volume and nearly all their liquid and hold a firm, crisp shape when removed from the oil. (The cooking time will vary depending on the thickness and moisture of the mushrooms. They should sizzle vigorously as they cook.) Remove the mushrooms from the oil and let cool, then set aside or store with enough of the frying oil to cover until needed.

Land of Mushrooms

Summer in Yunnan is mushroom season. Mushrooms take over the wet markets, displacing the usual bok choy and carrots. They rise in small mountains in the backs of vendors' vans. They even cover the sidewalks as foragers just in from the countryside lay down tarps and line up baskets piled high with so many different kinds of mushrooms it's nearly impossible to keep count.

Yunnan Province is home to more than 800 different varieties of mushrooms. Porcinis, chanterelles, summer truffles, even prized matsutakes all come out of Yunnan's mountains and are shipped to markets around the world. While these famous varieties carry the highest prices, local cooks particularly love the many kinds of mushrooms that most foragers outside the province might never hear of. Among them are *ganba jun*, or "dried beef mushroom," a white and gray coral-like mushroom that is named for its chewy texture (similar to the local dried beef)

and has a piny flavor; *huang you jun*, or "yellow oil mushroom," a type of boletus with large, thick spongy caps, stout stems, and a deep golden color; *qing tou jun*, or "blue head mushroom," which has a round, moss-green cap; and the ribbon-like *chongcao hua*, or "cordyceps flower" (*Cordyceps militaris*), a golden fungus that grows up from the ground like grass and has a rich, chanterelle-like flavor. At dedicated mushroom restaurants, which specialize in all things fungi, diners feast on massive hot pots filled with dozens of different varieties, and specially trained waitresses help prepare trickier specimens like *lao ren tou*, "old people's heads," which can be poisonous if not cooked properly. But most mushrooms are cooked at home, stir-fried with a handful of fresh or dried chiles, or poached in soups, the simplest and often best ways to celebrate the unadulterated flavors of these elusive and delicious ingredients.

炒灰树花

Maitake Mushrooms with Dried Chiles

This way of preparing mushrooms—stir-fried quickly with some garlic and dried chiles—is very popular in restaurants in Kunming during summer and fall, when local mushrooms are harvested all across Yunnan. It's a great way to prepare any mushroom varieties that have a rich, earthy flavor; even prized porcinis are cooked this way. The instructions below are specific to maitake mushrooms, called *hui shu hua*, or "ash tree flowers" (also known in the United States as "hen of the woods"). To substitute different mushrooms, cut them into thick slices and try using just half the soy sauce; once the mushrooms are almost done, taste them and add more as needed.

7½ oz. maitake mushrooms

2 tbsp. vegetable oil

10 dried Thai chiles

3 small garlic cloves, thinly sliced

1½ tsp. light soy sauce

Pull the maitakes apart into small clusters, about 2 inches at the widest spot. (You will have about 3 cups.) In a wok, heat the oil over a high flame until very hot. Add the chiles and stir and flip until they begin to darken, about 5 seconds. Add the mushrooms and garlic and stir-fry, stirring and flipping constantly, until the mushrooms are soft and have begun to brown, about 3 minutes. (If working on a regular stove, press the mushrooms against the side and bottom of the wok and let them sit for 20 to 30 seconds at a time to brown.) Drizzle in the soy sauce and continue to cook, stirring and flipping constantly, until the flavors have melded, 1 minute.

春天炒饭

Fried Rice with Ham, Potatoes, and Peas

Light, fresh fried rice is a perfect vehicle for Yunnan's famous air-cured hams. This recipe comes from Zhu Bo (page 38), who makes the dish with ham that she brings home from her parents' farm. For this dish, Zhu Bo seasons the rice with only salt and white pepper (rather than adding soy sauce) so that the flavors of the peas, the potatoes, and the rich, earthy ham shine through. The amounts listed below make a very generous portion of fried rice, which can be served in place of plain rice with other meat and vegetable dishes.

¼ cup vegetable oil

1 cup shelled peas, fresh or thawed

2 medium waxy potatoes, such as Yukon gold, peeled and cut into ½-inch dice (about 1¾ cups)

2½ oz. Yunnan ham or Spanish Jamón Serrano, rind and any large layer of fat removed, cut into ⅓-inch dice (about ½ cup)

1 tsp. salt

¼ tsp. ground white pepper

4 cups cold cooked white rice, preferably prepared the day before

In a wok, heat the oil over a high flame until very hot. Add the peas, potato, and ham to the oil and stir and toss to coat. Add the salt and pepper and stir-fry, stirring and flipping constantly, until the seasonings are mixed well and the fat on the ham has become translucent, about 1 minute.

Add 1 cup of water to the wok (enough to cover the vegetables and ham by about ¼ inch) and cover the wok with a lid. Cook the ingredients until tender, 8 to 10 minutes, then remove the lid and let any remaining water bubble away for a few seconds if necessary.

Add the rice to the wok and stir-fry everything together until the ingredients are well mixed and the rice is heated through. Taste the rice and adjust the seasonings as needed.

Everyday Meals with Zhu Bo

Zhu Bo's tiny kitchen overflows with ingredients. Tangles of fresh rice noodles share the counter with a pile of lotus root cut into wedges and a handful of ruby-red tomatoes. A bag of sweet pea greens sits in the sink, ready to be washed. A whole leg of ham hangs against the back wall, and two rice cookers set on a low table, next to the single-burner wok stove, are simmering away, one filled with jasmine rice, the other with chicken soup. Even the floor is crowded with toy trucks belonging to Zhu Bo's young son.

Zhu Bo clears some space on her round cutting board, which is made from a three-inch-thick slice of a pine tree trunk, and begins slicing a block of *er kuai* (Yunnan's famous rice cakes) to make stir-fried rice cakes with ham, tomato, and sweet pea greens. She works quickly and efficiently, cutting a few dozen nearly identical slices with the practiced ease of a professional. When Zhu Bo first moved to Kunming from her family's farm a couple of hours away, she took a job in the kitchen of a small restaurant, where she quickly learned to make all of the city's most famous dishes. When her son was born a few years later, she left the restaurant to cook at a handful of schools (where the hours were better), and learned to make a variety of Italian and American dishes.

But despite her professional training, Zhu Bo's favorite foods are still the simple, home-cooked dishes she grew up on. These days, when she is not working, Zhu Bo often invites friends to her small fifth-floor walk-up. Most of the apartment is dedicated to her husband's leather workshop, where he makes purses to sell online, so diners sit informally around the low coffee table in the family's living room. There, Zhu Bo serves dishes she learned to make at home, like fried rice lightly flavored with fresh peas and pieces of Yunnan ham, alongside local favorites like *xiaochao rou*—stir-fried pork and scallions with local pickles, chiles, and Sichuan peppercorns—all accompanied by simple, flavorful soups like chicken with sweet, crunchy pieces of lotus root or Yunnan's famous Steam Pot Chicken with Ginger and Goji Berries. With each dish, she keeps the preparation as simple as possible, letting the subtle flavors of the local vegetables and meats shine through.

clockwise, from top left: Pea greens, fresh from the market, are a popular ingredient in spring; Zhu Bo uses them in everything from simple soups (see recipe, page 41) to elaborate stir-fries. Ham and green chiles are sliced and ready to be cooked together into a simple, flavorful stir-fry. Zhu Bo, who always acts as host at any gathering, cracks walnuts for family and friends at nearby Green Lake Park. The market near Zhu Bo's apartment complex carries a wide variety of rice and wheat-based noodles, which she adds to leftover soups to make a hearty breakfast. Her version of Yunnan's famous Steam Pot Chicken Soup is flavored with ginger and bright red goji berries (see recipe, page 45).

老奶洋芋

Grandma's Potatoes

These mashed potatoes cooked with dried chiles, garlic chives, and pickled greens are Yunnan's ultimate comfort food. Known as "grandma's potatoes" because it is soft enough for even a grandma without teeth to eat, the dish is popular throughout Yunnan. Cooks use a wide variety of ingredients to flavor the potatoes: You can skip the pickled greens and just use garlic chives; throw in a handful of thinly sliced scallions; add a dollop of Dried Chile Oil; or simply cook the potatoes in lard with nothing more than dried chiles and salt. (In fact, a little bit of bacon grease added to the vegetable oil is a wonderful addition to any version of the dish.) Just make sure your potatoes are tender and cooked with plenty of oil and salt, and you can't go wrong.

8 small red-skinned potatoes (1¾ lbs.)

¼ cup + 1 tbsp. vegetable oil

6 dried Thai chiles, cut into 1-inch pieces

¼ cup Pickled Mustard Greens (page 272)

½ cup garlic chives cut into 1½-inch pieces

¾ tsp. salt

Bring a medium pot of water to a boil. Add the potatoes and boil until very tender, about 20 to 25 minutes. Drain the potatoes and set them aside to cool. When the potatoes are cool enough to handle, peel them and use your hands to break them into small pieces. (You will have about 3½ cups.)

In a wok, heat ¼ cup of the oil over a high flame until very hot. Add the chiles and stir for 5 seconds, then add the Picked Mustard Greens and stir just until they're coated with oil. Add the smashed potato and stir well, then add the garlic chives. Stir-fry the mixture for 3 minutes, stirring and flipping frequently, using a wok spatula to break the potatoes into smaller pieces, and spreading the potato mixture along the side and bottom of the wok for a few seconds at a time to brown. Add the remaining 1 tbsp. of oil and mix well, then add the salt and mix. Taste the potatoes and add more salt if needed, stirring well. Transfer to a serving plate.

Pea Greens Soup

豌豆尖汤

In Yunnan and all across China, the simplest way to prepare vegetables is to boil them for a few minutes and serve them in their boiling water as a lightly flavored soup. These dishes play two roles: they provide a palate-cleansing vegetable and a warm broth to drink (an important element of meals in the past, when clean drinking water was scarce). Both the broth and the vegetables are also considered good for digestion, a counterbalance to the richness of fried and stir-fried dishes. Tender pea greens are particularly delicious prepared this way, as boiling softens their leaves and stems but doesn't take away any of their sweet flavor. This version of the dish comes from home cook Zhu Bo (page 38), who uses a bit of salt and a spoonful of flavorful lard to fortify the broth.

1 tbsp. flavorful lard or rendered bacon fat

2 tsp. salt

4 cups lightly packed pea greens, leaves and tender parts of stems only

In a medium pot, bring 4 cups of water to a boil, then add the lard and the salt. When the fat has dissolved into the water, add the pea greens. Cook, occasionally stirring and flipping the greens in the water with chopsticks, for 2 minutes, until they are dark green. Pour the vegetables and broth into a serving bowl.

Yunnan Grilled Cheese Slices with Ham

锅贴乳饼

The only way to get your hands on some of Yunnan's famous *ru bing* cheese is to go there and try it at the source. But this mild goat cheese, which is often cooked on a griddle, has a texture similar to Greek Halloumi, which can serve as a stand-in. This method of preparing *ru bing* with slices of Yunnan ham comes from Lao Fangzi (Old House) restaurant, which has been open for decades in one of the last remaining old courtyard houses in Kunming. Other restaurants around the city sometimes serve pieces of the griddled cheese accompanied by little bowls of salt, sugar, or Sichuan Peppercorn Powder to dip them into (see alternate recipe below). Halloumi is noticeably saltier than *ru bing*, so it's best not to serve it with additional salt.

6 oz. *ru bing* or Halloumi, cut into 20 squares about ⅛ inch thick and 2 inches wide

1½ oz. Yunnan ham or Spanish Jamón Serrano, sliced very thin and cut into 10 squares a little smaller than the squares of cheese

Vegetable oil, for cooking

Sandwich each slice of ham between two slices of cheese. Wipe the bottom of a wok with a bit of vegetable oil, heat it over a high flame until very hot, then reduce the heat to medium. Carefully place the ham and cheese "sandwiches" into the oiled wok and toast them, using chopsticks to flip them once, until they have just browned on both sides but still hold their shape.

ALTERNATE RECIPE: **Vegetarian Grilled Cheese Slices**

Cut the cheese into ¼-inch-thick slices and toast them in a wok as described above. Serve with a small bowl of white sugar to dip them into.

紫薯饼

Purple Sweet Potato Pancakes

Kunming's bright-purple, silver-dollar-size sweet potato pancakes are as delicious as they are beautiful. The potatoes that are mixed into the batter give the pancakes their lovely color, a sweet, earthy flavor, and a slightly sticky, chewy texture reminiscent of a sticky rice dumpling. This recipe (pictured on page 43) comes from Lao Fangzi (Old House) restaurant in Kunming, where another, golden version of pancakes is also served, made from locally grown "bitter" buckwheat (also known as Tartary buckwheat), which has a unique flavor and a deep yellow color when cooked.

½ lb. purple sweet potatoes

1¼ cups all-purpose flour

¼ cup + 2 tbsp. granulated sugar

1 tsp. baking powder

2 eggs

Vegetable oil, for cooking

Bring a medium pot of water to a boil and add the sweet potatoes. Boil the potatoes until they are soft all the way through, about 20 minutes. Drain the potatoes and set them aside to cool.

When the potatoes have cooled, peel them and use your hands to mash them until there are no hard pieces left. (You will have about ¾ cup.) Mix the potatoes, flour, sugar, and baking powder together, breaking up any chunks of potato. Put the mixture into a blender with 1½ cups of water and the eggs and blend well, stopping the blender to stir as needed. The batter should be thick but runny; if you dip a chopstick in, the batter should run off it in long drips rather than in a continuous line. Add water a couple of tablespoons at a time as needed until you have the right consistency.

Heat a large cast-iron skillet over a high flame. When the pan is hot, rub a bit of vegetable oil on the surface with a brush or paper towel, then reduce the heat to medium. Use a ladle to pour silver-dollar-size rounds of batter onto the skillet; each should be about 3 inches in diameter once the batter spreads out. Cook the pancakes until bubbles appear on top and the edges are beginning to firm up. Flip the pancakes and cook the other side until done. (The pancakes should cook slowly, so that only the edges turn golden brown by the time they are cooked through; adjust the heat accordingly.) Remove the finished pancakes from the skillet and repeat, adding a bit more oil to the skillet for each batch, until the batter has all been used.

汽锅鸡

Steam Pot Chicken with Ginger and Goji Berries

The Yunnan steam pot is a thing of beauty. Brick-red with a curved bowl, small handles, and an upturned funnel in the middle, it is one of those rare cooking tools that deserve to be displayed prominently. But the real magic of the steam pot is the way it gently cooks anything you put in it. When the steam pot is set over boiling water, it acts like a double boiler, slowly heating the contents, while the funnel in the middle of the pot allows a small amount of steam into the bowl, keeping everything moist.

This gentle heating and steaming can be used to cook everything from vegetables to delicate egg custards, but it is most often used to prepare rich chicken soups full of medicinal herbs, which respond well to slow cooking. This version of Steam Pot Chicken Soup (pictured on page 39), from home cook Zhu Bo, is flavored with a thick slice of ginger and a handful of sweet-sour goji berries, both of which are considered good for the immune system in winter.

½ chicken (about 2 lbs.), cut across the bone into 1- to 2-inch pieces

1 tbsp. dried goji berries

Slice of unpeeled ginger, about 2 inches by ¾ inch

1 to 2 tsp. salt

EQUIPMENT:

2-quart traditional Yunnan steam pot (about 8½ inches in diameter) (optional; page 23)

IF USING A TRADITIONAL YUNNAN STEAM POT: Put the chicken, goji berries, ginger, and 2 cups of water into the steam pot. Fill a medium pot (6 to 7 inches in diameter) halfway with water and bring to a boil over high heat, then set the Yunnan steam pot on top of the boiling pot and reduce the heat to low. Allow the ingredients in the steam pot to cook slowly for 2 to 3 hours. Check the water in the lower pot during cooking and add more if necessary.

IF USING A REGULAR SOUP POT: Put the chicken, goji berries, ginger, and 2 cups of water into the pot and heat over a low flame so that the ingredients cook slowly for 2 hours.

When the soup is ready, stir in 1 tsp. salt, taste the broth, and add more salt if needed. Serve the soup as is, or pour it through a cheesecloth-lined strainer, pull the chicken meat off the bone, and serve with just the meat and the goji berries in the broth.

Yunnan Rice Cakes Stir-Fried with Ham and Chives

饵块炒火腿

The Guandu Er'kuai Techniques Exhibition Center offers visitors a glimpse of the traditional way of making Yunnan's unique *er kuai* rice cakes. The small space in Guandu Old Town (a tourist spot filled with shops and food stands just south of downtown Kunming) displays a massive wooden board suspended horizontally on ropes, with a large pestle attached to one end. A few times a day, visitors are invited to help make *er kuai* the old way—by stomping on the board rhythmically so that the pestle crushes and kneads cooked rice that is placed into a stone basin below.

To taste the finished *er kuai*, head to one of the town's nearby eateries. In this dish, it is stir-fried with Xuanwei ham, from eastern Yunnan, along with local pickled mustard greens, scallions, and garlic chives. The combination is rich and salty and wonderful.

3 tbsp. vegetable oil

1¾ oz. Yunnan ham or Spanish Jamón Serrano, cut into thin slices and then into 1-inch squares (¼ cup)

¾ lb. Yunnan rice cakes (er kuai), cut into slices ⅛ inch thick (2½ cups), or the same amount of sliced Korean rice cakes, sometimes labeled "ovalettes" (page 268)

3 scallions, white and light green parts only, cut into ½-inch pieces

¼ cup Pork Broth (page 280)

¼ cup garlic chives cut into 2-inch pieces

2 tbsp. Pickled Mustard Greens (page 272)

2 tsp. light soy sauce

In a wok, heat the oil over a high flame until very hot. Add the ham and stir-fry, stirring and flipping constantly, until the meat begins to brown a bit, about 30 seconds.

Add the rice cakes and scallions and stir to mix for a few seconds, then add the Pork Broth and stir-fry, stirring and flipping the ingredients frequently and using a wok shovel to break apart any pieces that stick together, until the rice cakes begin to soften, about 30 seconds.

Add the garlic chives, Pickled Mustard Greens, and soy sauce and stir-fry until the chives begin to wilt and the rice cakes are tender, about 30 seconds. Transfer to a serving plate and drain away any excess oil.

永平黄焖鸡

Dali-Style Yellow Stewed Chicken

Rich and aromatic, this dish of stewed chicken is very popular in Dali. The chicken is cooked using a method similar to the Chinese technique called "red cooking," in which sugar and dark soy sauce give meat a rich, brown color (see Red-Cooked Beef, page 50). In this case, a bit of sugar is cooked with star anise and chiles; then the chicken is added along with a generous pour of light soy sauce. The meat is stewed with spices and aromatics until it is deeply flavorful and has a lighter, more golden color than a traditional red-cooked dish. This chicken also showcases the flavors of three of central Yunnan's most popular spices—star anise, Sichuan peppercorns, and black cardamom—each of which adds a distinctive note.

In a wok, heat the oil over a high flame until very hot. Add the star anise, sugar, and dried chiles and cook, stirring, for few seconds, until the chiles are slightly fragrant. Add the chicken, salt, soy sauce, Ground Black Cardamom Seeds, and garlic and stir-fry, stirring and flipping frequently, until the chicken no longer looks raw, 3 to 5 minutes. Add 2 cups of water and the Sichuan Peppercorn Powder and bring the mixture to a boil.

Let the chicken boil for 3 minutes, stirring occasionally so that all the pieces cook evenly, then cover the wok with a lid, and continue to cook for 3 to 5 minutes. Remove the lid, add the scallions, and cook, stirring occasionally, for another 3 minutes, until the scallions are limp and the broth has thickened slightly. Transfer the stew, with the broth, to a serving bowl.

¼ cup vegetable oil

1 whole star anise

1 tbsp. granulated sugar

¼ cup whole dried Thai chiles

½ chicken (about 2 lbs.), cut across the bone into 1-inch pieces (or 1¾ lbs. boneless thighs and breasts cut into 1-inch-wide pieces)

2 tsp. salt

¼ cup light soy sauce

¼ tsp. Ground Black Cardamom Seeds (page 274)

5 garlic cloves

¼ tsp. Sichuan Peppercorn Powder (page 274)

2 scallions, both white and green parts, cut into 2-inch pieces

Dali-Style Cucumber with Vinegar and Chile Sauce

大理涼拌黃瓜

The cold cucumber salads served in Dali are some of the richest and most flavorful in China, slathered with spicy chile sauce and sticky-sweet dark soy in addition to the vinegar, garlic, and cilantro that are commonly used to dress cucumbers in other parts of the country. This version comes from a young woman named Yang Haxiang, who lives in Old Town Dali with her family in a cozy house just a few steps from the city's famous West Gate.

Peel the cucumbers, then smash them with the flat side of a cleaver and cut them into 1½-inch chunks. Add the garlic, cilantro, and seasonings to the cucumber and mix well.

2 cucumbers, preferably bumpy-skinned Chinese cucumbers or thin English "seedless" cucumbers

1 garlic clove, roughly chopped

2 tbsp. thinly sliced cilantro leaves and stems

1 tbsp. Zhenjiang vinegar

1 to 2 tsp. chile sauce (*lajiao jiang*)

½ tsp. salt

½ tsp. dark soy sauce

RED-COOKED BEEF TWO WAYS

Beef is the specialty at Hui Minority Restaurant in Jingdong, a quiet county seat. Every day the restaurant's two cooks, Li Yan and Ma Chunye, serve a variety of beef soups, stews, and stir-fries to locals and farmers who have traveled from the countryside to visit the regional government offices, buy tractor parts, or sell vegetables. These two dishes—both of which begin with a flavorful stewed beef shank—blend this signature Hui beef with flavors that are popular throughout central Yunnan.

The base recipe is made with a boneless beef shank—a long, thin muscle sometimes called a "banana" beef shank because of its shape. The cut is available in Asian markets and from some butcher counters; if you can't find it, use a cross-cut shank (the kind used to make osso buco). Just remove the bone and separate the attached muscles before cooking. One batch of red-cooked beef will make enough for two of the dishes on the following pages.

红
烧
牛
肉

Red-Cooked Beef

1½ lbs. beef shank, cut crosswise into 2-inch-long pieces, or 2½ lbs. cross-cut beef shank, bone removed, cut into roughly 2-inch-wide pieces

1 garlic clove

½ inch of unpeeled ginger, smashed with the side of a cleaver

¾ tsp. salt

¼ tsp. Ground Black Cardamom Seeds (page 274)

1 tbsp. rendered suet or vegetable shortening

2 tsp. rock sugar or granulated sugar

Put the beef, garlic, ginger, salt, and Ground Black Cardamom Seeds into a medium pot and add just enough water to nearly cover the meat; set aside. In a wok, melt the fat over high heat, then add the sugar and cook, stirring and breaking up any chunks of sugar as it bubbles and browns. When the mixture has a dark, molasses-like color, add it to the pot of beef. Cover the pot, bring the liquid to a boil, then reduce the heat to low and simmer for 2 hours. (Check the pot occasionally, and add water if more than a tiny bit of the meat is not covered by the liquid.) When the meat is done, remove it from the liquid and refrigerate to cool.

Cold Beef with Cilantro, Chiles, and Vinegar

凉拌牛肉

1 cup thinly sliced Red-Cooked Beef, cold (opposite)

½ tsp. salt

½ to 1 tsp. dried chile flakes

½ tsp. white sesame seeds

1 tbsp. Zhenjiang vinegar

1 tbsp. light soy sauce

4½ tsp. minced peeled ginger

1 scallion, white and light green parts only, thinly sliced

1 tbsp. thinly sliced cilantro leaves and stems

1 tsp. Pickled Chiles (page 271) (optional)

Pile the beef slices onto a small serving plate and sprinkle with the salt, chile flakes, sesame seeds, vinegar, and soy sauce. Top the pile with the ginger, scallion, cilantro, and pickled chiles and serve.

Stir-Fried Red-Cooked Beef with Garlic, Chiles, and Scallions

炒红烧牛肉

3 tbsp. vegetable oil

3 dried Thai chiles

3 garlic cloves, thinly sliced

2-inch knob of peeled ginger, sliced lengthwise and cut into thin slivers

2 cups ½-inch-thick slices of Red Cooked Beef (page 50)

1 tbsp. light soy sauce

2 scallions, dark green parts only, cut crosswise at an angle to make long rings

In a wok, heat the oil over a high flame until very hot. Break the chiles in half, add them to the oil, and cook them until just fragrant, about 15 seconds. Add the garlic and ginger and stir-fry, stirring and tossing constantly, until fragrant, about 15 seconds. Add the meat, stir and toss for a second, then drizzle in the soy sauce. Continue stir-frying until the meat begins to brown at the edges, about 1 minute. Add the scallions and cook, stirring constantly, until they are just wilted, 20 to 30 seconds. Remove from the heat and serve.

Sugar-Coated Deep-Fried Peanuts

This crunchy snack (pictured on page 67) is a wonderful accompaniment to afternoon tea and will add a sweet counterpoint to an otherwise spicy, salty Yunnan-style meal. The nuts are often served at the Old Theater Inn in Shaxi, where you can sit on the terrace overlooking rapeseed fields, and while away a quiet afternoon watching horses graze and small trucks with two-stroke engines rumble along the distant road. If you can't find raw peanuts that have already been shelled and peeled, remove the nuts' red jackets before cooking by rubbing them with a dish towel.

¾ cup vegetable oil

2 cups shelled, peeled raw peanuts

1 cup granulated sugar

Heat the oil and peanuts together in a wok over a very high flame, stirring occasionally. When the oil gets hot and the peanuts start to boil furiously, reduce the heat to medium-high and continue cooking, stirring and flipping constantly with a wok shovel, until the peanuts are golden brown, about 2 to 3 minutes. (The oil should be hot enough that the peanuts sizzle and foam, but not hot enough to burn them.) Remove the nuts from the wok and drain off all the oil.

Return the wok to the stove over high heat. Add ½ cup of water to the wok and pour in the sugar. Stir the mixture to melt the sugar and let it come to a boil. Continue stirring constantly until it begins to thicken into a syrup—the bubbles will become bigger and the mixture will slide down the side of the wok more slowly.

When the sugar has thickened (about 3 minutes), turn off the heat and return the peanuts to the wok. Mix the peanuts into the sugar syrup, stirring and flipping constantly. As you stir, the sugar will begin to cool and thicken, coating each nut. Continue stirring until the sugar has cooled completely and the nuts are coated in a crumbly, snowy-white crust.

清汤牛肉

Hui Beef and Vegetable Soup

This soup comes from Hui Minority Restaurant in Jingdong (page 50), where the cooks simply call the combination of summer squash, green beans, and bright celery greens and scallions *qing tang*, or "clear soup"—a term that is used for any soup with a clear, clean broth as its base. The name gives a good indication of the dish's flavor; it is light and clean tasting, made with a mild beef broth that lets the subtle flavors and faint sweetness of the vegetables shine. Because this is Yunnan, the soup is also served with a dipping sauce of chiles and herbs that you can use to give the vegetables a little kick.

FOR THE SOUP:

1 large waxy potato, peeled

5 oz. very firm green summer squash (ideally a round variety like "eight ball" squash)

20 large Romano beans or green beans

4 cups Beef Broth (page 280)

1 tsp. salt

½ cup roughly chopped celery greens (ideally from Chinese celery)

½ cup finely sliced scallions, both green and white parts (from about 8 scallions)

FOR THE DIPPING SAUCE:

1 tbsp. finely chopped celery greens, ideally from Chinese celery

1 tbsp. finely chopped scallions, both green and white parts

1 or 2 fresh Thai chiles, roughly chopped

½ tsp. salt

2 tsp. dried chile flakes

Cut the potato and squash into angled chunks about 2 to 3 inches long and 1 inch thick; if using a round squash, discard its seed-filled center. Trim the ends of the Romano beans and snap the beans in half.

Put the potato, squash, beans, Beef Broth, and salt into a wok or a medium pot and cover. Bring the broth to a boil, then reduce the heat to medium and boil the soup gently until the potatoes are tender, about 15 minutes. Add the celery greens and scallions to the wok and let them cook for 2 minutes. Transfer everything to a large serving bowl.

Mix the ingredients for the dipping sauce in a small bowl and stir in a small ladleful of broth from the soup (about 6 tbsp.). Serve the sauce next to the soup to dip the vegetables into.

White Beans Stir-Fried with Pickles

炒白云豆

In this simple recipe (pictured on page 55), tender white beans are fried until they're soft and covered with a delicate, crisp crust, then mixed with pickles. The dish is a popular choice in restaurants around Jingdong, in central Yunnan, where local Yi minority cooks use large "white cloud beans" (white kidney beans), which are roughly an inch long when cooked and have thick skins that help the beans keep their shape and crisp nicely when fried. Dried white kidney beans can be found in many Asian markets, and cannellini beans also work well in this recipe. If you're in a rush, you can use canned beans, but they will break apart a bit as they cook.

½ cup dried white kidney beans or cannellini beans, soaked overnight in water and drained

¾ cup vegetable oil, plus a little more as needed

2 dried Thai chiles

¼ tsp. salt

¼ cup Pickled Mustard Greens (page 272)

Put the soaked beans into a medium pot and add water to cover by about 4 inches. Bring the water to a boil, then reduce the heat to medium so that the beans are simmering with small bubbles rising from the bottom of the pot. Cook until the skins of the beans are tender and the insides are soft but the beans still hold their shape, about 3 hours (or about 1½ to 2 hours for cannellini beans), keeping an eye on the pot to ensure that the water doesn't come to a full boil, and add water as needed to keep the beans submerged. Check the beans frequently toward the end of the cooking to make sure that they cook through but don't become mushy. Drain the beans and set aside.

In a wok, heat the oil over a high flame until very hot, then add the beans, dried chiles, and salt; the oil should nearly cover the beans (add a little more oil if necessary). Stir the beans a bit, then allow them to cook until they are very soft and their skins have started to crisp, about 3 to 4 minutes (1½ minutes for cannellini beans). Stir in the pickled greens, cook for about 30 seconds, and remove the beans and Pickled Mustard Greens from the wok, leaving the oil behind.

洋芋焖小瓜

Yi-Style Squash with Black Cardamom

This recipe comes from the tiny roadside Yi Kang Restaurant, in the very center of Yunnan. The family-run spot has just a few outdoor tables on a patio a couple of yards from Regional Expressway 222, a small, winding mountain road that connects Dali and Jingdong. The food at Yi Kang Restaurant is as simple as can be, but it's redolent of the flavors and spices typical of Yi food in the area, particularly ground black cardamom, which is a perfect partner for mild summer squash. In Yunnan, cooks use round, squat squash, which is much harder than the long, thin squash usually found in the United States. Fortunately, farmers' markets and well-stocked stores in the U.S. now offer many varieties of squat, star-shaped squash that work perfectly in this dish. In winter, cooks in Yunnan use pumpkin as a substitute.

1 lb. squat, hard, star-shaped summer squash or sweet orange pumpkin, such as kabocha

1 large slightly waxy potato, such as Yukon gold

¼ cup vegetable oil

1 dried Thai chile, broken in half

1½ tsp. salt

½ tsp. Ground Black Cardamom Seeds (page 274)

Cut the squash into angular pieces 1½ to 2 inches long and about 1 inch thick, cutting around the edges and discarding the softer, seed-filled center, for about 3 cups total. (Summer squash can be used with the skin on; pumpkin should be peeled.) Peel the potato and cut to match the squash.

In a wok, heat the oil over a high flame until very hot. Add the dried chile and cook until the chile has blackened. Add the squash and potatoes and stir-fry for a few seconds. Add the salt and cardamom and mix until they are thoroughly distributed. Pour 1 cup of water into the wok and cover with a wok lid. Let the squash stew with the lid on for 8 to 10 minutes, stirring halfway through. Remove the lid and check to make sure the potatoes and pumpkin (if using) are tender. (If using pumpkin, you may need to add a little more water and let everything cook another minute or two.) Stir to ensure the seasoning is well distributed and cook 1 to 2 more minutes, with the lid off, to boil away most of the remaining water before serving.

烧烤

Kunming-Style Barbecue

The *shao kao* shops on Jiexiao Alley, one of Kunming's last old-fashioned walking streets, come to life in the early evening, as soon as the daylight begins to fade. Shopkeepers roll up their metal service doors and set out trays full of skewered meats and vegetables, and by the time it gets dark, they are hard at work, bending over narrow gas-fueled grills, charring skewers of fatty pork belly and fragrant garlic chives.

Shao kao, Chinese barbecue, is popular throughout the country, often enjoyed as a late snack by people coming home from drink-fueled nights. A wide variety of meats and vegetables can be used for *shao kao*, so this recipe is designed to be flexible in its ingredients and to expand or contract with the number of guests. A good rule of thumb is to prepare three or four skewers of meat and three skewers of vegetables per person, plus a helping or two of the Grilled Eggplant Stuffed with Spiced Pork (page 61) or the Stuffed Lotus Root with Shao Kao Spices (page 62), if you like.

2 cups vegetable oil

3 tbsp. salt

Dried ground chile (optional)

Shao Kao Spice Mix (page 275), ideally in a shaker with large holes

ASSORTED MEATS AND VEGETABLES, SUCH AS:

Green beans (15 to 20 per skewer, depending on size)

Whole scallions, roots trimmed (10 to 15 per skewer, depending on size)

Button mushrooms (5 to 8 per skewer, depending on size)

Oyster mushrooms (6 to 8 per skewer, depending on size)

Garlic chives with thick stems (roughly 30 per skewer)

Okra (8 to 10 per skewer, depending on size)

Zucchini, cut crosswise into thick slices (4 to 5 per skewer, depending on size)

Pressed tofu squares (three 3-inch-wide squares per skewer)

Pork belly, skin removed, cut into cubes or rectangles ¾ inch thick (about 2¼ oz. per skewer)

Thinly sliced pork, beef, and/or lamb (about 1½ oz. per skewer)

TO PREPARE WHOLE VEGETABLES: Slide the skewers through the green beans, scallions, mushrooms, okra, and other long vegetables at a 90-degree angle so that you can fit as many pieces as possible on each skewer; leave at least 3 inches at either end to serve as handles.

TO PREPARE THIN, WIDE INGREDIENTS, SUCH AS PRESSED TOFU AND ROUND PIECES OF ZUCCHINI: Skewer the pieces through the side so that they will lie flat on the grill.

TO PREPARE THE MEAT: Sliced meats can be folded up accordion-style, put on a skewer, and then stretched out so that they will lie relatively flat on the grill. Pieces of pork belly should be skewered through the center. To make the meat a little bit spicy, rub some dried ground chile onto the skewered pieces and set them aside for at least 10 minutes to absorb the flavor.

In a jar, mix the vegetable oil with the salt and set it aside with a pastry brush or small paintbrush.

If using a charcoal grill, heat a large pile of coals until very hot, and heap them up on one side of the grill so that they are as close to the grate

(recipe continues)

Extra-thin 12- to 13-inch-long bamboo skewers

Charcoal or gas grill

Handheld fan if using charcoal (electric or manual—even a piece of cardboard will do)

as possible. If using a gas grill, heat one side of the grill to the highest possible temperature.

Grill the skewers over high heat, flipping them frequently and brushing them with the salted oil. (If using a charcoal grill, use a small handheld fan or a piece of cardboard to fan the coals to keep them hot.) Cook the meats until they are cooked through and have a nice crust; cook the vegetables until they are soft and pliant and have a bit of char. As each skewer is finished, move it over to the cooler side of the grill to keep warm.

When all the skewers have been cooked, transfer them to a large plate or tray and dust them with a generous shake of the Shao Kao Spice Mix.

Yunnan's Role in World War II

Somewhere in the depths of Dianchi, the 118-square-mile lake to the south of Kunming, lies the wreckage of a Curtiss P-40 Warhawk airplane. The aircraft is the only remaining piece of equipment used by the Flying Tigers, the pilots who operated out of Kunming during World War II.

The Flying Tigers were part of a small volunteer force organized by a retired U.S. Army Air Corps major, Claire Chennault, who had become an advisor to Chiang Kai-shek. Chennault used a series of shell corporations to purchase American warplanes, and President Franklin D. Roosevelt signed an order allowing pilots to resign their commissions in the U.S. forces in order to volunteer with the group. Between December 1941, when the pilots arrived in Kunming (just days after the attack on Pearl Harbor), and July 1942, when the group was incorporated into the U.S. forces, they bombed Japanese bases and brought down nearly three hundred Japanese planes.

Kunming played other critical roles during the war. When the Japanese had taken control of all of China's ports, the 700-mile Burma Road—built by the British from Lashio, Burma, to Kunming—became China's sole land route to the outside world and the only means of supplying Chiang Kai-shek's army. And starting in 1942, when the Japanese conquered Burma, Allied pilots flew supplies over "the Hump," a dangerous air route from Assam, India, to Kunming that required them to weave their way through the Himalayas.

In 1944, the Office of Strategic Services (the forerunner of the CIA) established an office in Kunming. The staff included a young Julia Child (then Julia McWilliams), who worked in the Registry and, during her off hours, ate Crossing the Bridge Rice Noodles (page 157) and Steam Pot Chicken (page 45) with her future husband, Paul Child.

肉末烤茄子

Grilled Eggplant Stuffed with Spiced Pork

This delicious dish (pictured on page 59) is a specialty of Kunming's *shao kao* or barbecue cooks, but it is not cooked on a skewer. Instead, stir-fried pork is mixed with *shao kao* spices and a bit of fresh chile, then stuffed into a whole grilled eggplant. To make the dish, be sure to use a seedless eggplant such as one of the shorter, thicker Japanese varieties; a couple of regular Asian eggplants will also work. (Italian varieties are generally too bitter and may have too many hard seeds.) If you don't have a grill, the eggplant can be cooked under a broiler.

1 large or 2 small fat seedless eggplants

1 tbsp. vegetable oil

1 dried Thai chile

¼ lb. ground or finely chopped pork (about ½ cup)

¼ tsp. salt

1 scallion, white and light green parts only, thinly sliced

1 fresh Thai chile, thinly sliced (optional)

Shao Kao Spice Mix (page 275)

Prepare a gas or charcoal grill or heat a broiler and cook the eggplant, turning it frequently, until the vegetable has completely collapsed on itself and the skin is browned and slightly charred.

In a wok, heat the oil over a high flame until very hot. Add the dried chile and cook for 5 seconds. Add the ground pork and the salt and stir-fry the pork, breaking it up with a wok spatula, until it is cooked through and some bits of meat have begun to brown. (If working on a regular stove, press the meat up against the side of the wok and let it sit for 30 seconds at a time to brown.) Add the scallion and the sliced fresh chile (if using) and stir-fry for another few seconds. Remove the meat from the wok and drain away the oil, then dust it with a very generous amount of the Shao Kao Spice Mix and toss so that everything is well combined.

With a pair of kitchen scissors, cut a long, narrow rectangle in the top of the eggplant and remove the strip of skin to create an opening. Lowering the tips of the scissors through the opening, cut up the flesh of the eggplant, making sure plenty of flesh is detached from the vegetable's skin, then fill the eggplant with the spiced pork, mixing everything up inside the eggplant's skin with a pair of chopsticks before serving.

五香糯米藕

Stuffed Lotus Root
with Shao Kao Spices

Sweet and spicy, crunchy and sticky, this dish of fried lotus root slices stuffed with sticky rice and dusted with barbecue spices (pictured on page 59) is addictively delicious. The lotus–sticky rice combination is commonly found at Kunming's *shao kao* (barbecue) stands. The stuffed lotus can be grilled, like any other *shao kao* ingredient, but it's best fried, because the hot oil crisps the edges of the sticky rice filling, adding a wonderful texture to the already complex combination of chewy rice and crunchy vegetable. Barbecue restaurants that offer this preparation usually thread the lotus onto skewers, like their other offerings, and cook them in a deep-fat fryer, but it's easiest to fry them in a wok if you add the slices to the oil two or three at a time. **Makes six to eight skewers.**

2 lobes of lotus root, joint ends intact (each about 5 inches long)

½ cup sticky rice, soaked overnight in water

2 cups vegetable oil (if using a wok), or enough to fill a deep-fat fryer

Shao Kao Spice Mix (page 275)

EQUIPMENT:

Toothpicks

Deep-fat fryer (optional)

Peel the lotus roots and cut off about ½ inch at each end, to remove the joints. Wash the lotus roots well. Drain the sticky rice and use a chopstick to push the soaked rice into the holes in the lotus roots until they are filled. Reattach the joint pieces to the lotus root lobes with toothpicks to seal the ends so that the rice won't fall out.

Put the lotus roots into a pot and add water to cover by at least 2 inches. Bring the water to a boil, then reduce the heat to medium and cook, partially covered, for 1 hour, until the lotus is just tender and the rice is cooked through. (Add more water if necessary to keep the lotus submerged.) Remove the stuffed lotus from the pot and let cool. Remove the joint pieces and cut the stuffed lobes of the lotus root into ½-inch-thick slices.

Heat the oil in a wok over a high flame until very hot. (To check the temperature of the oil, submerge the tip of a wooden chopstick; it should produce a strong cloud of little bubbles.) Carefully fry two or three slices of lotus root at a time, turning once or twice until they are golden and lightly crisp, 2 to 4 minutes, adjusting the heat as needed. Repeat until all the slices have been fried.

Before serving, dust the lotus root slices with a generous helping of Shao Kao Spice Mix.

糖
醋
排
骨

Home-Style Sweet and Sour Pork Ribs

Sticky sweet and sour pork ribs are a staple on Kunming restaurant menus, popular with adults and children, locals and expats alike. In most restaurants, the flavor on the ribs comes from a thick sauce that coats the meat, but this version, which chef Li Bing Zhi makes at home, is subtler, sweetened with sugar, doused with dark vinegar, and stir-fried until the flavors just come together.

Li has been making and serving high-end Yunnan dishes since 1982, when he became a cook at the Kunming Fandian Hotel, one of only two fancy hotels in the city at the time. There, he cooked for Chinese political leaders and even Queen Elizabeth II of England, and he learned to make Cantonese food and Western dishes in addition to local favorites.

1 rack baby-back ribs or St. Louis–style pork ribs (about 2½ to 3 lbs.), separated and cut across the bone into 1½- to 2-inch pieces

1 whole scallion

Slice of unpeeled ginger, about 1½ inches by ½ inch

1 cup vegetable oil

¼ cup granulated sugar

¼ cup + 1 tbsp. Shanxi vinegar

1 tsp. light soy sauce

¼ tsp. dark soy sauce

Put the ribs, scallion, and ginger into a medium pot and add water to cover by about 1 inch. Bring the mixture to a boil over high heat, skimming the foam that rises to the surface, then reduce the heat to medium and boil the ribs gently for 10 minutes. Drain the ribs and set aside until they have cooled a bit and dried. Discard the scallion and ginger.

In a wok, heat the oil over a high flame until very hot. Add the ribs and carefully stir-fry, pushing them back and forth in the oil and flipping occasionally, for 5 minutes. Carefully pour off and discard all but about 1 tbsp. of the oil, then return the wok with the meat in it to the stove.

Add the sugar and ¼ cup of the vinegar to the meat. Mix well and cook for 2 minutes, stirring and flipping occasionally so that all the pieces have a chance to simmer in the sauce at the bottom of the wok while the sugar bubbles and browns. Add both soy sauces and stir-fry until just mixed, 10 to 15 seconds. Add the remaining 1 tbsp. of vinegar, mix for 10 to 15 seconds, and transfer the ribs to a serving plate before the vinegar boils away.

Home-Style Stir-Fried Pork with Garlic Chives

云南小炒肉

This dish of stir-fried pork with scallions, dried chiles, and Sichuan peppercorns is an everyday recipe, one of the easiest and most basic dishes you'll find in Yunnan. Every cook in the province makes a version of it, and each has his or her own way of flavoring it. Most recipes call for large local scallions (*da cong*), but some cooks in central and eastern Yunnan like to use long pieces of bright, fragrant garlic chives instead. This version uses both, and the combination is utterly delicious.

12 oz. lean pork, such as boneless pork chop

1 tbsp. light soy sauce

¼ tsp. dark soy sauce

¼ cup vegetable oil

1 tbsp. thinly sliced peeled ginger

4 dried Thai chiles

4 garlic cloves, thinly sliced

2 tsp. whole Sichuan peppercorns

5 large scallions, both white and green parts, cut into 1½-inch pieces (about 1 cup)

2 tbsp. garlic chives cut into 1½-inch pieces

1 tsp. salt

Cut the pork into very thin slices. (The easiest way to do this is by pulling the meat away from the knife slightly with one hand while slicing with the other hand so that there is tension between the knife and the meat. You will have about 1½ cups.) If the slices are more than ½ inch wide, cut them in half lengthwise to make long, thin pieces. Mix the pork with the light and dark soy sauces in a small bowl and set aside to marinate for 5 minutes.

In a wok, heat the oil over a high flame until very hot. Add the ginger, chiles, garlic, and Sichuan peppercorns and stir once or twice. Add the pork and stir-fry the mixture, stirring and flipping frequently, until the meat is just cooked through, about 1 minute. Add the scallions and garlic chives and stir-fry until the scallions start to wilt, about 1 minute. (If working on a regular stove, press the meat and greens against the side of the wok and let them sit for 30 seconds at a time to brown.) Add the salt, mix well, and transfer the mixture to a serving plate.

蒜芯炒猪肉

Pork with Garlic Scapes and Sichuan Peppercorn Oil

12 oz. lean pork, such as boneless pork chop

1 tsp. light soy sauce

15 garlic scapes, each about 15 inches long

¼ cup vegetable oil

5 dried Thai chiles, broken in half

½ tsp. Sichuan Peppercorn Powder (page 274)

2 tsp. Sichuan Peppercorn Oil (page 277)

The small villages of the Shaxi Valley are spread out among fields of rice and wheat, each one about a 20-minute walk from the next. The Bai villagers here live a fairly traditional life, farming their family plots and raising much of their own food. The largest town, Sideng, was once a major trading stop on the ancient Tea Horse Road, and the local market is still a center of trade for Bai and Yi villagers from across the county who come down from the mountains in fancy ethnic dress to buy livestock, farming supplies, and household goods.

This springtime recipe comes from the owner of the Old Theater Inn, which overlooks rapeseed fields in Duan Village. The hotel, built around an old theater dating from 1782, was one of the first in the valley, opened by Wu Yunxin, a teacher from Chengdu, and his wife, Duan Janpin (a local Bai woman who grew up in the village), who did all the cooking for their guests, making dishes like this combination of pork and garlic scapes.

Cut the pork into ¼-inch-thick slices, then cut the slices lengthwise into ½- to ¾-inch-wide strips (about 1½ cups). Mix the pork with the soy sauce and set aside. Trim the ends and the dark green parts of the tips from the garlic scapes and cut them into 2-inch pieces. (You will have about 1¾ cups.)

In a wok, heat the oil over a high flame until very hot. Add the dried chiles and pork and stir-fry, stirring and flipping frequently and separating the meat if the pieces stick together, until the meat is just cooked through, about 3 minutes. Remove the pork and chiles from the wok with a perforated scoop, draining away the oil, and set aside.

Discard about half of the oil and reheat the remaining oil over a high flame. Add the garlic scapes and stir-fry, stirring and flipping constantly, for 30 seconds. Return the meat to the wok along with the Sichuan Peppercorn Powder and Sichuan Peppercorn Oil and cook everything until well mixed, about 30 seconds, then transfer to a serving plate, draining away any excess oil.

opposite, clockwise from top left: corn and chiles drying in a farmhouse courtyard; a gate in Sideng; the town square in Sideng; Stir-Fried Fern Shoots and Fava Beans (recipe on page 68); Sugar-Coated Deep-Fried Peanuts (recipe on page 53); a Bai minority woman coming home from the market

茴香炒蚕豆

Stir-Fried Fern Shoots and Fava Beans

All home cooking in Yunnan is seasonal. Cooks use a wide variety of locally grown ingredients, and the vegetables available in markets change significantly with the seasons. Yunnan is also home to an astonishing array of wild ingredients, and foraged vegetables and herbs make up a large part of the local pantry. This dish of fern tips and fava beans (pictured on page 67) embodies the fresh, vegetal flavors of spring. It is served at the Old Theater Inn in the Shaxi Valley when fresh fern tips are in season and local foragers bring them to the Friday market.

In Yunnan, this dish is made with the tips of bracken ferns. These are not readily available in U.S. markets because they contain a potentially carcinogenic chemical, but you can sometimes find them frozen in Korean markets, where they may be labeled "fernbrake." The recipe also works well with ostrich fern fiddleheads, which are available at farmers' markets and specialty stores in spring. When preparing fava beans, local cooks don't bother to boil the shelled beans before they peel off the outer skins, so in this recipe the beans are peeled and then boiled to make them tender.

3 oz. Yunnan ham or Spanish Jamón Serrano (a piece with alternating striations of meat and fat), or bacon

1 cup fiddlehead fern shoots, ends trimmed; if using bracken ferns, cut into 2- to 3-inch-long pieces

1 cup shelled, peeled fresh fava beans (from 1½ to 3 lbs. of fava bean pods, depending on their contents)

2 tbsp. vegetable oil

2 whole dried Thai chiles

½ tsp. salt

¼ cup garlic chives cut into 1-inch lengths

Thinly slice the ham across the grain (so each piece has striations of meat and fat), then cut each slice into ¼-inch-wide strips, each with rows of fat and meat, about ½ cup. Soak the ferns in cool water for a few minutes to clean them, rub off any fuzzy or papery outer coverings, and drain.

Fill a wok with 1½ inches of water and bring to a boil over a high flame. Add the fava beans and boil until tender, about 5 minutes. Using a spider or perforated scoop, remove the fava beans from the water and rinse well with cold water to stop the cooking.

Add the ferns to the boiling water and cook, stirring occasionally, until tender, about 10 minutes. Drain and set aside. Discard the cooking water and dry the wok.

In the wok, heat the oil over a high flame until very hot. Add the chiles and ham and cook for a little over a minute, stirring, to let the meat render some of its fat. Add the fiddlehead ferns and stir-fry, stirring and flipping occasionally, until the ferns are well cooked, about 3 minutes.

Add the fava beans and the salt and stir-fry, stirring and flipping constantly, until the beans are cooked, about 1 minute. Add the garlic chives to the wok and stir-fry, stirring and flipping, until the chives are just wilted, about 30 seconds, then transfer the vegetables and meat to a serving plate, draining off any excess oil.

Traveling Along the Tea Horse Road

The old market square in Sideng, the main town in the Shaxi Valley, is quiet during the day. The large, cobblestoned courtyard is often empty, with just the occasional shopkeeper passing through. But an ornate wooden theater and a large Buddhist temple on either side of the space are reminders of a busier time, back when Shaxi was a major stop on a network of trading routes now known as the Tea Horse Road.

Also called the Southern Silk Road, the Tea Horse Road connected Sichuan and Yunnan to Tibet, India, Burma, and Southeast Asia, as well as to southern China. Though less famous than the northern Silk Road, which connected China to the Middle East, some version of this southern trading network may have been in use as far back as the Bronze Age, and it was a busy corridor up through the mid-twentieth century; during World War II, these same roads were a crucial means of supplying Chinese troops after Japan occupied the country's ports.

The route is named for two of its most important commodities—horses raised in Tibet, and tea from Sichuan and the *pu'er* growing regions of southern Yunnan—but caravans through Yunnan also carried jade from Burma, opium from the Burmese border regions, and a wide variety of other goods from across China and Southwest Asia. They also carried foods, from spices and medicinal herbs to staples like rice and salt, and introduced cooks throughout Asia to the flavors of distant lands.

砂
锅
米
线

Clay Pot Noodle Soup

3 oz. ground or finely chopped pork (about ½ cup)

2 cups Pork Broth (page 280)

½ cup Napa cabbage sliced crosswise into ⅛-inch strips

5 tbsp. Pickled Mustard Greens (page 272) or ¼ cup Quick Pickled Cabbage (page 271)

Large handful of fresh or cooked rice or wheat noodles (the weight will depend on the kind of noodles)

½ tsp. salt

2 tbsp. garlic chives cut into 1-inch pieces

½ tsp. Dried Chile Oil, plus more for serving (page 276)

Zhenjiang vinegar, for serving

EQUIPMENT:

Yunnan sand pot with handle (optional; page 23)

Kunming is a city fueled by noodle soup. Walk down any street, and you'll see shops packed with people slurping down warm, nourishing soups for breakfast or lunch. There isn't a lot of variety among these soups—they are made with a basic pork broth, ground pork, pickled vegetables, chile paste, cabbage, and noodles. The real variation is in the noodles themselves: you can order your soup with rice noodles as thin as angel hair pasta or as wide as handkerchiefs, or with toothsome wheat noodles that are twice the width of linguine.

This recipe comes from a small storefront in Jiexiao Alley in the center of Kunming. The women who run the shop are well-known for their *shaguo mi xian*, or "sand pot" rice noodles, which are cooked in an individual-sized clay pot with a short handle that can be put directly over the flame and then brought to the table still bubbling and spitting. A similar soup can be found in Dali, where cooks use pickled cabbage instead of the mustard greens favored in Kunming. If you don't have clay pots, you can make this soup in a regular pot, but it's best if prepared one serving at a time. You can also use dried noodles instead of fresh—before making the soup, soften them, following the instructions on their packaging. The noodles should be al dente before they're added to the soup. Makes one serving.

Fill a medium pot with water and bring it to a boil. Blanch the ground pork in the boiling water for 5 to 10 seconds, breaking up the meat with chopsticks or a spoon, then drain the meat and set it aside; it will still be quite pink.

Put the Pork Broth into a Yunnan sand pot or a small conventional pot, place it on the stove over medium-high heat, and bring it to a boil. Add the pork, the Napa cabbage, and 3 tbsp. of pickled vegetables to the pot. Return the soup to a boil and cook for 2 to 3 minutes, until the stems of the Napa cabbage soften slightly. Add the noodles and cook until they are soft (about 30 seconds for rice noodles and 2 minutes for wheat noodles).

When the noodles have softened, stir the salt into the broth, then top the soup with the garlic chives, Dried Chile Oil, and the remaining pickled vegetables. Cook for another 30 seconds, remove from the heat, and serve with the vinegar and more Dried Chile Oil on the side.

酸菜炒牛肉

Stir-Fried Beef with Pickled Greens and Garlic Chives

This satisfying combination of beef, pickled greens, and fragrant garlic chives is a staple at Dragon Phoenix Muslim Restaurant. The hole-in-the-wall spot on the main road in Sideng, in the Shaxi Valley, is the busiest eatery in town even though it has no fancy sign or inviting courtyard and sits a few steps down from the road, in view of any passing truck or motorbike. The owner, a middle-aged Hui woman, does all the cooking herself in a little alcove that is open to the street, preparing rich beef soups and quick stir-fries in a large wok built into the counter and fired by traditional cakes of pressed carbon and coal dust. Other family members help clear tables or prep vegetables in a small courtyard behind the kitchen.

This stir-fry is traditionally made with finely chopped beef, which the cook ages herself, hanging it on hooks on the back wall of the kitchen, but grass-fed ground beef has a similarly rich flavor. If using regular ground beef, add a little extra soy sauce to boost the umami.

¼ cup vegetable oil

2 dried Thai chiles

2 garlic cloves, cut into thick slices

1 lb. ground or finely chopped beef (about 1¾ cups)

3 tbsp. light soy sauce

1 cup garlic chives cut into 1-inch pieces

2 heaping tbsp. Pickled Mustard Greens (page 272)

In a wok, heat the oil over a high flame until very hot. Add the chiles, garlic, and beef and stir-fry the mixture, stirring and flipping frequently and using a wok shovel to break up any large pieces of meat. When the meat begins to brown, add the soy sauce by pouring it across the side of the wok in an arc. Continue to stir-fry the mixture until the meat is fully browned. (If working on a regular stove, press the meat up against the side of the wok and let it sit for 30 seconds at a time to brown.) Add the garlic chives and Pickled Mustard Greens and stir-fry for another minute, until the chives have wilted slightly, then remove the mixture from the wok, draining off the oil.

Lotus Root with Pickles

酸菜炒藕

This simple but wonderful stir-fry combines crunchy, slightly sweet lotus root with sour pickled mustard greens. The dish is a popular choice at Dragon Phoenix Muslim Restaurant in Sideng, where it is often served alongside Stir-Fried Beef with Pickled Greens and Garlic Chives (opposite) and the restaurant's version of Potato Pancake with Chile Powder (page 99).

The cooks at Dragon Phoenix Muslim Restaurant are able to make this dish with slightly thicker slices of lotus root than are used here because their coal-fired stove cooks the vegetable much more quickly. If you have a stronger-than-average stove, you might try making the dish with slightly thicker slices, which would give it a nice, crunchy texture. Additionally, while this dish is usually made with beef broth (because beef is the only meat served at the restaurant), chicken broth or vegetable broth also works well.

3 tbsp. vegetable oil

4 dried Thai chiles

8- to 10-inch lotus root, peeled and very thinly sliced into 1/16-inch rounds (about 3 cups)

1/2 cup Beef Broth (page 280)

3 scallions, white and light green parts only, cut into 1/2-inch pieces

3/4 tsp. salt

1/2 tsp. Dried Chile Oil (page 276)

1/2 cup Pickled Mustard Greens (page 272)

In a wok, heat the oil over a high flame until very hot. Add the chiles and lotus root and stir-fry, stirring and tossing, for 30 seconds. Add the broth to the wok and let it boil, stirring and tossing the lotus root, until the liquid boils away, about 2 minutes. Add the scallions, salt, and Dried Chile Oil, and stir-fry, stirring and tossing everything frequently, for another minute, until the lotus root is tender but still crisp. Add the Pickled Mustard Greens to the wok, stir to mix, then transfer the mixture to a serving plate.

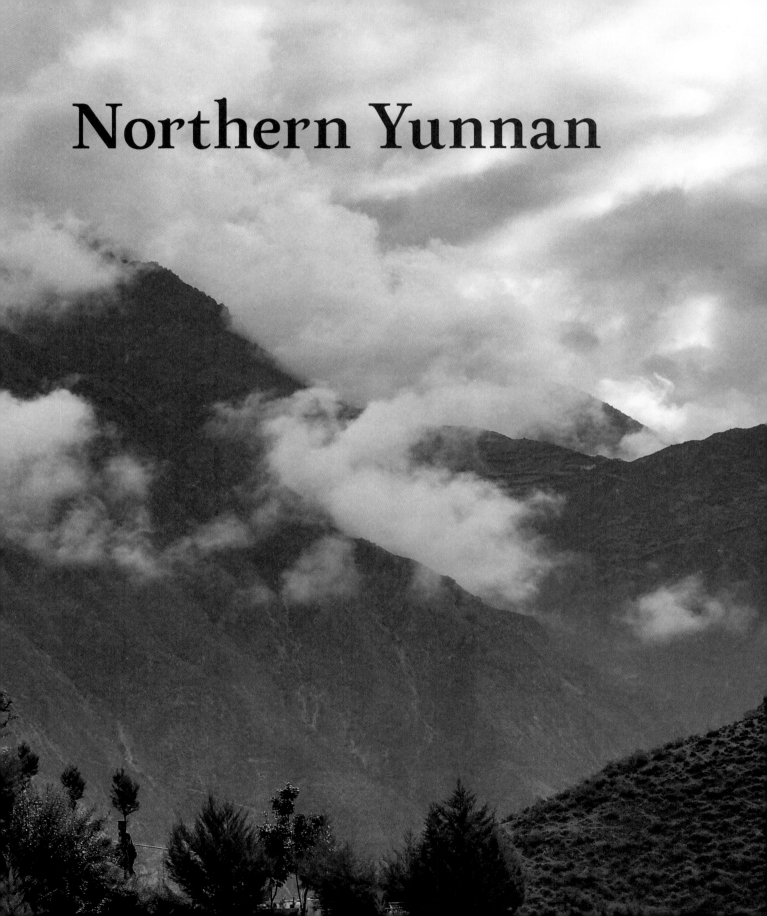

Northern Yunnan

IN THE TINY VILLAGE OF RONGDING, in the northern reaches of Yunnan, a few elderly Tibetan pilgrims are preparing to begin a *kora*, or meditative pilgrimage, around the peak of glacier-topped Kawakarpo, or Meili Snow Mountain. They circle a small temple, spinning handheld prayer wheels, counting their revolutions with small piles of rocks set along the side of the path. The temple is a modest structure draped with colorful prayer flags and covered in thick layers of whitewash that hundreds, if not thousands, of pilgrims have added as kind of a purification ritual before beginning their journey. Inside the windowless room, the altar is illuminated by dozens of small butter candles.

This part of Yunnan, known as Diqing (or Dechen in Tibetan), is the southern tip of the Kham region of historical Tibet. The area is a landscape of nearly impenetrably high mountains and deep valleys, and the Tibetans here, the Khampa, were historically independent from rulers in both Lhasa and China and developed a reputation as formidable warriors and, at certain moments in history, fearsome bandits.

Kawakarpo (sometimes pronounced Kawagebo in Chinese) sits on Yunnan's northern border with the Tibetan Autonomous Region. It is the Khampas' most important mountain peak and their most important territorial god. Pilgrims from across the Tibetan regions of China come here every year to make the two-week trek around the mountain; some return repeatedly, hoping to complete as many as thirteen trips during their lifetime.

The largest Tibetan community in Diqing is about 130 miles southeast, in and around the city of Shangri-la (historically called Zhongdian in Chinese and Gyalthang in Tibetan). Shangri-la is set in the middle of a wide plain where locals work small farms and horses and yaks roam freely across open meadows. At its center is an old Tibetan town, a warren of streets filled with ornate wooden buildings. For centuries, this area was a

clockwise, from top left: a flag-draped stupa in Shangri-la; a traditional Mosuo feast near Lugu Lake; horseback riding is a popular tourist activity near Shangri-la; Dongzhulin Monastery, north Benzilan; clouds settle on the tops of the mountains along Yunnan's northern border; villagers in Gu Jiu village; prayer wheels at Dongzhulin Monastery

major stop on the Tea Horse Road that connected Tibet to Yunnan, India, Burma, Nepal, and Southeast Asia, and the Tibetans here have long had close relationships with other minorities in the vicinity, especially the Naxi, who live just south, in and around Lijiang. Through their influence, many of the other minorities in northern Yunnan converted to Tibetan Buddhism over the centuries, and Tibetan-style *stupas* and prayer flags are common across the region.

Shangri-la is still a major center for business for Tibetans and others in Yunnan. It is also a popular tourist spot. In Old Town, visitors from all over the world browse for Tibetan handicrafts in souvenir shops and relax in small restaurants, nibbling on *momos* and sipping from steaming cups of sweet, milky chai or salty butter tea. Outside the old quarter, Shangri-la is a small modern city, a sprawl of blocky three- and four-story buildings designed to echo the local architecture with brightly painted faux beams over the windows. The city is in a state of perpetual construction, with new buildings and roads going in every day, and there's a palpable feeling of ambition here as Chinese and Tibetan entrepreneurs come from across the country to try to cash in on the area's mythic beauty. Taken all together, the place feels like a Tibetan version of the Wild West.

Farther south, at the foot of another snowcapped peak—Jade Dragon Snow Mountain—is Old Town Lijiang, Yunnan's best-known tourist attraction. The hamlet of traditional Naxi-minority wood and stone houses is a UNESCO World Heritage Site; it draws more than 30 million visitors a year who come to carouse in the hotels, bars, and shops that have taken over the town. In the main square, McDonald's, Pizza Hut, and Starbucks franchises sit across from the city's famous wooden waterwheels, and tourists fill the town's narrow lanes, snacking on sticks of grilled yak meat, tall jars of fatty yak milk, and fluffy pieces of French toast topped with melted cheese and sweet red beans.

But walk around early in the morning, along the back streets, and you'll find the charming side of the town. Small streams carrying water from Black Dragon Pond babble softly next to winding cobblestone streets; wisteria and flowering bougainvillea climb up the sides of doorways and onto gray tiled roofs; and local vendors fry fresh *baba*—the city's signature flatbreads—to sell from carts at street corners.

The Lijiang Plain has long been the center of Naxi life. The tribe migrated to the region from the north centuries ago and built a wealthy civilization, cultivating the fertile land and running caravans from central Yunnan up into Tibet. During the Ming Dynasty, the Mu family, members of the Naxi elite, were chosen to serve the government in Beijing as *tusi*, or "native leaders," de facto rulers of the Kingdom of Mu, which stretched from central Yunnan all the way up through Sichuan to the Tibetan border and west to the edge of Burma. As a result, the Naxi became one of the best-educated groups in Yunnan and developed close ties with the Imperial government; later some Naxi became government officials.

To the northeast of Lijiang sits Lake Lugu, home of the Mosuo minority (or Na in the local language). According to legend, the lake was created by the goddess Gamu, who is embodied in the nearby Lion Mountain. A mountain god, Waru Bula, came to visit Gamu but found her with another lover and left, stomping his feet in anger. When Gamu discovered he had gone, her tears filled his footprints, becoming the lake.

The Mosuo are considered a branch of the Naxi, but they have their own distinctive history and culture that has long fascinated outsiders. Because Mosuo families are unlike Han families, the Mosuo are often misunderstood by both Chinese and Westerners and mischaracterized in popular media. The Mosuo are traditionally a matrilineal society, and most Mosuo live in their mothers' homes. In many families, the grandmother is the titular head of the household and has her bed in the main room, next to the hearth where the family gathers for meals.

Mosuo relationships also allow for more flexibility than traditional Chinese marriages. While some Mosuo marry, others practice what are called "walking marriages." In these arrangements, men and women both live at their own mothers' houses, but men visit their girlfriends at night, and relationships can be short-lived or last for many years. In walking marriages, children maintain a relationship with their fathers, but uncles also serve an important role, helping to raise and provide for their nieces and nephews.

Though many Mosuo are still farmers, villagers around Lugu have begun to build up the tourism infrastructure. Many young women participate in nightly dance performances in the local squares, dressed in traditional silk jackets, white skirts, and headdresses decorated with colorful beads. Older men and women spend part of the day ferrying tourists around the lake in brightly painted wooden boats. Others have opened small lakeside restaurants where visitors can order meat from suckling pigs roasted on

opposite, top to bottom: the hearth in a traditional Mosuo home; a winding lane in Old Town Lijiang

below: Black Dragon Pool in Lijiang

a spit or cook their own vegetables and meat over coal fires built into the center of the tables.

~

Beyond these populated centers, the mountains of northern Yunnan are home to a number of other minorities, including some of China's smallest groups: the Pumi, the Nu, and the Dulong. The Dulong, also called the Drung, are the smallest and most isolated, a group of fewer than 7,000 people named for the valley where they live, in the northwestern corner of the province. The Dulong are known primarily for the facial tattoos women used to wear, and though the custom is no longer practiced, the oldest women still bear the markings they received when they became old enough to marry.

The Dulong were largely cut off from the rest of China until 1999, when the first real road to the region was built, and until recently many villages were accessible only via dirt paths, narrow suspension bridges, and the area's famous "rope bridges." These "bridges" were really nothing more than sturdy ropes strung across unfordable areas of river—to cross, you attached yourself to the rope in a sling and slid down like a zip line or pulled yourself along hand over hand.

South of the Dulong, scattered in pockets along the Salween River, live the Nu, who claim to be the original inhabitants of northern Yunnan. The group is not homogeneous—the term "Nu" comes from the Chinese name for the Salween, so two different groups living along different parts of the river, as well as a third group living nearby, along the Mekong, have all been grouped into this official designation. The Nu in the northernmost part of Yunnan may actually be the same group as the Dulong, separated when the Dulong left these valleys, and their culture has been influenced by the nearby Tibetan communities and the Catholic missionaries who built churches in the area. The Nu in the south are more influenced by the culture of the nearby Lisu.

The area east of Lijiang is also home to small communities of Pumi (or Premi, as they call themselves). China's Pumi primarily live in the neighboring areas of Sichuan, but some came to Yunnan as part of Kublai Khan's army and were given land here. The Pumi speak their own distinct language and identify strongly as a unique ethnic group, but in Yunnan their traditional costumes, religion, foods, and way of life resemble those of the Naxi.

below: a Tibetan pilgrim in Rongding Village

The largest group in the mountains and valleys along the Salween and Lancang Rivers is the Lisu, who also live in Myanmar, India, and northern Thailand. The Lisu proudly identify themselves as mountain people, but they also have strong rice-farming traditions and control some of the best agricultural land in the area. Pigs are extremely important in Lisu society; while other nearby groups, like the Tibetans, traditionally eat beef or yak, the Lisu prefer pork and distribute pieces of cooked pork as favors at weddings and funerals and as payment at community house-building events. The Lisu even distinguish between "Lisu pigs" and "Han pigs": according to the Lisu, "Han pigs" are fed hormones and grow quickly, while the Lisu pigs eat grass, cornmeal, and local vegetation and grow slowly, so that they are not ready for slaughter for at least two years. The result, according to locals, is much tastier, firmer meat.

While the foods found in different parts of northern Yunnan reflect local groups' histories and traditions, they are all generally simple and straightforward, made without many of the spices and sauces used in other parts of the province. Many dishes are hearty and filling, sustenance for high-altitude living and cold winters. Meats and vegetables are often deep-fried, and filled breads of various kinds are popular. Warming chicken soups are a specialty in many towns.

Many groups in the area have developed unique ways of preserving meat. Around Lugu Lake, the Mosuo preserve whole pigs, which are gutted, salted, and pressed flat with heavy weights until the meat is dense, smooth, and tender; it can then be stored for years. In Lijiang you'll find "waxed" pork ribs with meat that has been completely dried out; the dried ribs are then boiled or cooked in hot pots so that the meat softens and becomes edible again.

In some places, the local food reflects the proximity to Sichuan, flavored with the same dried chiles and Sichuan peppercorns you find across the border, but the dishes are generally less spicy here than in central Yunnan. And in Shangri-la, Tibetans who have moved to the region from Lhasa and other Tibetan areas of China have introduced locals to traditional Tibetan dishes like fried stuffed breads and hearty noodle soups, which have become popular in restaurants all over town.

top to bottom: butter tea and snacks in Weixi; yak meat hot pot in Shangri-la

牛肉包子

Meat-Filled Momos

Meat-stuffed *momos* are one of the traditional Tibetan dishes that have become popular in restaurants in Shangri-la Old Town—even though they were not historically part of the local cuisine. This simple recipe comes from Lhasa Restaurant, a small eatery opened by two young women from the Tibetan Autonomous Region who serve traditional Tibetan dishes alongside sweet, fragrant chai tea in a second-story spot in the center of town. They fill their *momos* with yak meat, but the seasonings in this recipe have been adjusted for regular beef; if you have access to yak meat, cut back on the soy sauce. Either way, be sure to use fatty meat so that the *momos* will be juicy and tender. Makes 24 momos. (Follow the steps in the bottom row of the photo grid, opposite, to make the meat dumplings.)

1 lb. ground or finely chopped beef (1¾ cups)

3 scallions, white and light green parts only, cut in half lengthwise and finely sliced crosswise

1½ tsp. light soy sauce

1 tbsp. vegetable oil

1½ tsp. salt

¾ tsp. Sichuan Peppercorn Powder (page 274)

1 recipe All-Purpose Tibetan Dough (page 275)

EQUIPMENT:

Steamer lined with cabbage leaves

Dumpling rolling pin or wooden dowel (page 22)

Prepare the beef by breaking it up with a fork or chopping it lightly, then mix in the scallions, soy sauce, oil, salt, and Sichuan Peppercorn Powder until evenly distributed. Set the filling aside.

Divide the prepared dough into quarters and lightly flour a work surface. Working with one quarter of the dough at a time, knead the dough a couple of times and then use your hands to roll it into a rope about 1½ inches thick. Cut the rope into six small, even pieces.

Take one small piece of dough, roll it into a ball in your palms, and then use the heel of your hand or the bottom of a measuring cup to smash it into a flat, even circle. Use a dumpling rolling pin or wooden dowel to further flatten the circle into a 3½-inch wrapper with a thick center. The best way to do this is to use the rolling pin on just the bottom third of the circle, then turn the dough counterclockwise a bit and repeat; this way the edges of the wrapper will receive even pressure, while the center stays untouched. (The finished wrapper should have the shape of a very flat flying saucer or a fried egg.) Repeat with the remaining dough, setting the wrappers aside on a floured surface and making sure they don't touch each other.

(recipe continues)

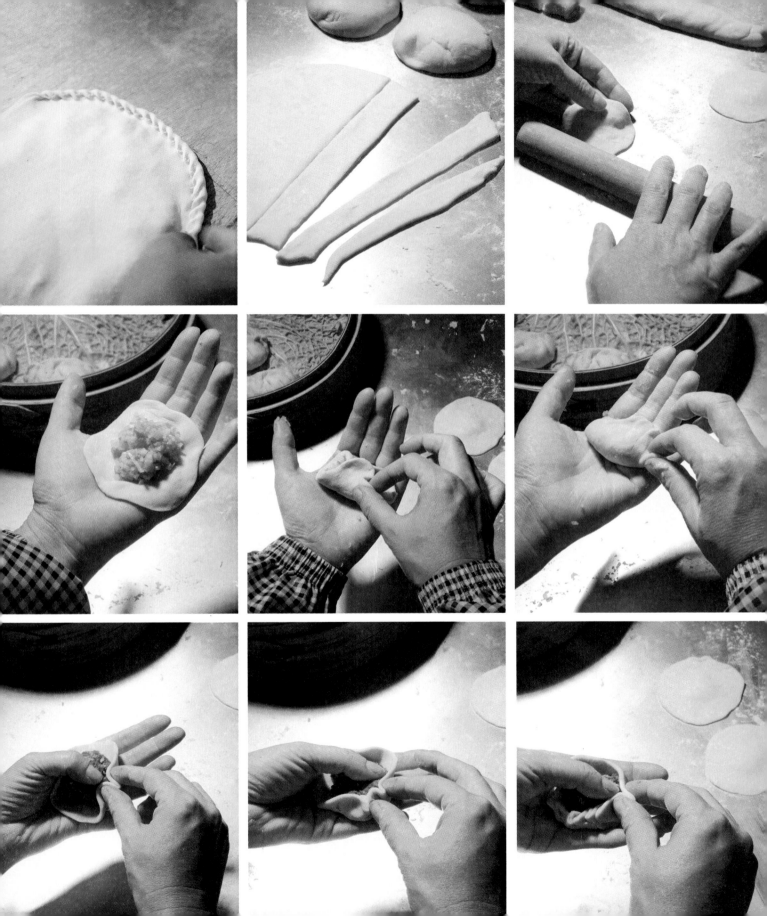

When all the wrappers have been prepared, fill the momos: place a wrapper in the palm of one hand and top with a small mound of filling (approximately 1 tbsp.). With your other hand, bring the right edge of the wrapper up toward the center of the filling. With your thumb on that edge of the wrapper, use your index finger to grab the edge of the wrapper about ½ inch from your thumb, then pinch the two parts of the edge together, to create a small fold. Repeat the pinching motion, bringing more and more of the dumpling's edge into the middle, and rotating the dumpling in your hand, creating pleats all around the dumpling. (The dough is flexible, so if you need to, pull and stretch the dough over the filling.) When all the edges of the wrapper have been secured together, pinch the top of the dumpling, where they meet, to ensure that they are stuck together well.

Fill a large pot that will fit under the steamer with water and bring it to a rolling boil. Place the momos on the steamer lined with cabbage leaves and steam them over the pot for 8 to 10 minutes, until the dough looks slightly translucent. (If using a steamer with stacked trays, the momos on the bottom may be done before those on the upper levels.)

Vegetable Momos

蔬菜包子

The recipe for these *momos*, filled with a simple, light mixture of vegetables and thin rice noodles, comes from Lhasa Restaurant (page 84). The vegetables are flavored with both a hint of aromatic ground cumin and just enough Sichuan peppercorn powder to give the *momos* a touch of citrusy flavor. The cooks at Lhasa Restaurant use fresh rice noodles in the filling, but very thin dried rice noodles, such as Vietnamese rice vermicelli—boiled, drained, and rinsed with cold water—will also give you the right consistency. (Follow the steps in the middle row of the photo grid on page 85 to make the dumplings.)

Mix the vegetables, rice noodles, oil, salt, Sichuan Peppercorn Powder, and cumin well, then set the filling aside.

Divide the prepared dough into quarters. Lightly flour a work surface. Working with one quarter of the dough at a time, knead the dough a

¾ cup minced Napa cabbage

¼ cup minced carrot

½ cup cooked rice vermicelli, finely chopped (from about 1⅓ oz. dried noodles)

1½ tsp. vegetable oil

1 tsp. salt

¼ tsp. Sichuan Peppercorn Powder (page 274)

¼ tsp. ground cumin

1 recipe All-Purpose Tibetan Dough (page 275)

EQUIPMENT:

Steamer lined with cabbage leaves

Dumpling rolling pin or wooden dowel (page 22)

couple of times and then use your hands to roll it into a rope about 1½ inches thick. Cut the rope into six small, even pieces.

Take one small piece of dough, roll it into a ball in your palms, and then use the heel of your hand or the bottom of a measuring cup to smash it into a flat, even circle. Use a dumpling rolling pin or wooden dowel to further flatten the circle into a 3½-inch wrapper with a thick center. The best way to do this is to use the rolling pin on just the bottom third of the circle, then turn the dough counterclockwise a bit and repeat; this way the edges of the wrapper will receive even pressure, while the center stays untouched. (The finished wrapper should have the shape of a very flat flying saucer or a fried egg.) Repeat with the remaining dough, setting the wrappers aside on a floured surface and making sure they don't touch each other.

When all the wrappers have been prepared, fill the momos and shape them into a "pleated crescent" shape: place a wrapper in the palm of one hand and top it with a small mound of filling (approximately 2 tsp.). Fold the wrapper in half, bringing the bottom edge up toward the top, and use your other hand to pinch the wrapper closed just in the center, leaving the sides open. Grab the front edge of the wrapper ½ inch to the right of the center, where you pinched the wrapper shut, and fold it almost all the way to the center to create a pleat; pinch the pleat closed. Take the front edge of the wrapper ½ inch to the right of your new pleat and fold it toward the center, stopping before you get to the first pleat, so that your folds sit next to each other. Make another pleat or two on the right to close that side of the dumpling, then repeat the procedure on the left, folding in the opposite direction, so that all the pleats face the center of the dumpling. (The dough is flexible, so if you need to, pull and stretch the dough over the filling.) When all the edges of the wrapper have been secured together, pinch all the folds closed to ensure that they are stuck together well.

Fill a large pot that will fit under the steamer with water and bring it to a rolling boil. Place the momos on the steamer lined with cabbage leaves and steam them over the pot for 8 to 10 minutes, until the dough looks slightly translucent. (If using a steamer with stacked trays, the momos on the bottom may be done before those on the upper levels.)

牛肉饼

Fried Bread Stuffed with Curried Meat

This Tibetan-style meat-filled bread offers a culinary glimpse into the changing population of Shangri-la. The recipe comes from the owner of a short-lived restaurant called the Silent Holy Stones, a Tibetan man from Sichuan who had studied in India and then moved to Yunnan to take advantage of the influx of tourists that has turned Shangri-la into something of a boomtown. The combination of curry powder, cumin, turmeric, and Sichuan peppercorns he uses in the dish draws flavors from all of these places. This bread is traditionally stuffed with yak meat, but the seasonings here have been adjusted for regular beef; if you have access to yak meat, cut back on the amount of soy sauce in the filling.

½ lb. ground or finely chopped beef (scant 1 cup)

2 cups + 3 tbsp. vegetable oil

2 tsp. light soy sauce

½ cup finely chopped bell pepper (ideally a mix of red and green peppers)

1½ tsp. curry powder

¼ tsp. ground cumin

¼ tsp. ground turmeric

¼ tsp. ground coriander

¼ tsp. Sichuan Peppercorn Powder (page 274)

1 recipe All-Purpose Tibetan Dough (page 275)

EQUIPMENT:

Dumpling rolling pin or wooden dowel (page 22)

Prepare the beef by breaking it up with a fork or chopping it lightly. In a wok, heat 3 tbsp. of the oil over a high flame until very hot. Add the beef and stir-fry, stirring and flipping frequently and using a wok shovel to break up any large pieces. When the meat is no longer pink, add the soy sauce by pouring it across the side of the wok in an arc. Add the bell peppers and continue to stir-fry until the meat has browned and the peppers are tender, about 2 minutes. Add the spices and continue to cook, stirring and flipping constantly, until the powder is fully mixed into the meat, about 1 minute. Remove the mixture from the wok, draining away any excess oil, and set aside.

Pull off two small pinches of the prepared dough (to test the oil temperature for frying), then divide the remaining dough into quarters and roll each into a ball. Set two aside, under plastic wrap.

Rub a clean work surface with a little bit of vegetable oil, flatten two of the balls into disks with your hands, then use a dumpling rolling pin or wooden dowel to roll them into thin disks 7 inches in diameter. (They should be as uniform as possible.)

Put half of the meat filling (¾ cup) on top of one of the disks and spread it out in an even layer, leaving a 1-inch border of dough around the filling. Top with the second disk of dough and press the edges together.

Seal the dough disks firmly together by creating a rope pattern along the edge: take a pinch of dough from the bottom edge of the bread between your thumb and forefinger. Stretch it away from the rest of the bread just a bit, then twist it and pinch it back onto the dough, creating a very thin twisted edge. Continue pinching and twisting the dough until the entire circle has a wavy edge.

Heat the remaining 2 cups of oil in a wok over a high flame until very hot. (To test the temperature of the oil, submerge the tip of a wooden chopstick; it should produce a cloud of little bubbles. If the chopstick bubbles, drop one pinch of the reserved dough into the oil; it should pop to the surface, bubbling. If it doesn't, wait a couple of minutes and try again with the second pinch.)

Using a perforated scoop or a spider, lower the filled bread into the oil; you can use a pair of chopsticks to help remove it from the scoop. Let the bread fry in the bubbling oil until the bottom is golden brown, then very carefully flip it over. Continue to deep-fry the bread until the other side is also golden brown; it should cook for 2 to 3 minutes total. Remove the fried bread from the wok, draining away any excess oil.

Repeat with the remaining dough and filling. Before serving, cut each bread into six wedges.

Family-Style Cooking in Laza Village

Lanrong Zhancang bends over a small pile of logs and dried leaves, blowing on them to create a fire under the large iron stove where his wife, Jashi Yangzong, will cook dinner. The young couple live in a traditional wood-and-stone Tibetan house in the village of Laza, outside Shangri-la, with Jashi's parents. Jashi works for the government, planting trees, Lanrong has a business driving tourists to local sights, and the two also help out on the family farm. In addition to growing vegetables and raising pigs, cows, and chickens, the family grows wheat and grinds it into flour; processes rapeseed into rich, golden oil; and makes their own fresh cheese and butter. Over the course of the year, the family produces nearly every bit of food they consume, and they often have enough left over to sell at local markets.

Jashi has been doing nearly all the cooking for her family since she was fourteen, and she easily negotiates her way around the wood-fired stove, adding just enough fuel as she goes so that each dish is cooked at the ideal temperature. Strips of fragrant aged yak are fried until crisp and mixed with scallions, chiles, and garlic. Homegrown potatoes are shredded, then turned into a plate-sized pancake seasoned with chiles and Sichuan peppercorns. Local mushrooms and greens are stir-fried until cooked through. As she finishes each dish, Jashi puts it in a metal bowl and sets it on top of the stove to keep warm. She also warms a small bowl of butter mixed with soft sweet-and-sour local cheese, then stirs them together into a dip—a special treat to serve to guests.

While she cooks, her mother, Najie Zhuowu, makes *baba*, a traditional flatbread, to serve with the cheese dip. She gently mixes the family's homemade flour with sour whey left over from cheese making, then rolls out rounds of dough and toasts them in an electric skillet until they puff up slightly and have a crisp crust. When everything is ready, the family sits down to eat at a coffee table surrounded by large, comfortable couches. The dishes are all hot from the stove and perfectly seasoned—the fruits of months of work and centuries of tradition.

clockwise, from top left: The family's dinnerware is kept in a hutch in a corner of the main living room, next to the wood-fired stove where Jashi cooks meals. To prepare vegetables like chrysanthemum greens and amaranth greens, Jashi takes them outside to the enclosed yard in front of the house to wash them with a hose. She then trims and peels the vegetables before bringing them back inside (see recipe, page 104). Rich, flavorful fried yak meat is served with fresh lettuce (see recipe, page 94). Water offering bowls stacked by the fire. Lanrong and Jashi pose outside their front gate.

炸牛肉

Fried Beef with Fresh Lettuce

This rich dish (pictured on page 93) is popular around Shangri-la. The meat is cut into strips and fried until it is dense and chewy, almost like a flavorful jerky, then served with fresh leaves of lettuce. Like most dishes in the region, this is traditionally made with yak meat; if using yak meat, skip the step of marinating the meat in soy sauce.

1½ lbs. lean cut of beef, such as top sirloin

1 tbsp. + 4 tsp. light soy sauce

4 cups vegetable oil

4 scallions, white and light green parts only, smashed with the side of a cleaver and cut at an angle into thin slices

2 garlic cloves, thinly sliced

10 dried Thai chiles, cut crosswise into ¾-inch pieces

¼ tsp. dried ground chile

½ tsp. Sichuan Peppercorn Powder (page 274)

6 large lettuce leaves (preferrably Green Leaf)

Cut the beef into strips approximately ¼ inch thick. (The easiest way to do this is by pulling the meat away from the knife slightly with one hand while slicing with the other hand so that there is tension between the knife and the meat. You will have about 3 cups.) If the slices are more than 4 inches long, cut them in half crosswise. Put the beef into a small bowl, sprinkle with 1 tbsp. of the soy sauce, and mix well. Set the meat aside to marinate for 10 to 15 minutes. While the meat marinates, stack the lettuce leaves in layers on one side of a serving plate.

In a wok, heat the oil over a high flame until very hot. (To test the temperature of the oil, submerge the tip of a wooden chopstick; it should produce a strong cloud of little bubbles. If the chopstick bubbles, drop a tiny piece of the meat into the oil; it should pop to the surface, bubbling.) Use a spider to carefully put all the meat into the oil; the oil should bubble vigorously. Fry the meat, pushing it back and forth with the spider constantly, until the pieces no longer stick to one another, then stirring every couple of minutes, for a total of 10 minutes. The meat should be extremely well done, browned, and chewy. Remove the meat from the oil, drain, transfer it to a bowl, and mix in the remaining 4 tsp. soy sauce.

Set aside 2 tsp. of the sliced scallions to use as garnish; put the remaining scallions, the garlic, and the dried chiles into a fine-mesh sieve or spider. Lower the sieve into the oil and fry the aromatics, stirring a bit with chopsticks, for 1 minute. Remove the sieve from the oil, drain the aromatics, put them on top of the meat along with the chile powder and Sichuan Peppercorn Powder, and mix everything together. Just before serving, arrange the meat mixture next to the lettuce on the plate and top it with the reserved scallion. The meat is best eaten wrapped in a bit of lettuce.

香格里拉式炒香菇

Stir-Fried Shiitakes with Chiles and Sichuan Peppercorns

Mushrooms grow wild throughout Yunnan's mountainous areas, and many of the most famous ones come from the northern part of the province. In summer, when mushroom growth is at its peak, foragers move into little wooden shacks built along the sides of the area's main roads so that they can spend the day searching for mushrooms and then sell their finds to middlemen who travel along the road, buying up the day's haul to sell to international distributors.

This recipe for stir-fried shiitakes (pictured on page 97) comes from home cook Jashi Yangzong. Her recipe includes dried chiles and Sichuan peppercorns—traditional Yunnan flavorings—and a bit of butter, a notably Tibetan touch that gives the whole dish a luxurious, silky texture.

¾ lb. shiitake mushrooms (6 cups)

¼ cup vegetable oil

10 dried Thai chiles, broken in half

1 garlic clove, roughly chopped

1 to 1½ tsp. salt

½ tsp. dried ground chile

½ tsp. Sichuan Peppercorn Powder (page 274)

½ tbsp. butter

Thoroughly wash the mushrooms; then, working with one at a time, squeeze each mushroom gently to release any excess water, trim the hard end of its stem, and pull it apart lengthwise, first splitting it in half and then dividing it into wedges measuring ¾ inch to 2 inches across at the widest point of the cap. (For the best results, start pulling the mushrooms apart at their stems; ideally many pieces will have both cap and stem.)

In a wok, heat the oil over a high flame until very hot. Add the dried chiles, garlic, and mushrooms and stir-fry for 30 seconds, stirring and flipping frequently. Cover the wok with a lid, reduce the heat to medium, and continue to cook for 3 minutes, stirring occasionally. Uncover the wok, add 1 tsp. of the salt, the ground chile, and the Sichuan Peppercorn Powder, mix the ingredients together, then re-cover the wok and cook the mixture for about 10 minutes, stirring occasionally, until tender. If the mushrooms don't release much moisture as they cook, add a bit of water or broth to the pan halfway through cooking. And if the mushrooms release a lot of liquid, remove the wok lid halfway through cooking and let it bubble away. Turn off the heat and add the butter to the mushroom mixture. Mix until the butter has melted and coated all the mushrooms, then remove everything from the wok.

Potato Pancake
with Chile Powder

土豆饼

The potatoes grown in Yunnan are things of beauty. Some have deep-purple skin and and starburst patterns in their flesh; many have a rich, almost buttery flavor, and they are all shockingly good stir-fried with just a bit of salt and dried chile. Cooks all over the province also use these potatoes to make a wonderful dinner plate–sized pancake. In the absence of Yunnan's potatoes, the pancake can be made with any low-starch, flavorful potatoes. When cooked, the edges of the pancake will be crisp, but the center will remain soft and pliant. (When frying this pancake, make sure your wok is well seasoned so that the potato won't stick.) When the pancake is finished, it is usually topped with bits of chives and smoky dried ground chile, but some cooks prefer to mix these ingredients into the potato before cooking. Both versions are delicious.

1¼ lbs. (2 to 3 medium-size) low-starch all-purpose potatoes, such as Yukon gold

1 tsp. salt

½ cup vegetable oil

2 tsp. dried ground chile with a pinch of paprika added

1½ tsp. sesame seeds

2 tsp. finely sliced chives

Wash and peel the potatoes, setting them aside in a bowl of cool water as you work to keep them from browning. Using a mandoline or a grater, shred the potatoes into strips approximately ⅛ inch wide. (You will have about 3 cups of potato.) Sprinkle the salt onto the shredded potatoes, mix them together with your hands, and let sit for 5 minutes. (If you'd like to mix the ground chile, sesame seeds, and chives into the potatoes, add them after the potato rests.)

In a wok, heat the oil over a high flame until very hot. Pour the potato mixture into the wok, and use a wok spatula to flatten it into an even disk along the bottom and sides of the wok. (The pancake should be about 11 inches in diameter.) Cook the potatoes over medium heat for approximately 10 minutes, running the spatula along the bottom of the pan once or twice to ensure they're not sticking.

When the potato shreds are no longer raw and the bottom of the pancake has turned gold, increase the heat to high and cook the pancake until the bottom potatoes have begun to crisp, about 2 minutes. Carefully flip the pancake over. (If it comes apart while flipping, or you need to flip it in

(recipe continues)

two pieces, use the spatula to mash it back together.) Continue to cook over high heat for 3 to 5 minutes, until the other side of the pancake is golden brown and crisp.

Carefully slide or flip the pancake onto a large plate, draining away the excess oil. Sprinkle the pancake with the ground chile and sesame seeds, then top with the chives (if they haven't been mixed into the potatoes). Use the back of a spoon to press the toppings into the potatoes. Before serving, cut the pancake into chessboard-like square pieces.

Christianity Comes to Yunnan

The square brick steeple of the Cizong Catholic Church rises high above the homes in the rural town of Cizong. The building is a mix of Western and local styles, with high arched windows and decorative Ionian columns on the façade and a swooping Chinese-style tile roof crowning the tower. Inside, the walls of the sanctuary are painted with curly Chinese and Tibetan designs, and pictures of saints hang on the walls.

The congregants of the Cizong church are Tibetan, Naxi, and Nu Catholics, from groups that were originally converted to Christianity by French and Swiss missionaries who came to Yunnan in the mid-nineteenth and early twentieth centuries. The first was Père Charles Renou, who managed to disguise himself as a Chinese merchant and spend two years at Dongzhulin Monastery, ingratiating himself with local religious leaders. Renou established a church in Bonga, just over the border in Tibet, and another church in Weixi, Yunnan (a version of which still stands), but after a few years the church in Bonga was burned by local Buddhist leaders who expelled Renou and the priests with him from the region. In the next half decade, a number of other churches were established, but priests were still often harassed (and sometimes killed), and in 1905 Tibetan lamas destroyed churches and murdered priests in a concerted campaign to drive them from the area. Despite these setbacks, Catholic missionaries continued to make inroads in the region until the Communist revolution, converting many locals, building churches, and also planting small vineyards of wine grapes that would eventually serve as the foundation for Yunnan's new commercial wineries (page 105).

Other Western Christian groups also sent missionaries to Yunnan to convert the local minorities. The Protestant missionary James Fraser, of the British China Inland Mission, arrived in 1910 and converted many Lisu. Around the same time, English Methodists and missionaries from the Free Church of Scotland began baptizing the Miao. And in the southwest, many Jingpo (and the Kachin in Burma) became Baptists after Dr. Ola Hansen, an American minister, developed a written language for the Kachin and then translated the Bible for them. The missionary tradition continues in Yunnan today, with groups sending doctors and aid workers to impoverished areas to help with community health initiatives or to tackle local infrastructure projects.

Oyster Mushrooms with Sichuan Peppercorn Oil

炒平菇

Mushrooms of all kinds respond wonderfully to seasoning with Sichuan peppercorn oil, soaking up the flavor, which marries perfectly with their savory woodiness. Oyster mushrooms, which have a very delicate flavor of their own, are a particularly good canvas for the oil. This recipe adds red bell pepper to the mushrooms, but the cook at the Dali Special Clothing Restaurant in Benzilan, who makes this dish, says that it is included just for color and can be omitted if you're not concerned with presentation.

8 oz. oyster mushrooms (3½ cups)

¼ cup vegetable oil

½ oz. fresh pork fat (from fresh pork belly or bacon), roughly chopped (1 tbsp.)

¼ cup diced red bell pepper

3 scallions, white and light green parts only, cut into ½-inch pieces

1 garlic clove, minced

½ tsp. salt

¼ tsp. dried ground chile

2 tsp. Sichuan Peppercorn Oil (page 277)

Thoroughly wash the mushrooms, then, working with one at a time, squeeze each mushroom gently to release excess water, and pull it apart lengthwise into wedges measuring ¾ inch to 2 inches across at the widest point of the cap. (For the best results, start pulling the mushrooms apart at their stems; ideally many pieces will have both cap and stem. You will have about 2 cups, depending on the size and shape of the mushrooms.)

Heat the oil and pork fat in a wok over a high flame until the pork fat shrinks and crisps, about 2 minutes. Add the mushrooms and bell pepper and stir-fry, stirring and tossing frequently, for 1 minute. Add 2 tbsp. of water and continue to stir-fry for another minute. Add the remaining ingredients and stir-fry until everything is cooked through, about 1 minute.

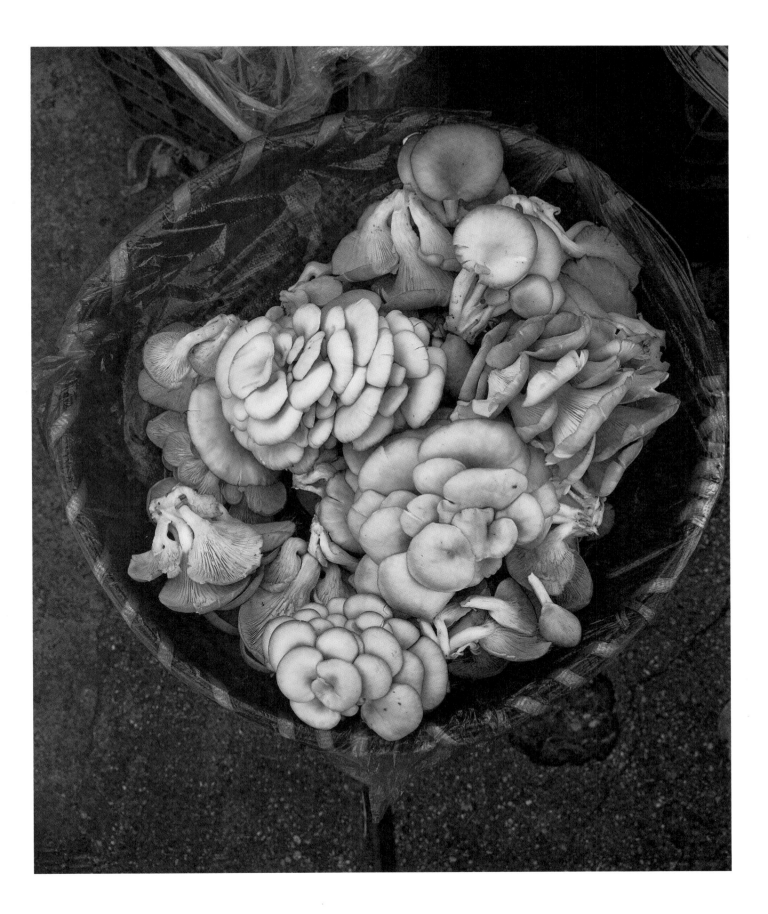

炒皇帝菜

Stir-Fried Chrysanthemum Greens with Chile

Lacy chrysanthemum greens are a popular vegetable throughout Asia. The greens, which come from the garland chrysanthemum (*Glebionis coronaria*), have a uniquely wonderful flavor that is somewhat similar to celery leaves and can be eaten raw, in a Chrysanthemum Greens Salad (page 244), or cooked, as they are in this recipe. In Asian markets they are usually found labeled "crown daisy," "*tongho*," "*shinguku*," or "*ssukgat*." This way of preparing them—with garlic, Sichuan peppercorn powder, and two kinds of dried chiles—comes from Jashi Yangzong (page 92), who cooks them in oil left over from frying meat to give the greens a little added flavor.

3 tbsp. vegetable oil

3 garlic cloves, smashed with the side of a cleaver and roughly chopped

9 cups chrysanthemum greens, cut crosswise into 1¼-inch pieces, with stems thicker than ⅓ inch removed (1 lb.)

5 dried Thai chiles, broken in half

1 tsp. salt

1 tsp. dried ground chile

1 tsp. Sichuan Peppercorn Powder (page 274)

Boil about 1 cup of water in a kettle or small pot and set it aside. In a wok, heat the oil over a high flame until very hot. Add the garlic, stir once, then add the chrysanthemum greens and stir and flip a couple of times. Add the dried chiles and sprinkle in the salt, chile powder, and Sichuan Peppercorn Powder. Stir and flip just to mix, then add ⅓ cup of the hot water. Cook the greens, without stirring (unless anything begins to burn), until tender, 2 to 3 minutes. Transfer to a serving bowl and drain away any excess water.

¼ cup vegetable oil

3 garlic cloves, smashed with the side of a cleaver and roughly chopped

9 cups amaranth greens (½ lb.)

5 dried Thai chiles, broken in half

1 tsp. salt

1 tsp. dried ground chile

1 tsp. Sichuan Peppercorn Powder (page 274)

AMARANTH GREENS VARIATION

With just a few adjustments to the cooking method, this dish can be made with amaranth greens (or other tender leafy greens, such as spinach). Beautiful red-veined amaranth leaves lose their dramatic color when they're cooked, but the reddish hue seeps into the cooking oil, leaving a lovely pool of light-pink liquid on the plate.

In a wok, heat the oil over a high flame until very hot. Add the garlic, stir once, then add the amaranth greens and stir and flip a couple of times. Add the chiles, and sprinkle in the salt, chile powder, and Sichuan Peppercorn Powder. Stir-fry, stirring and flipping frequently, until the greens are thoroughly wilted and cooked through, 2 to 3 minutes. Transfer to a serving bowl.

From Ancient Vines to Modern Wines

China's young wine industry is starting to find its feet. Wine grapes are cultivated in at least fifteen different provinces, and leading French beverage companies have established vineyards in the country. But Yunnan's winemakers have a long history to call on to help market their beverages' unique terroir. Winemaking in Yunnan goes back over 100 years, when French and Swiss missionaries first planted grapes here to make communion wines. (Historical records show that some Tibetans also made wine from grapes in areas north of Yunnan five centuries earlier.) Though the priests taught only the locals who worked as their assistants to make wine, and many of the vines were pulled out after the revolution to make room for other crops, some of the grapes the missionaries planted survived.

These grapes, used by local vintners to make a sweet, light red wine, are called Rose Honey and are unknown outside Yunnan. Some experts think they may come from a varietal that was wiped out by *phylloxera* in France, while others think they were probably brought to the region long after Europe's *phylloxera* crisis or came from a different part of the world altogether. According to biologists at the University of California, Davis, the grapes may be a varietal that was planted in the eighteenth century throughout New England, where it was known as "Isabella."

Winemakers in Yunnan also plant cabernet sauvignon, cabernet franc, chardonnay, and vidal blanc. One winery even produces a sweet ice wine in the area just below the famed peaks of Meili Snow Mountain with cabernet and local grapes that are left to age and wrinkle until the mountain cold freezes them on the vine, giving them an intense sweetness and a heady flavor.

Chicken and Chestnut Soup

板栗炖鸡汤

The valleys around the town of Weixi, 50 miles west of Shangri-la, feel like little wedges of paradise—lush, sunny slivers tucked deep in the ridges of the Yunling Mountains, between the Jinsha and Lancang Rivers. The Lisu, Nu, and Pumi villagers in the region raise nearly everything they need on their small, fertile farms and gather honey from local bees to sell at market.

This rich soup combines free-range chicken with chestnuts, which give the broth a uniquely rich, sweet flavor, and is usually made at parties so that guests can help peel the chestnuts as the soup begins to simmer. This version of the dish comes from a Weixi native known as He Ayi, or "Auntie He." To make the soup, He carefully chooses chestnuts that are relatively easy to peel—such as Italian chestnuts, whose inner skins aren't as firmly attached to the meat of the nut—and dries them in the sun for a couple of days to loosen the shells. While her guests shell the nuts, He sears the chicken in a wok, then cooks the meat and chestnuts in a rice cooker.

2 black cardamom pods

2½ lbs. chicken, cut across the bone into 2-inch pieces

2 tbsp. salt

2 lbs. small raw Italian chestnuts, shelled (4½ cups; see shelling methods, next page)

Using the side of a cleaver, smack the cardamom pods until they begin to split, then break them up into 3 to 4 pieces each with your hands. (If they're very hard, cut them open instead.) Place them in a wok and toast them over high heat, stirring occasionally, for 2 minutes, until they are very fragrant. Add the chicken and cook, flipping the meat occasionally and spreading it out along the bottom and sides of the wok so that it sears evenly, for 5 minutes, until the pieces have just begun to brown. Transfer the chicken and cardamom to a large soup pot.

Add 2 cups of water to the wok and use it to scrape up any browned bits from the side and bottom, then add it to the pot. Add the salt and 6 more cups of water to the pot and bring it to a boil over high heat. Cover the pot with a lid and simmer the soup over a very low flame, without stirring, for 30 minutes.

Add the chestnuts to the pot, stir to mix them with the chicken, then re-cover the pot and continue to simmer for another 45 minutes. (Add a little water if needed to cover all the ingredients.) Before serving, check

(recipe continues)

one of the chestnuts to make sure it is cooked and tender all the way through, and simmer for a few more minutes if necessary.

SHELLING CHESTNUTS

Boiling Method:

Using a small, sharp knife, cut a tiny X in the shell of each chestnut (to keep the nuts from exploding while they are cooking). Fill a large pot halfway with water and bring it to a boil. Add the chestnuts to the water and boil them for 10 minutes to soften the shells and skins. Turn off the heat, but leave the chestnuts in the water to keep them hot.

Remove one or two chestnuts at a time from the water and peel them as soon as they are cool enough to handle, discarding both the shells and the fibrous skin. The hotter the nuts are, the easier they will be to peel; you may want to use a dish towel to hold them so that they can be peeled before they cool. If the skins will not peel off easily, try rubbing them with the towel.

If the chestnuts don't peel easily, turn the heat back on under the pot and boil the nuts for another few minutes, testing one or two occasionally to see if they are ready. If the chestnuts peel easily but a few of them won't shed their inner skins, set those nuts aside and boil them, without the outer shells, for a minute or two, then try again to peel the skins.

Microwave Method:

Using a small, sharp knife, cut a tiny X in the shell of each chestnut (to keep the nuts from exploding while they are cooking). Working with a few chestnuts at a time, set them on a microwave-safe dish and microwave them in 30-second intervals. Check the chestnuts after each interval to see if the shells and fibrous skin can be peeled off.

Remove the chestnuts from the microwave and peel them as soon as they are cool enough to handle, discarding both the shells and the fibrous skin. The hotter the nuts are, the easier they will be to peel; you may want to use a dish towel to hold them so that they can be peeled before they cool. If the skins will not peel off easily, try rubbing them with the towel.

Repeat with the remaining nuts. If the chestnuts peel easily but a few of them won't shed their inner skins, set those nuts aside and microwave them for 10 to 15 seconds, then try again to peel the skins.

Northern-Style Cucumbers with Vinegar and Chile

维西凉拌黄瓜

This variation on the classic Chinese dish of cucumbers in vinegar comes from He Ayi, a cook from the Weixi Valley (page 107). The cucumber is dressed with a generous scoop of dried chile flakes and a few Sichuan peppercorns heated in oil until fragrant; then the chiles' heat is offset with dark vinegar, soy sauce, and a hint of sugar.

2 cucumbers, preferably bumpy-skinned Chinese cucumbers or thin English "seedless" cucumbers

2 tsp. salt, plus more to taste

1-inch-square piece of rock sugar or 1 tsp. granulated sugar

¼ cup dried chile flakes

¼ tsp. whole Sichuan peppercorns

¼ cup vegetable oil

2 tbsp. Zhenjiang vinegar

2 tsp. light soy sauce

Peel the cucumbers, then smash them with the flat side of a cleaver and cut them into 1½-inch chunks. In a medium bowl, mix the cucumbers with the salt. Let them sit for 15 minutes, stirring occasionally.

Scatter the sugar on top of the cucumbers. Place the chile flakes and Sichuan peppercorns in a small heatproof bowl. Heat the vegetable oil in a wok over a high flame until it is smoking, then pour half of the oil into the bowl with the chiles and the other half onto the cucumbers.

Stir the chile mixture, then add it and the vinegar and soy sauce to the cucumbers and mix well. Taste and add a little more salt if needed.

Lijiang "Baba" Filled Flatbreads

Lijiang's most famous food is a flatbread known as *baba*. But *baba*, which is served as a hearty breakfast, is a type of food, not a specific recipe. The *baba* found in Lijiang Old Town and the surrounding plain range from thin, fried flatbreads served as part of a larger meal to thick disks filled with layers of minced ham, flavored with a thick paste made from rendered lard, and fried in oil.

This simple but hearty version—a thick bread filled with layers of meat or nuts and cooked on a flat griddle with only a minimum amount of oil—is inspired by the one made by Xi He, a Naxi woman who has been selling her *baba* from a small table on the streets of Old Town for fifteen years. Like most cooks in Lijiang, Xi uses a bit of the previous day's dough as a starter, and over the years, her *baba* has developed a complex flavor, similar to a mild sourdough. This version is leavened with yeast but has a small amount of yogurt worked in to give it a more complex flavor. (The same dough can be used to make small flatbreads for Naxi sandwiches; see page 115.) It can be filled with salty ham or a mixture of flavorful beef and scallions, as are Xi's popular *baba*, or with a sweet combination of nuts and sugar that is also popular in the area. **Makes four baba.**

⅓ cup plain yogurt

1 tsp. active dry yeast

3 cups all-purpose flour, plus more for dusting

1 cup pastry flour

Beef, ham, or nut and sugar filling (see methods on pages 112–113)

Chile sauce (*lajiao jiang*) (optional)

Vegetable oil, for cooking

EQUIPMENT:

Dumpling rolling pin or wooden dowel (page 22)

In a large bowl, mix the yogurt and yeast with 1¾ cups of lukewarm water and stir until the yeast is dissolved and the liquid is well-mixed. Add 2 cups of the all-purpose flour and stir until everything is incorporated into a sticky mass. Let the dough rest in a warm place, covered with plastic wrap, for 1 hour.

Add the remaining 1 cup all-purpose flour and the pastry flour to the dough and stir to incorporate. Flour a clean work surface and knead the dough, continuing to incorporate flour as needed so that the dough has a sticky texture but doesn't come off in clumps on your hands (this can mean adding ¼ cup of flour or even a bit more, depending on the weather and how your dough has risen). Knead for 5 minutes, until the dough is fairly smooth, then put it back into the bowl, cover with plastic wrap, and set aside to rise until it has doubled in size, about 2 to 3 hours.

(recipe continues)

Pull the dough away from the side of the bowl and knead it lightly so that it deflates. Divide the dough into quarters.

Heat a large cast-iron pan over a low flame. Lightly oil a work surface with a bit of vegetable oil, and oil a dumpling rolling pin or wooden dowel, letting the oil also coat your hands. Take one quarter of the dough and roll it out on the oiled work surface into a long, thin oval—the dough will be very springy and bounce back; keep rolling until you have an oval about 20 inches long and 6 inches wide. Top the dough with one portion of your chosen filling (see below), distributing the ingredients evenly and pressing them gently into the dough. Starting at one of the short ends, roll the dough up into a tight spiral, then stand the spiral on its end and press it down with your hands to form a circle with the filling rolled up like a spiral. Press the spiral into a flat circle with the palm of your hand, then use the rolling pin to flatten the circle until it measures about 9 inches across, flipping the circle over once as you roll.

Coat the pan with a light film of vegetable oil and put the filled dough into the pan. Cover the pan with a wok lid and cook the bread, flipping it once or twice and re-covering it, until it is browned on both sides and the edges look completely cooked through, about 8 to 10 minutes for the nut filling, 10 to 12 minutes for the ham, and 12 to 15 minutes for the beef. Cut each baba into quarters and serve hot with a bit of chile sauce to spread on top, if desired.

Beef Filling

8½ oz. ground or finely chopped beef (scant 1 cup)

1 tbsp. vegetable oil

1½ tsp. light soy sauce

7½ tbsp. fragrant chile sauce (*xiangla jiang*)

1 tsp. salt

1 tsp. Sichuan Peppercorn Powder (page 274)

4 tbsp. very thinly sliced scallions, white and light green parts only

Set aside 4 tbsp. of the meat to use raw in the baba. In a wok, heat the oil over a high flame until very hot. Break up the remaining beef with a fork and add it to the wok. Stir-fry the meat, breaking it up with a wok spatula, until it is cooked through, 1 to 2 minutes. Add the soy sauce and fragrant chile sauce to the meat and stir-fry, stirring and flipping frequently, until the ingredients are well mixed, 2 to 3 minutes; use the back of a wok shovel to smash the beans in the chile sauce against the side of the wok so that they become part of the sauce. Remove the meat and sauce from the wok, draining off the excess oil, and let the mixture cool to room temperature before using.

Fill each baba with ¼ tsp. of salt, a large pinch of the Sichuan Peppercorn Powder, 3 tbsp. of the cooked meat mixture, 1 tbsp. of the raw beef, and 1 tbsp. of the sliced scallions.

Ham Filling

2¼ oz. Yunnan ham or Spanish Jamón Serrano, with very little fat on it, rind removed

Sweet Nut and Sesame Filling

½ cup raw walnuts

¼ cup raw peanuts

2 tbsp. black sesame seeds

2 tbsp. sugar

Cut the ham into small dice; you should have ½ cup. Fill each baba with ¼ of the ham.

Toast the walnuts and peanuts together in a hot cast-iron pan, stirring constantly, until the nuts are fragrant and a little brown on all sides, 1½ to 2 minutes. Using a mortar and pestle or a small food processor, crush and grind the nuts, sesame seeds, and sugar into a fine powder. Fill each baba with ¼ of the mixture (a little less than ¼ cup).

藏式牛肉面

Tibetan Noodle Soup

This classic combination of hand-torn noodles, beef broth, and bright vegetables, which is called *thenthuk* in Tibetan, has become a staple in Shangri-la and is served at many restaurants in Old Town. This version comes from Lhasa Restaurant (page 84), where the noodles are made from the same soft wheat dough that's used for the restaurant's dumpling wrappers. The thick noodles simmer in the broth until they are both tender and springy and have absorbed the meat's rich flavor. This version of the soup also includes a handful of very thin rice noodles, which have a smooth, slick texture and contrast nicely with the wheat noodles. **Makes four to six servings.**

1 recipe All-Purpose Tibetan Dough (page 275)

3 tbsp. vegetable oil

1 yellow onion, diced

2 garlic cloves, roughly chopped

2 cups diced tomato

½ lb. meat left over from making the Beef Broth (page 280), sinews discarded, torn into bite-sized pieces (2 cups)

10 cups Beef Broth (page 280)

2 tbsp. light soy sauce

2½ oz. yu choy or choi sum leaves (about 24 leaves) or other Chinese leafy greens, stems cut into 1½-inch pieces, leaves cut into ½-inch-wide slices (3 cups)

1 cup cooked rice vermicelli (from about 2⅔ oz. of dried noodles)

1 bunch of chives, sliced into ½-inch pieces (3 tbsp.)

EQUIPMENT:

Dumpling rolling pin or wooden dowel (page 22)

Divide the prepared dough into quarters and roll each into a ball. Working on a lightly floured surface, flatten the balls into disks, then use a dumpling rolling pin or wooden dowel to roll them out until the dough is ⅛ inch thick (the circles will be about 7 inches in diameter).

Heat the vegetable oil in a large wok or pot over high heat for 1 minute, then add the onion, garlic, tomato, and meat and cook, stirring and flipping frequently, until the onion is cooked through, 2 minutes. Add the broth and the soy sauce to the wok.

While the broth is heating, cut the circles of dough into strips 1 inch wide. When the broth comes to a boil, add the yu choy, then start tearing the noodles: working with one strip of dough at a time, stretch it slightly to make it a tiny bit thinner, then tear it into 1- to 2-inch-long pieces and toss them into the broth. Repeat until all the noodles are in the wok.

Continue to cook the soup, stirring occasionally, until all the noodles are cooked through, 3 to 5 minutes, then add the rice noodles and simmer for 30 seconds to warm them through. Divide the soup among serving bowls and top each with the chives.

Naxi Sandwich

纳西三明治

⅓ recipe of dough for Lijiang "Baba" (page 110) or 2 very fresh pieces of pita bread

1 tbsp. vegetable oil

1½ cups all-purpose potatoes, such as Yukon gold, peeled and shredded on a mandoline

1 tsp. salt

2 slices buffalo mozzarella, each about ½ inch thick and cut along the length of the ball so that the slices are as long as possible (if your ball of mozzarella is less than 4 inches long, use 2 additional half slices)

3 slices of ripe, flavorful tomato, each about ½ inch thick and cut along the length of the tomato so that the slices are as long as possible (if your slices are less than 3 inches long, use 2 additional slices)

Chile sauce (*lajiao jiang*) (optional)

EQUIPMENT:

Dumpling rolling pin or wooden dowel (page 22)

Baisha Village, half an hour south of Lijiang, is a beautiful Naxi town on a wide, fertile plain. This was the original home of the Mu family, the Naxi Dynasty that ruled an enormous area of northern Yunnan on behalf of the Chinese imperial government for nineteen generations as an officially designated *tusi*, or "local chief." The Mu family eventually moved to Lijiang and built a mansion there, and Baisha remained a small farming settlement.

Baisha is now a tourist town, but it is also a thriving local community and is much quieter and more laid-back than Lijiang. It is a lovely place to spend a day admiring local architecture, watching master artisans work in embroidery workshops, and browsing in stores that sell old odds and ends like small teapots or carved wooden screens, along with woven shawls and costume jewelry.

The recipe for this delicious sandwich-like dish, made with *baba* bread, a thatch of fried potato, creamy local cheese, and flavorful tomato, comes from the restaurant of Baisha Times Guesthouse, a popular spot in the center of town that offers an English menu for tourists but still cooks dishes with a decidedly local flavor. Featuring a soft yak cheese whose texture is similar to very creamy mozzarella, the sandwich is seasoned with a chile sauce called *zhu gan zha* that combines local Qiubei chiles and meat from preserved pork ribs. The restaurant also prepares its own *baba* to order on a large, flat cast-iron pan; if you don't want to take the time to make the dough and shape the bread, high-quality pita toasted until soft and golden is an excellent substitute. These quantities will make two sandwiches, which is enough for four small servings.

If making the bread, wipe a bit of oil on a clean work surface and on a dumpling rolling pin or wooden dowel. Divide the dough into two softball-sized handfuls and roll them into balls. Use the rolling pin to roll each ball into a thin circle about 8 inches in diameter.

Heat a large cast-iron pan over medium heat, place the pieces of dough on the pan, and cover with a wok lid. Cook the dough until a few brown spots appear on the bottom and parts of the dough have puffed up,

(recipe continues)

about 2 minutes. Flip the dough, sprinkle 1 tsp. or so of water into the pan, and re-cover the wok with the lid. Continue cooking until the baba are cooked through and toasty on both sides, another 2 minutes. Remove the baba from the pan, cut each piece in half (into two half-circles), and set aside.

Alternatively, if using pita, heat a cast-iron pan over high heat and toast the pita until both sides are slightly blistered and browned. Remove the pita from the pan, cut them into two half-circles, and set aside.

Add the vegetable oil to the pan and swirl it to coat the surface, then reduce the heat to medium-high. In a bowl, mix the shredded potato with the salt, divide it into two large clumps, and put them into the pan, keeping them a few inches apart so that they won't stick together. Cook until the potatoes are browned and crispy on the bottom, about 2 to 4 minutes, then flip them. While the potatoes are browning on the second side, heat the slices of cheese in the pan just until they begin to melt, about 20 seconds, then put them on top of the cooking clumps of potato.

When the potatoes have browned on the second side, put the stacks of potato and cheese onto two halves of the baba (or pita). Top each stack with a slice (or two) of tomato, spread a bit of chile sauce (if using) onto the two remaining pieces of baba, and top the sandwiches with them. Cut each sandwich in half and serve.

All The Cheese in China

Outside the entrance to the food market on Long March Avenue, in Shangri-la, a young woman in a traditional Tibetan head-wrap and a blue down vest sits at a low table under a striped umbrella. On the table is a beautiful array of cone-shaped cheeses. Some are fresh with bumpy white rinds and have a soft, creamy texture and a flavor that is somehow both sour and sweet. Others have been set over a wood fire and smoked; their rinds range from lightly toasted to a rich, deep brown, and the cheese inside is much firmer, best cut into irregular chunks with a sharp knife.

For centuries, most Chinese people have avoided dairy products; cheese, especially, was seen as foreign, something only European "barbarians" ate. But in many parts of Yunnan, where minorities have cultivated their own food traditions and taboos, cheese is a prized ingredient. Just south of Shangri-la, in Lijiang, cooks cut thick slices of creamy mozzarella-like cheese to eat between slices of flatbread with shredded potato and fresh tomato. Farther south, in Dali, Bai cooks prepare a firmer cow's-milk cheese into *rushan*, or "milk fans," thin slices that are stretched, wrapped around sticks, then dried until they are firm and can be toasted over coals and spread with rose petal jam. And in Kunming, restaurants offer funky goat's-milk *ru bing* ("milk cakes") stir-fried with vegetables.

香肠炒花椒

Stir-Fried Sausage with Sichuan Peppercorn

Life is quiet at Hongpo, a Tibetan monastery high in the mountains of northern Yunnan. A few dozen monks live here, praying and working in traditional two-story Tibetan homes with brightly painted roof beams and a fresh coat of white paint on the walls. When they look out across the mountains, they can see Kawakarpo, one of Tibetan Buddhism's most sacred peaks. A few miles below the monastery, down a winding narrow road, is a tiny town where pilgrims stop to buy bright silk prayer flags and bundles of cedar-scented incense. There is also a little restaurant where a quiet young woman cooks Tibetan-Chinese fusion dishes, like this stir-fry made with a type of sausage that has Sichuan peppercorn powder mixed into the meat.

This sausage is popular with Tibetan nomads across the northern areas of Yunnan and Sichuan. It is used in soups, added to hot pots, or stir-fried, as it is in this dish. While it is not available outside China, you can substitute Spanish chorizo, which has a similar flavor and texture; a dusting of freshly ground Sichuan peppercorns added as the sausage cooks will give the dish its distinctive flavor.

1½ cups vegetable oil

½ lb. Spanish (dry-cured) chorizo, cut at an angle into very thin, long slices (about 1¾ cups)

4 scallions, white and light green parts only, cut crosswise into 1-inch pieces

¼ green bell pepper, seeded and cut into ⅓-inch-wide strips

½ tsp. Sichuan Peppercorn Powder (page 274)

In a wok, heat the oil over a high flame until very hot. (To test the temperature of the oil, submerge the tip of a wooden chopstick; it should produce a cloud of little bubbles.) Carefully add the chorizo and deep-fry, stirring occasionally, until the meat is well cooked and the slices are curling up into crescents, about 3 minutes. Remove the chorizo and oil from the wok, ideally by pouring everything through a strainer or perforated scoop set over a metal bowl; set the drained chorizo aside.

Add 2 tbsp. of the oil back into the wok and stir-fry the scallions and bell pepper over high heat, stirring and tossing constantly, until they are tender and beginning to brown slightly, about 1 minute. Add the chorizo back into the wok and sprinkle with the Sichuan Peppercorn Powder. Stir-fry, mixing the ingredients well so that the peppercorn powder is evenly distributed, for 1 minute. Transfer to a serving plate.

鱼香茄子

Eggplant with Garlic and Chiles

The restaurant of the Tibetan Family Inn sits perched on the edge of the road in the tiny village of Shu Song. From the dining room, guests can look out over the village's small fields and vegetable plots, where the inn's owner grows nearly all the food she serves. Most visitors to the restaurant are long-distance cyclists who ride from Lijiang or Shangri-la all the way to Lhasa, a strenuous trip through high mountain passes that takes at least twenty-one days to complete.

The Chinese name for this dish translates to "fish-fragrant eggplant," a term that is used to describe eggplants cooked with the same spices that local cooks would use when cooking fish. This version is flavored with mild fresh chiles and just a hint of soy sauce.

3 Asian eggplants, each about 14 inches long

1 tbsp. salt

¼ cup vegetable oil

1 Anaheim chile, de-stemmed, seeded, and cut into ½-inch squares

2 tsp. light soy sauce

8 garlic cloves, smashed with the side of a cleaver and roughly chopped

6 thin scallions, white and light green parts only, cut into ½-inch pieces

Peel the eggplants and cut them crosswise into 2-inch pieces, then cut each piece lengthwise into wedges about ½ inch thick at the widest part. Mix the eggplant with the salt, and massage them together for a few seconds to work the salt into the flesh. Let the eggplant sit for 10 minutes, then firmly knead it again, squeezing the wedges to wring out the moisture; set them aside.

In a wok, heat the oil over a high flame until very hot. Add the eggplant, chile, and soy sauce and stir-fry, stirring and flipping frequently, for 1 minute. Add the garlic and cook, stirring and flipping, for 1 minute, then add the scallions and cook one more minute before removing everything from the wok.

凉拌香菇

Dried Mushroom Salad

The recipe for this salad comes from Gaozuo Zhima, a young Mosuo woman who lives near Lugu Lake in a traditional Mosuo household. Like many Mosuo, Gaozuo's family refers to their main living room as the "grandmother's room," and her seventy-two-year-old grandmother sleeps in an alcove to the side of the main hearth, while Gaozuo's mother and aunts and uncles all live in other parts of the house. Gaozuo and her husband, Zhu Wenqing (an entrepreneur originally from Shanghai), also live in the family home. Their large room is organized like a separate apartment, with a sleeping loft and a sitting area, but they share the home's main kitchen, cooking and eating with the rest of the family.

2 oz. sliced dried mushrooms, such as porcinis or shiitakes (about 3½ cups)

7 to 8 tsp. Zhenjiang vinegar

3 to 4 tsp. light soy sauce

2 to 3 tsp. Dried Chile Oil (page 276)

¼ tsp. salt

¼ cup roughly chopped cilantro leaves and stems

Place the dried mushrooms in a medium bowl, add cool water to cover by about 3 inches, and let sit until the mushrooms are softened all the way through, 10 to 20 minutes. Drain the softened mushrooms and squeeze them to remove any excess water. Toss the mushrooms with the smaller amounts of the vinegar, soy sauce, and chiles, then add the salt and cilantro. Taste and add more seasoning if needed. The salad can sit for up to 1 hour before serving.

Southern Yunnan

THE MEKONG RIVER flows slowly through the small city of Jinghong, winding its way toward Yunnan's borders with Myanmar and Laos, just 40 miles or so to the south. Along the banks, thickets of palm and banana trees partially obscure the apartment buildings and shiny new high-rises that make up the capital of Xishuangbanna Dai Autonomous Prefecture. This city feels far more like a part of Southeast Asia than of China. Nearly every building in town nods to the architectural motifs of nearby Laos and Thailand with decorative peaked roofs and curlicues shaped like stylized flowers or peacock feathers. Even the roofs of covered bus stops are topped with golden tiles that look like peacock heads.

Lush trees and enormous flowering hibiscus plants line streets full of electric bikes, tuk-tuks, and imported cars that hurry past small hotels built for the tourists who come here to enjoy the tropical climate and explore the local wildlife. At noon the sidewalks are oddly empty as everyone heads indoors to escape the heat and humidity, but by sundown the streets are alive with barbecue restaurants serving fish stuffed with herbs and chiles, squares of tofu wrapped in chives, and small spatchcocked chickens, all cooked over large charcoal grills and served alongside piles of dried beef and piquant salads of raw, thinly shaved eggplant.

The hills surrounding the city are covered in dense subtropical jungle made up of massive clumps of bamboo and tall trees practically smothered in climbing vines. Below, a variety of animals—including endangered species like mouse deer, black bears, and Asian golden cats—roam in protected nature reserves along with wild elephants that sometimes break out of the jungle and storm through nearby farmland, trampling everything in their path.

An hour east of Jinghong, the jungle gives way to neat rows of rubber trees on the hills and small farms and stands of banana trees in the valleys. The villages in the area are a mix of old-style wooden Dai minority houses on

clockwise, from top left: buying squash blossoms in Jinping; crossing the river in Menglun; a vegetable seller in Menghai; eggs for sale at a Hani minority market; roadside fruit stands in Honghe; an Ake minority cook; Xishuangbanna Wild Elephant Valley; Bulang minority women at the market in Menghai

stilts, with double-peaked shingle or corrugated-metal roofs, and more modern versions of the same design built with bricks and faced with colorful tiles. At nearby intersections on the highway, fruit sellers from these towns sit under little lean-tos and sell bright fuchsia dragon fruit, spiky jackfruit, piles of jewel-like mangosteens and rambutans, and four or five different varieties of mangoes.

⌖

The largest ethnic group in this region is the Dai minority. For centuries, Xishuangbanna was an autonomous kingdom ruled by the Dai (known outside China as the Tai), a branch of the ethnic group that populates Laos and Thailand. The kingdom, called Sipsongpanna, was established in the twelfth century, and even after it was conquered by Kublai Khan's army (along with the rest of Yunnan), the local elites continued to govern the region as a relatively autonomous area until the establishment of the People's Republic of China.

The Theravada Buddhist monarchy had a unique social institution called *huoxi*, in which each village in a particular administrative district was responsible for a specific task or service for the monarchy and nobility: one village cooked for the nobility, while a second made clothing, a third maintained boats and ferried people across the river, a fourth raised the ruler's peacocks and elephants, and yet another provided people to blow trumpets during processions.

The Dai are now the third-largest minority in Yunnan, and they are still the most visible group in the south, where their traditions are considered the key to Xishuangbanna's unique culture. The Dai also maintain strong connections with Tai communities in Southeast Asia, and a large percentage of the area's tourists are visitors from Thailand.

⌖

Xishuangbanna's most famous commodity comes from the region's tea mountains, where *pu'er* (or *puerh*) tea grows. Terraces planted with neatly trimmed tea shrubs wind around mountainsides in the western part of the prefecture, and forests hide the ancient trees—some more than 1,000 years old—that produce the most coveted and expensive leaves. *Pu'er* has been produced for over 2,000 years and has always been a prized commodity. It has been popular with royalty, including both Tibetan princesses and Chinese emperors, since the Ming Dynasty, and for centuries it was one of the main commodities traded on the Tea Horse

Road. These days, high-quality *pu'er* has something of a cult following, and the best teas are as sought after (and as expensive) as the world's best wines.

Some of the oldest tea trees may have been planted by the Bulang minority, who have lived in the high-altitude areas where tea flourishes for centuries. The Bulang (or Blang) also live in mountainous areas of Laos, northern Thailand, and Myanmar, but most live in the southwestern part of Xishuangbanna, around Menghai. Bulang in this area have historically had more contact with the lowland Dai than other mountain tribes, and their cultures are very similar, from the construction of their wooden houses to the flavors of their sour, spicy foods. (According to one Bulang legend, they are the older brother of the Dai.)

In recent decades, Bulang farmers who live at lower elevations have planted rubber trees, and their communities have become relatively wealthy. But for those living at altitudes of 1,600 to 2,000 meters above sea level (where rubber will not grow), their connection with tea is still a fundamental part of their identity. Instead of trimming their tea into rows of low bushes, as most producers around the world do, they let the trees grow tall, so that they have to climb up into the branches to pick the prized buds and young leaves. The Bulang drink fresh (*sheng*) *pu'er*, which hasn't been aged, and they also eat sour fermented tea, which is made by cooking the tea, packing it into pieces of bamboo, and burying it in the ground for a couple of months or even years—a technique that is similar to the way pickled tea is made in Burma. The leaves can be eaten on their own or mixed with chile, garlic, and salt.

The Jinuo minority, who live in the mountains around Jinghong, also cultivate tea, but their plantations weren't established until the 1990s, when the government determined that their traditional slash-and-burn agricultural practices were damaging the local environment. The Jinuo are among China's smallest minority groups, with about 22,000 people. According to one of their legends, they were born from the belly of an enormous gourd planted by a brother and sister who were the only people on earth to survive a great flood.

⌒

Xishuangbanna is home to some branches of the Hani minority, including members of the Ake and Akha subgroups who live in rural areas near the Myanmar border, in small villages of traditional wooden houses built on stilts. But the majority of Yunnan's Hani live a few hours to the northeast,

opposite, top to bottom: a shrine among the trees at the Xishuangbanna Tropical Botanical Garden; the Guanyin Cave Temple in Ming Jiu Zhen

below: making pu'er tea from freshly harvested tea leaves on Nannuo Mountain

top to bottom: sliced bananas drying in the sun in Man Hui Suo Village; eating breakfast noodles in Yuanyang

in the Honghe Hani and Yi Autonomous Prefecture. Here, in an area of steep mountains and narrow valleys, they have built one of the most stunning and famous farming landscapes in the world: the Honghe Hani Rice Terraces. These rows of winding terraces stretch for more than 620 miles, rising from the banks of the Hong River almost all the way to the tops of the Ailao Mountains, and some portions have been farmed since the Tang Dynasty, or for roughly 1,300 years.

The Hani have a long history of rice farming—according to Hani myth, rice has existed since the universe was established—and the step terraces take advantage of unusual geographical and meteorological conditions to turn what was once a harsh environment into a productive agricultural system that has scarcely changed for more than a millennium. Because the mountains are so steep, the river valley is hot and dry, while the tops of the mountains are cold; according to a local saying, "One mountain is four seasons at once." As a result, evaporation from the rivers turns to heavy fog at the highest elevations, and the area receives more than 55 inches of rain a year. The mountains, made of sand covered with granite, are uniquely suited to absorb water, and there are enough streams, waterfalls, ponds, and springs to keep the entire system irrigated. The terraces have proven remarkably sustainable, in part because the Hani are very focused on water conservation and in part because they have protected large swaths of water-saving forest at the mountaintops.

The terraces are not entirely populated by Hani (there are Yi villages too), but they make up the majority of people in the area. Farmers grow dozens of varieties of rice, including the region's famous red rices, which are remarkably adaptable to the different climates found on the mountains, require little fertilizer, are unaffected by pests, and produce delicious grains with a reddish-brown hue.

A couple of hours east of the terraces, the city of Mengzi is much more tropical and humid, with flowering trees and swaying palms. Mengzi is best known as the home of Crossing the Bridge Rice Noodles, Yunnan's most famous dish, and the site of the newly discovered bones of the Red Deer Cave people, a prehistoric group of archaic humans similar to Neanderthals. These days the area's main industry is tin mining, and farmers export pomegranates from the two million acres of orchards just to the north of town.

In the late 1800s, the city was one of the most important stops on the narrow-gauge railway line that the French colonial government built from Hanoi to Yunnan in 1888. A handful of bright-yellow French colonial-era buildings can still be found in Mengzi city, but the clearest vestiges of French trade are in the small town of Bisezhai, a few miles north, where a train station was built. The French-constructed buildings, including the station, a customs house, and a small hotel, have been rehabilitated and painted bright gold with green shutters.

The food in Xishuangbanna resembles that of northern Laos; it includes lots of grilled dishes flavored with fresh herbs and searingly spicy chiles, salads made from fresh green papaya, and mashed *larb*-like dishes of minced meat and herbs that are eaten with sticky rice. Near Mengzi, the local foods reflect the region's proximity to Vietnam; the dishes are significantly less spicy than those in Xishuangbanna and are often full of herbs and flavorful wild greens. Local soups, in particular, taste very similar to Vietnamese *pho*, their broth flavored with the distinctive warmth of star anise and the licorice-like notes of fennel seeds. In the mountainous areas just along the Vietnamese border, where small communities of Hani live alongside Miao and Yao minority villagers (see Eastern Yunnan, page 170), smoked meats are also very popular. Restaurants serve slices of peppery smoked pork stir-fried with green chiles and scallions, and at roadside markets old Hani women in traditional blue and black embroidered jackets hang tiny quail on bamboo poles and smoke them all day, constantly replenishing the coals and rotating the birds so that they will be perfectly cooked for any local farmers or travelers who might stop by for a snack.

below: cooking and serving a post-funeral feast in Jinping

Dai Grilled Chicken with Herbs

傣味烤鸡

2- to 3½-lb. whole chicken, ideally with the head still attached

1 tbsp. + 1 tsp. salt

½ cup roughly chopped cilantro leaves and stems

½ cup roughly chopped sawtooth herb

4 scallions, both white and green parts, thinly sliced

2 to 4 fresh Thai chiles, thinly sliced

1 lemongrass stalk or 2 whole scallions, roots trimmed

½ cup vegetable oil

EQUIPMENT:

Charcoal grill

Square metal grill basket

Outside Menglun Town, in Xishuangbanna, on a winding country road, is a small restaurant called Red Bean Garden Fish Farmstead. The space is simple and relaxing, just an open-air pavilion next to a banana farm and a couple of fishponds. The food there is simple local fare like this flavorful grilled chicken (pictured on page 141), which is often served with eggplant slices fried until soft; squares of local riverweed; and sticky rice mixed with fresh pineapple and banana.

The restaurant is owned by a Dai woman named Mi Zhuang who spent the first part of her career as a nurse, traveling through the countryside to rural villages to administer vaccines. Though Mi Zhuang lives in the tiny town of Man'e—a hamlet of Dai-style wooden houses on stilts surrounded by rubber farms—her work gave her an important role in the county and enabled her to provide an excellent education for her children; her daughter was the first Dai student in China to earn a Ph.D. With her children grown, Mi Zhuang retired and opened her restaurant as a place for local families to gather. She cooks everything herself, occasionally enlisting the help of her daughter-in-law when feeding large groups. Guests call ahead and let her know how many people to expect, and she prepares whatever she has found at the market that day.

This grilled chicken is one of Mi Zhuang's specialties. She makes it with very small chickens that she raises herself and allows to roam through nearby banana farms and alongside fishponds, eating whatever greens and bugs they find. The key to making the dish is to cook the chicken slowly over hot coals while poking the skin, so that all of the fat runs off. Vegetable oil mixed with salt is brushed onto the chicken as it cooks to add flavor and help the skin crisp.

Butterfly the chicken by cutting it down the center of the breastbone. Rub the chicken inside and out with about 1 tsp. of the salt and set it on the counter, skin side down. Fill the chicken's exposed cavity with the herbs and chiles. With a large wooden pestle or the handle of a cleaver, pound the lemongrass until it's soft and pliable, place the stalk (or, alternatively, the whole scallions) over the herbs, folding it into a zigzag shape so that it holds them inside the chicken. If the chicken's head is attached, fold the head over to help hold everything in place. Put the chicken, herb side up, into the grill basket; it should fit snugly. Pour the vegetable oil into a small jar or cup, mix in the remaining 1 tbsp. of salt, and set aside.

Heat charcoal in a grill until the coals are hot. Poke the chicken all over with the point of a sharp chopstick to pierce its skin, then cook the chicken a few inches from the coals, keeping it far enough from any flames so that it doesn't burn. Flip the chicken repeatedly as you cook, use a pastry brush to brush it with a bit of the salty oil every few minutes, and continue to poke the chicken and tilt it occasionally so that the fat under the skin drains out and the skin becomes crisp. Grill the chicken for about 30 to 50 minutes, depending on the size of the chicken, and the heat of the grill; the skin should be a deep, singed brown, and when the meat in the breasts and thighs is pierced, the juices should run clear. Remove the grill basket from the grill and set aside to cool. When the chicken is cool enough to handle, remove it from the grill basket and use a cleaver to cut it across the bone into 12 pieces.

菠萝饭

Dai Pineapple Rice

Whole pineapples hollowed out and filled with a sweet mixture of sticky rice and fruit are an integral part of Dai meals all over Xishuangbanna and are often served alongside the regions' spicy grilled dishes. This very simple version, made with just pineapple, banana, and a bit of white sugar added to the rice, comes from Red Bean Garden Fish Farmstead restaurant (page 134).

1 cup white sticky rice

2½-lb. whole pineapple (about 7 inches tall and 13 inches in circumference)

4 inches of banana

1 to 3 tbsp. granulated sugar

Prepare the sticky rice according to the instructions on page 281. Set aside to cool.

Remove the top of the pineapple, cutting about 1 inch below the leaves; set the top aside. Hollow out the pineapple by cutting into the flesh about ½ inch from the skin, then angling the knife to cut the flesh out in chunks. Cut out and discard the firm core, and cut the rest of the chunks into pieces ½ inch wide or smaller. Set the hollowed-out pineapple aside.

When the rice is still warm, but cool enough to handle, transfer it to a mixing bowl. Add ½ cup of the cut-up pineapple, squeezing the fruit with your hands to break it into small pieces and release its juices into the rice. Add the banana and 1 to 3 tbsp. of sugar, depending on the sweetness of the pineapple (1 tbsp. if the fruit is candy-sweet, 3 tbsp. if it is fairly tart). Use your hands to mix everything together, kneading the mixture a bit to evenly distribute the fruit throughout the rice. Pack the mixture into the hollowed-out pineapple, filling it to the top. (You may have some excess rice mixture, depending on the size of the pineapple and the amount of flesh you removed; if so, you can steam it in the same kind of banana leaf packet used for Vegetables Grilled in Banana Leaves, page 247.)

Put the top of the pineapple back onto the body and secure it with toothpicks, or cover the filling with foil. In a tall pot fitted with a wire rack or a steamer basket, steam the stuffed pineapple for 10 minutes, until the rice inside is nice and sticky, and the flavors have blended. Let cool slightly and serve warm or at room temperature, in the pineapple. (If you don't have a steamer pot deep enough to fit an upright pineapple, arrange a small cake pan or pie tin upside down in a large stockpot. A wok lid can be useful to cover a pot containing a too-tall pineapple.)

Green Papaya Salad

傣味凉拌树木瓜

The crunchy, tart green papaya salad eaten in Xishuangbanna is somewhat similar to papaya salads found in northern Thailand (just 75 miles south of the province), but without the fish sauce and palm sugar that give the Thai versions their funky sweet flavor. Instead, Yunnan's salad is lightly dressed, flavored with lime juice, salt, fresh cilantro, and searingly spicy Thai chiles, and it is best eaten right after it's made, when it is still bright and crunchy. This recipe comes from the small Dai village of Man'e, just outside Menglun. On hot afternoons, the young women of the village often gather in the shade under one of the wooden houses, built on stilts, to chat and share the dish as a snack.

These days, cooks making this salad rely on a mandoline grater with little teeth that produces perfectly even strips of papaya. If you don't have a mandoline, you can make it the traditional way, cutting the papaya into thin slices, then cutting the slices into long, thin strips. (Note: When adding the chiles, be aware that a little goes a long way in this dish, as the chiles' oil will infuse the lime juice and spread to every strand of the papaya.)

1 small green papaya, about 1⅓ lbs.

1 to 3 fresh Thai chiles, thinly sliced

1 tbsp. roughly chopped cilantro leaves

4 to 6 tbsp. fresh lime juice

1 to 1½ tsp. salt

Use a vegetable peeler to remove all the papaya's peel, then trim off the stem. Cut the papaya in half lengthwise, and scoop out the seeds.

Using a mandoline, grate the papaya lengthwise into long, thin strips (you will have about 4½ cups). Put the strips into a medium bowl along with the chile and cilantro.

Add 4 tbsp. lime juice and 1 tsp. salt and mix well. Taste the mixture and add the remaining lime juice and/or salt if needed. (The salad should be quite tart and salty.) Let the salad sit for a few minutes before serving so the flavors can blend.

CELTUCE VARIATION

This salad can also be made with celtuce. Sometimes called stem lettuce or celery lettuce, celtuce is a common Chinese vegetable that is essentially the thick stalk of a head of a specific type of lettuce that is allowed to grow very tall as the bottom leaves are removed. It has a lovely tender but crunchy texture.

15-inch-long, thick piece of celtuce

1 to 3 fresh Thai chiles, thinly sliced

1 tbsp. roughly chopped cilantro leaves

1½ to 2 tbsp. lime juice

¾ to 1 tsp. salt

Remove the leaves from the celtuce stem, and use a vegetable peeler to remove all the fibrous outer peel. (If you have a more mature celtuce with a thicker stem, you may need to peel a few layers off to remove all the fibrous parts of the plant.) Using a mandoline, grate the celtuce into thin strips, grating lengthwise so that the strips are as long as possible. Put the strips into a medium bowl along with the chile and cilantro.

Add 1½ tbsp. lime juice and about ¾ tsp. salt and mix well. Taste the mixture and add the remaining lime juice and/or salt if needed. (The salad should be quite tart and salty.) Let the salad sit for a few minutes before serving so the flavors can blend.

Tilapia Stuffed with Herbs and Chiles

香草烤鱼

At Red Bean Garden Fish Farmstead (page 134), most dishes are cooked over wood on a small cement stove called a *huotang* that is set on the restaurant's back porch. The owner, Mi Zhuang, crouches over the stove and slowly cooks over hot embers, turning the foods and fanning the fire until everything is perfectly done. The stove looks out over the restaurant's fishponds, and Mi Zhuang begins to prepare this dish by catching a fresh fish and gutting and scaling it right on the bank. Back inside the kitchen, she washes the fish, butterflies it with a swift cut down the side of the spine (to keep the tender belly meat intact), and fills it with fresh herbs and chiles that perfume the meat as it cooks.

Rub the fish inside and out with about ½ tsp. of the salt. Mix the herbs, chile, and another ½ tsp. of salt, and use the mixture to stuff the fish, then close the fish and put it into the grill basket. Pour the vegetable oil into a small jar or cup, mix in the chile flakes and the remaining 2 tsp. of salt, and set aside.

Heat charcoal in a grill until the coals are hot. Cook the fish over direct heat for 5 minutes, then flip the grill basket and grill the other side for another 5 minutes. Use a pastry brush to coat the fish with the prepared oil, and grill for 5 more minutes on each side. The fish's skin should be partially blackened and crispy, and the flesh should be firm, flaky, and no longer translucent.

1½-lb. whole tilapia, cleaned and cut open so that it lies flat on the cutting board (ideally cut along the spine rather than through the stomach)

3 tsp. salt

3 scallions, both white and green parts, smacked with the side of a cleaver and roughly chopped

2 tbsp. roughly chopped cilantro leaves and stems

1 to 3 fresh Thai chiles, thinly sliced

¼ cup vegetable oil

¼ tsp. dried chile flakes

EQUIPMENT:

Charcoal grill

Square metal grill basket

炸
丝
瓜
尖

Fried Squash Leaves

Simple dishes of greens fried in egg batter are the unsung staple of southern Yunnan meals. Home cooks across Xishuangbanna use this forgiving frying technique to cook all kinds of greens (as well as eggplant; opposite page). It is particularly useful for preparing local nettles and other plants with small spines, such as the squash greens in this recipe, because the frying softens the bristles and turns the thick leaves tender and velvety. Leaves from the vines of the bottle gourd (*Lagenaria siceraria*, or *hulu* in Mandarin), which are sold in Asian markets during summer, are especially good in this recipe.

6 large eggs

1 tsp. salt

2 tbsp. cornstarch or potato starch

2 cups vegetable oil

4 cups squash leaves, ideally bottle gourd greens (from about 14 oz. of leaves and vines), or similar greens

Combine the eggs, salt, and cornstarch in a medium bowl and whisk them together until thoroughly mixed.

Heat the oil in a wok over a high flame until it is very hot. (To test the oil, use a chopstick to drop a bit of the egg mixture into the oil; it should bubble up to the surface and expand immediately.) Reduce the heat to medium-high.

Working with one or two leaves at a time (depending on their size), dip the squash leaves into the egg mixture to coat them, then fry them in the oil until golden brown, using chopsticks to spread them out to their full size and flipping them over a few times to brown evenly on both sides. Adjust the heat between high and medium as needed so that the leaves turn golden brown within 1½ to 2 minutes. Put the cooked leaves into a strainer set over a bowl to drain away the excess oil. Repeat until all the leaves are cooked, then transfer them to a serving plate.

Fried Eggplant Slices

炸茄子

In this simple recipe (pictured on page 141), slices of eggplant are dipped in egg and fried in oil until they become soft and develop a custard-like texture. The dish is served at Red Bean Garden Fish Farmstead, outside Menglun, usually alongside local favorites like Dai Grilled Chicken with Herbs (page 134) and Dai Cucumber Salad with Herbs and Peanuts (page 148), and the eggplant's soothing flavor is an excellent foil for the searingly spicy fresh chiles in those dishes. Mi Zhuang makes this dish with eggplants that have a distinctive light purple and green skin, often sold in the United States as "Filipino eggplants." You can substitute regular Asian eggplants, but they won't have the same custardy texture. Although the recipe involves frying in oil, it is extremely forgiving—eggplant slices that may have cooked a bit too quickly or too slowly will still taste wonderful.

2 long Filipino eggplants (each about 14 inches)

3 large eggs

1½ tsp. salt

1 tbsp. cornstarch or potato starch

1 cup vegetable oil

Peel the eggplants with a vegetable peeler and cut them at an angle into long, ½-inch-thick slices. Combine the eggs, salt, and cornstarch in a medium bowl and whisk them together until thoroughly mixed.

Heat the oil in a wok over a high flame until it is very hot. (To test the oil, use a chopstick to drop a bit of the egg mixture into the oil; it should bubble up to the surface and expand immediately.) Reduce the heat to medium-high.

Dip four slices of eggplant into the egg mixture to coat them, then fry them in the oil until golden brown, flipping them a few times with chopsticks to brown evenly on both sides. Adjust the heat between high and medium as needed so that the slices turn golden brown on both sides within 1½ to 2½ minutes. Put the cooked slices into a strainer set over a bowl to drain away the excess oil. Repeat until all the eggplant is cooked, then transfer to a serving plate.

Pu'er—The Most Coveted Tea in China

High on the slopes of Nannuo Mountain, Long Bian Sheng prepares to turn freshly picked tea leaves into Yunnan's most famous export: *pu'er* tea. First, he piles the four-inch-long leaves onto the freshly swept concrete floor of his workshop and stokes the wood fire under his brick oven. When the flames are hot enough, he turns on a rotating metal tube that runs through the center of the oven and begins loading in armfuls of leaves. The tube tosses the leaves in the heated air for a few seconds, then deposits them, curled and steaming, onto the floor at the other end, where Long's eldest son, Long "Sheng Da," is waiting. Sheng Da spreads them out over the workshop's floor, sprinkling them by the handful so that they cool as they fall through the air. Once all the leaves have cooled, they will be massaged until they curl up into long spirals, left to dry a bit in the sun, then packed into round, flat cakes and wrapped in paper.

Pu'er (also anglicized as *puerh* in China's older transliterations) takes its name from the city of Pu'er, just north of Xishuangbanna, where it was historically traded. But authentic *pu'er* is all grown to the south, in the mountains of Xishuangbanna. It differs from other kinds of tea in that it is made from a variety of tree that produces much longer leaves (up to five inches long), and while other teas are all dried at some point during production, to keep their flavors from changing, *pu'er* is allowed to ferment for weeks or even years, becoming dark and flavorful.

Recently, tea connoisseurs from Hong Kong, Beijing, and Shanghai have fallen in love with *pu'er* (and its ability to increase in value over many years) and turned it into a luxury product. They buy the most famous teas, from the oldest tea trees on the most famous mountains, and carefully let them age until they develop a dark hue and a warm, mellow, earthy flavor that can have hints of wood, dates, and even molasses or caramel. Locals, however, prefer to drink the tea fresh and unaged. The flavor is bright, sharp, and grassy, a perfect eye-opening pick-me-up for Xishuangbanna's hot, humid weather.

opposite page: fresh green tea leaves are toasted, rolled, and pressed into firm cakes of pu'er, which are left out to dry

left: when the cakes are ready, they are wrapped in paper, then seven cakes are stacked together and wrapped into a bamboo leaf package called a *tong*

包烧鸡

Chicken Grilled in Banana Leaf

Foods cooked in banana leaves are popular across southern and western Yunnan, where the leaves are used not only for cooking over an open fire without a wok but also for infusing the ingredients with the leaf's vegetal flavor. But this recipe, from Dai home cook Wang Qiu (see page 150), is much more complex than most "banana packet" dishes. While most cooks limit the packet contents to relatively simple ingredients, Wang fills the leaves with chicken that has already been flavored with strong ingredients, including grilled chiles, galangal, and various herbs, a complex combination that reflects the tastes of people in this part of Xishuangbanna, which borders Shan State in Myanmar and is also just 100 miles from northern Thailand.

Grill or broil the red chiles until the skin is blackened and the flesh is very soft. Let the chiles cool, then peel off the skin and slice the chiles crosswise into ¼-inch-wide strips.

Using a large mortar and pestle, mash the grilled chiles (and their seeds) with the garlic chives, galangal, green Thai chile, dried chile flakes, and 1 tsp. of the salt until the ingredients have been crushed into a very rough paste; transfer to a large bowl. Peel the lemongrass stalk to remove the firm outer leaves and cut off the tough greens, leaving just the tender inner leaves. Smash these leaves with the side of a cleaver and thinly slice the bottom, tender parts (usually the bottom 2 or 3 inches of the stalk). Add the chicken, sliced lemongrass, sawtooth herb, and the remaining ½ tsp. of salt to the bowl and massage the meat and flavorings together until well mixed. Add the vegetable oil and mix.

Lay the large pieces of banana leaf flat on a counter and place the smaller pieces in their centers with the grain of the leaf running perpendicular to the grain of the larger leaf. Pile half of the chicken mixture onto each set of leaves. Fold the top and bottom edges of the banana leaves over to completely enclose the mixture like an envelope, then fold the sides over so that you have two rectangular packages about 6 by 8 inches. Secure each packet with toothpicks.

2 to 4 fresh red chiles, such as Fresno chiles

¼ cup garlic chives cut into 1-inch pieces

1-inch piece galangal, peeled and cut into thin slices

1 fresh green Thai chile

1 tsp. dried chile flakes

1½ tsp. salt

1 lemongrass stalk

2-lb. whole chicken or a combination of bone-in breast and whole legs with thighs, cut across the bone into 1- to 2-inch-wide pieces

½ cup thinly sliced sawtooth herb

1 tbsp. vegetable oil

2 14-inch square pieces of banana leaf and 2 10-inch square pieces of banana leaf

EQUIPMENT:

Gas or charcoal grill

Grill basket

If using a charcoal grill, heat a large pile of coals until very hot. Place the packets in a grill basket and grill on a gas or charcoal grill over direct heat, turning occasionally, until the banana leaves are browned on all sides and the chicken is cooked through, 20 to 30 minutes (the time will vary depending on how close the grate is to the flame). Unfold the packets to serve.

剁
生

Poached Pork with Herbs

This recipe's Chinese name—*dou sheng*, or "chopped raw"—is a holdover from the past, when the dish was made with raw meat, served uncooked. Eating raw meat was common in the southern and western parts of Yunnan until a few decades ago, when the government declared the practice a health hazard and encouraged people to cook the ingredients. This dish (shown on page 141) is served with fresh mint and sticky rice; a pinch of the sticky rice and a mint leaf can be used together to scoop up a bite of the pork mixture, the same way the region's mashed eggplant is eaten (see page 149).

On a large cutting board, combine the meat, scallions, cilantro, chiles, and garlic and chop together, using the knife to gather and fold the mixture as you go so that the meat is broken up and everything is well mixed. Put the mixture into a mixing bowl or large mortar, add the salt, and use a pestle to pound and mix everything together so that the herbs and chiles are crushed and mashed into the meat.

Put the mixture into a medium pot with just enough water to almost cover. Cook the mixture over high heat. When the water begins to boil, continue cooking, stirring every minute or so and breaking up any clumps, until the meat is just cooked through, about 3 minutes. Transfer the meat and cooking liquid to a serving bowl, draining off some of the excess liquid but leaving enough to keep the dish warm and porridge-like. Tuck the fresh mint sprigs into the side of the bowl.

1 lb. ground or finely chopped pork (scant 2 cups)

⅓ cup finely chopped scallions, light and dark green parts only

⅓ cup finely chopped cilantro leaves

4 fresh Thai chiles, finely chopped (ideally a mix of orange and red chiles)

¾ tsp. minced garlic

1 tsp. salt

Small handful of fresh mint sprigs

傣味涼拌黃瓜

Dai Cucumber Salad with Herbs and Peanuts

Winter is dry season in Xishuangbanna, and without rain, the afternoons become hot and sticky. Local cooks have two approaches for counteracting the heat: cool dishes of raw vegetables like cucumber, green papaya, or celtuce, and spicy dishes with lots of fresh red chiles that make everyone sweat. This bright, citrusy cucumber dish, served at Red Bean Garden Fish Farmstead (page 134), fulfills both roles. The cook, Mi Zhuang, uses a mix of fresh herbs that includes cilantro, sawtooth herb, and *yan xin*, a cilantro-like herb known as *bac lieu* in Vietnam.

⅓ cup roasted, skinless, unsalted peanuts

2 long cucumbers (each about 12 inches), preferably bumpy-skinned Chinese cucumbers or thin English "seedless" cucumbers

1 tbsp. roughly chopped cilantro (or ½ tbsp. cilantro and ½ tbsp. *yan xin*, if available)

2 tbsp. roughly chopped sawtooth herb (or another 1 tbsp. of cilantro)

1 to 2 fresh Thai chiles, thinly sliced

½ to ¾ tsp. salt

2 to 3 tbsp. lime juice

Crush the peanuts with a mortar and pestle until most of the nuts are crushed, or chop and smash them with a large knife; set aside. Using a vegetable peeler, peel the cucumbers, then cut them into large, triangular chunks, about 1½ inches long, by holding the knife at an angle to the cucumber (not directly perpendicular) and turning the cucumber approximately 45 degrees between each cut.

Put the cucumber chunks into a bowl, add the herbs, chile, ½ tsp. of the salt, and crushed peanuts, and stir to mix everything together. Just before serving, add 2 tbsp. of the lime juice and toss all the ingredients to coat them. Taste the salad and adjust the seasonings as needed.

Mashed Eggplant with Herbs and Chiles

傣味凉拌火烧茄子

2 long Asian eggplants (each about 14 inches), preferably Filipino eggplants (which are distinguished by their distinctive light purple and green skin)

2 to 4 fresh Thai chiles

¼ cup finely chopped cilantro

2 tbsp. finely chopped sawtooth herb

2 slender scallions, white and light green parts only, finely chopped

1 tsp. salt

This dish is a delicious reminder of eggplant's versatility. When grilled, the flesh of Asian eggplant quickly becomes soft enough to pound into a smooth, silky paste, which is then flavored with bright cilantro, scallions, and sawtooth herb along with fiery red Thai chiles. The result is a perfect complement to the region's crisp grilled foods such as Dai Grilled Chicken with Herbs (page 134). This dish (shown on page 141) should be eaten with sticky rice and scooped by hand, the way *larb* and similar dishes are eaten farther south in Laos and northern Thailand: grab a large bite of sticky rice with the tips of your thumb and first two or three fingers, and use it to scoop up some of the silken eggplant mixture.

Cook the eggplants on a hot grill or in a broiler, turning frequently, until they are brown on all sides, starting to blacken a bit, and the eggplant is saggy and looks deflated. Remove them from the heat, let them cool, then peel, cutting off the stems and discarding the skin. Roughly chop the eggplant flesh.

Put the eggplant, chiles, chopped herbs, and salt into a mixing bowl or a very large mortar and use a pestle to smash everything together until the mixture has a smooth texture.

The Indispensable Mortar and Pestle

One of the most important tools in a Dai cook's kitchen is a large mortar and pestle. Some cooks use a wooden bowl as large as a Western mixing bowl and a hefty, two-foot-long wooden pestle. Others use a hollow piece of bamboo instead of a bowl, or a massive stone mortar, which is heavier and boasts a rough surface that helps break down the ingredients. Whatever the materials, the mortar and pestle can be used in a variety of ways: to smash peanuts that will dress cucumber salads; mash fresh or roasted chiles, tomatoes, and herbs into a piquant sauce to serve with raw vegetables; crush raw meat into paste; or mash grilled eggplant until it is silky-smooth.

香茅草烤鱼

Fish Stuffed with Spice Paste

Wang Qiu crouches low to the ground, bending over a large wooden mortar with a pestle in her hands. She puts a knob of ginger, its skin still on, into the bowl, along with chiles and a handful of bright green garlic chives, and starts to carefully pound them into a paste. Although Wang, a Dai housewife from Menghai, cooks in a thoroughly modern kitchen, she still does much of her cooking while crouched down on the floor, where she cleans vegetables, makes a variety of herb and chile mixtures, and lays out squares of green banana leaves to stuff them with seasoned meat and fish before steaming or grilling them.

For this dish, Wang coats the skin and flesh of the cleaned fish with chile-herb paste, then stuffs more inside and folds the fish in half, nose to tail, holding it closed with a split piece of bamboo and some lemongrass that she wraps around the fish to secure it and give it a nice aroma. Then she grills the fish outdoors, on a long, low charcoal grill. The chile paste on the fish's skin chars and browns as the flesh cooks, adding another layer of smoky, spicy flavor to the finished dish.

3-inch knob of unpeeled ginger, washed well and smashed with the side of a cleaver

3 fresh Thai chiles

1 tbsp. dried chile flakes

1 tbsp. + 1 tsp. salt

1 cup garlic chives cut into 1-inch pieces

2 whole 1½-lb. firm-fleshed white fish, such as tilapia, cleaned and cut open so that they lie flat on the cutting board (ideally cut along the spine rather than through the stomach)

2 long lemongrass leaves pulled from the outside of a lemongrass stalk

2 tbsp. vegetable oil

1 to 2 tbsp. chile sauce (*lajiao jiang*)

EQUIPMENT:

Charcoal grill

Piece of split bamboo or a grill basket large enough to hold two fish

Using a large mortar and pestle, mash the ginger, chiles, chile flakes, and 1 tbsp. of the salt until the ginger and chiles have been shredded into small pieces. Add the garlic chives and smash everything until the ingredients are well-bruised and thoroughly mixed together.

Rub each fish inside and out with approximately ½ tsp. of the salt. Stuff the fish with the spice paste, then close the fish: if using split bamboo, fold the head of each fish over the tail, as if the fish were kissing the tip of its tail; if using a grill basket, close each fish back up so that it looks whole again. Smash the lemongrass leaves with the handle of a cleaver until they are pliable, wrap each fish in a leaf, and secure the fish with the bamboo or put them into the grill basket.

Heat charcoal in a grill until the coals are hot. Cook the fish over direct heat for 5 minutes, using a pastry brush to brush them with the oil a couple of times, then flip them and grill the other side for another 5 minutes. Use the pastry brush to coat the fish with the chile sauce and grill for 5 minutes on each side. The fish's skin should be partially blackened and crispy, and the flesh should be firm, flaky, and no longer translucent.

Crunchy Eggplant Salad

This piquant salad is a popular dish at Jinghong's *shao kao* (barbecue) stands. Every night, when the sun has set and the heat of the day begins to lift, these open-air eateries fill with families and large groups of friends who order generously, making sure that everyone at the table has enough grilled meat, seafood, and vegetables to keep them eating for hours. Men shrug off their shirts and enjoy the relative cool of the night air while they joke with friends, sharing cigarettes and countless bottles of the weak local beer. Groups of twenty-somethings and teenagers come directly from work, the women in heels and short skirts or lacy dresses, the men in polos or T-shirts printed with fancy logos or foreign phrases, everyone giggling and flirting as they eat. Babies sleep in carriers tied to their mothers' backs, and small children balance on their parents' knees, happy to stay up past bedtime and join in the fun.

The slight bitterness of the thinly sliced raw Thai eggplants used in this dish is balanced with salty pickled greens, a funky, slightly sweet chile-bean paste, a touch of vinegar, and the bright flavors of cilantro and garlic. In Jinghong it is made with beautiful mottled purple eggplants, each about 2 inches wide, but green Thai eggplants of the same size also work wonderfully.

5 round purple or green Thai eggplants (8½ oz.)

1 tbsp. minced garlic

2 or 3 fresh Thai chiles, cut into ⅓-inch-thick slices

1 tbsp. southern-style chile-bean paste (*douban jiang*)

1 tbsp. Pickled Mustard Greens (page 272), roughly chopped, plus 2 tsp. of the pickling liquid

1 tbsp. roughly chopped cilantro leaves and stems

1 tbsp. Chinese white rice vinegar

½ tsp. salt

Trim the stems from the eggplants, cut each eggplant in half, then use a mandoline or sharp cleaver to cut them into ⅛-inch-thick slices. (You will have about 1½ lightly packed cups.) Put the eggplant slices into a bowl and add cold water to cover. Wash the eggplant in the water for a few seconds to remove some of its bitterness, pressing it firmly with the palm of your hand, then drain away the water and any seeds that have dislodged from the slices. (The water may have turned slightly brown.) Repeat the washing process once again, then put the eggplant into a serving bowl. Add the remaining ingredients to the bowl and mix well.

The Grande Dame of Crossing the Bridge Rice Noodles

At seventy years old, Wang Lizhu still moves around her restaurant's kitchen with surprising ease, first checking the broth boiling away in a massive wok, then glancing over prepared soup ingredients before making her way out to the dining room to greet regulars and friends. She commands the attention of the room, a serene presence among her busy staff, a small army of waitresses who literally run around her to get the eatery's famous bowls of Crossing the Bridge Rice Noodles to hungry customers.

Wang's restaurant, Wangji Chrysanthemum Crossing the Bridge Rice Noodles, is the oldest continuously operating Crossing the Bridge Rice Noodles restaurant in Mengzi. Unlike most soup specialists in town, who have adopted a fast-food-style model, letting guests choose their soup ingredients from trays arranged behind a wall of glass, Wang is old-school, and serves her soup in a formal dining room with chandeliers and faux-silk covers on the chairs. All the options here, whether the 10 *kuai* bowl with twelve ingredients or the 40 *kuai* bowl with twenty-one ingredients, are served in the classic style, each ingredient brought to the table in its own separate saucer, ready to go into an enormous bowl of rich chicken and pork broth.

Wang herself originated this serving style. The third generation of her family to make Crossing the Bridge Rice Noodles, she started working in her father's restaurants at the age of fourteen. In 1986, she opened her own restaurant, in Kunming. At the time, all the other restaurants in town were bringing their ingredients on large plates, so Wang decided that to elevate her soup, she would serve each ingredient in its own small saucer and would add raw quail eggs to the usual offerings of ham, boiled and roasted meats, and assorted herbs and greens. Both of those new ideas proved wildly popular, and soon restaurants across the city were copying Wang's innovations.

Wang eventually returned to Mengzi, and in 1999 she opened her current restaurant, where she started adding golden chrysanthemum petals to her soups—another innovation that has become standard across the city. Most days the restaurant serves a few dozen regulars, but on big holidays, like Chinese New Year, they sell up to 3,000 bowls of soup a day to tourists who often wait for over an hour in a line around the block. While Wang is no longer in the kitchen every day, she has no plans to retire. "I don't think I'll ever stop," she says. "Even if my eyes stop working someday, I'll still be able to make noodles."

clockwise, from top left: golden chrysanthemums are Wang's signature touch; a waitress prepares soup ingredients for a crowd of regulars with a standing reservation; Wang inspects her soup broth, which is made from a combination of pork ribs and whole chickens and simmers for hours before it is served; servers carry huge stacks of prepared plates to tables; in Wang's famous serving style, which has been widely copied, each ingredient in its own saucer.

Crossing the Bridge Rice Noodles

过桥米线

This gorgeous soup from the city of Mengzi is Yunnan's most famous dish. According to popular legend, there was once a scholar who was studying for his exams on the island in the center of beautiful South Lake, a kilometer's walk from the old town. His wife (whose name is lost to antiquity) brought the scholar food for lunch every day, but it always got cold before she arrived. One day, when she hadn't had time to prepare a full meal, the wife grabbed a pot of rich broth, gathered all the raw ingredients she could find in her kitchen, and made her way to the lake. When she arrived, she realized that the fat in the broth had risen to the top of the pot and solidified, keeping the soup underneath piping hot, and she quickly added all her other ingredients to the bowl, where the heat of the broth cooked them perfectly. The scholar loved the resulting soup, and just like that, a delicious classic was born.

The soup is extremely impressive looking when served, with the ingredients displayed in tiny saucers or arrayed on a plate, ready to go into the bowl of hot broth. But that doesn't mean the dish is difficult to prepare. The key to making this soup in as quick and easy a way as possible is to embrace what is available. If you have a Chinatown nearby, grab some roast pork belly and see if you can hunt down some fresh tofu skin to cut into thin strips or small squares. If Chinese roast meats are not available, American-style bacon would not be out of place. Raw quail eggs can be replaced with a very thin, crepe-like omelet cut into strips. As long as you have five or more ingredients, the rich broth will carry all the flavors and bring them together in a cohesive whole. And as for the broth, if you don't eat pork, go ahead and try making the base with chicken and duck or even some goose. As long as there's plenty of meat—and, ideally, a few kinds of it— you'll end up with something fragrant and ambrosial.

In Mengzi, this soup is assembled in huge bowls nearly the size of a cooking pot. Diners choose how many ingredients they want to add to the broth (restaurants offer sets ranging from ten to twenty different toppings), then load it up with as many noodles as they like. This recipe is adapted to make four slightly smaller portions of soup (to fit in more conventional bowls), but if you have extra-large bowls, try making

FOR THE BROTH:

1 lb. pork bones

1 whole chicken, plus 2 whole legs with thighs and 2 more thighs (about 4½ lbs. total)

1 rack spareribs (3 to 3½ lbs.)

4 whole star anise

3 black cardamom pods

¼ cup light soy sauce

(recipe and ingredients continue)

FOR THE ADD-INS:

1 cup lightly packed bean sprouts

1 cup garlic chives cut into 2-inch pieces

8 quail eggs

3 oz. lean pork, such as a boneless chop, very thinly sliced (⅓ cup)

2 oz. Yunnan ham or Spanish Jamón Serrano, very thinly sliced and cut into 1-inch squares (⅓ cup)

3 oz. flavorful mushrooms, such as shiitake or trumpet, cut into thin slices (about 2 tbsp.)

½ cup fresh or rehydrated tofu skin, cut into strips about ⅓ inch by 2 to 3 inches

6 oz. Chinese roast pork with crispy skin, thinly sliced and cut into 1- to 1½-inch squares (1 cup)

¾ cup chicken left over from making the broth, shredded

2 lbs. fresh or cooked rice noodles (about 8 cups)

2 scallions, both white and green parts, very thinly sliced

4 tbsp. thin golden chrysanthemum petals (optional)

SEASONINGS ON THE SIDE:

Light soy sauce

Dried Chile Oil (page 276)

Dark Chinese vinegar

the original size by using eight cups of broth and twice the amount of noodles called for below. Cooks in Mengzi also keep their broth cooking for months or even years, adding more meat and water every day and building up a base of flavor. When starting from scratch, roasting some of the meat can help approximate the broth's rich, layered flavor. Makes four medium servings.

Preheat the oven to 450°F. Put the pork bones and the chicken legs and thighs on a rimmed baking sheet and roast until golden brown, about 25 minutes.

Transfer the cooked meat and bones to a large stockpot, add the ribs, whole chicken, star anise, and cardamom, and cover with 5 quarts of water. Cover the pot and bring to a boil, then reduce the heat to low and continue cooking, covered, at a low boil for 4 to 6 hours (the longer the broth cooks, the more flavorful it will be). When the broth is ready, stir in the soy sauce, then strain out the meat, bones, and seasonings. Reserve ¾ cup of the chicken meat, removing it from the bone, to add to the soup. (The broth can be made a day or two before you plan to serve the soup and refrigerated until use.)

Bring a medium pot of water to a boil. Boil the bean sprouts until tender, 1 to 2 minutes, then remove them from the pot with tongs or a perforated scoop, rinse with cold water, squeeze out as much moisture as possible, and set aside. Use the same pot to boil the garlic chives for 30 seconds, then rinse with cold water, squeeze out as much moisture as possible, and set aside. Divide all the soup add-ins into four servings and arrange them in little saucers or on a plate for each diner. Crack the quail eggs into small bowls or saucers, two eggs for each diner. If the tofu skin is folded into tight layers, pull them apart so that they resemble noodles, or cut them into small squares.

When the add-ins are all prepared, bring the broth back to a boil, then quickly divide the broth into four very large, deep soup bowls (4 to 5 cups each). Immediately serve with the rest of the ingredients on the side.

To assemble the bowls, diners should begin by stirring the broth with their chopsticks and adding the raw eggs (which should become wispy in the moving broth), followed by the raw pork or any other raw meats, the ham, tofu skin, mushrooms and any other ingredients that need to be cooked, and then the already-cooked ingredients, such as the roast pork, chicken, and cooked vegetables. Add the rice noodles to the bowl and stir, then garnish with the scallions and the chrysanthemum petals.

酸笋牛肉

Stewed Beef and Bamboo Shoots with Fresh Mint

Five hundred different species of bamboo grow in Yunnan, crowding along riverbanks and rising above the jungles and forests. Southern Yunnan is a particularly good spot for the fast-growing plant (which is technically a kind of grass), and farmers in the region cultivate various kinds to produce both wood for construction and edible shoots.

While bamboo shoots can be boiled and eaten right after they're picked, cooks in southern and western Yunnan also cut them into long, thin strips and pickle them until they have a distinctive sour, astringent, slightly funky flavor (page 16). In western Yunnan, the strong flavor of these pickles is often highlighted in dishes like Beef with Pickled Bamboo (page 253). But in this dish, made by Hani minority cooks near Yunnan's border with Vietnam, the pickled bamboo is cooked with chiles, stewed with beef until its flavor has mellowed, and then served over fresh mint. The combination of the meat's umami and the bright herbal flavor of the mint (along with a bit of spice from fresh chiles) perfectly balances the slightly sour flavor of the bamboo, and the dish manages to be both comforting and surprising.

7 oz. relatively lean beef, such as flat iron steak

4 tsp. light soy sauce

3 tbsp. vegetable oil

1 to 3 fresh Thai chiles, roughly chopped

⅓ cup thinly sliced Thai or Yunnan sour bamboo

1 tsp. salt

1½ tsp. whole Sichuan peppercorns

Large handful of mint, leaves and thin stems only

Cut the beef into very thin slices, cutting at an angle to get pieces at least 1 to 1½ inches wide. (The easiest way to do this is by pulling the meat away from the knife slightly with one hand while slicing with the other hand so that there is tension between the knife and the meat. You will have a scant 1 cup.) Mix the beef with 2 tsp. of the soy sauce in a small bowl, and set it aside to marinate for 5 minutes.

In a wok, heat the oil over a high flame until very hot. Add the chiles and bamboo shoots and stir-fry, stirring and flipping constantly, for 15 seconds. Add 3 cups of water to the wok along with the salt, Sichuan peppercorns, and the remaining 2 tsp. soy sauce and stir.

Bring the mixture to a boil and let it boil vigorously for 30 seconds. Add the beef, bring the broth back to a boil, and cook, stirring occasionally, until the beef is no longer pink, 30 seconds to 1½ minutes.

Put the mint in a serving bowl and use a perforated scoop to ladle the meat and bamboo shoots on top of the mint, then add as much of the broth as will comfortably fit in the bowl and serve.

Stir-Fried Beef with Mint

牛肉炒薄荷

This dish comes from a restaurant called Menghai Old Chicken Shop, which is located on the outskirts of Jinghong, Xishuangbanna, in a mall built to look like a collection of Dai-style houses with traditional peaked roofs and wooden details on the façade. While the restaurant is named for its famous roast chickens, many patrons order this stir-fry of rich beef, ginger, mint, and fresh chiles. Restaurants in Xishuangbanna traditionally use flavorful aged beef, so this recipe, made with fresh beef, calls for extra soy sauce to mimic the aged meat's natural umami.

¼ cup vegetable oil

1 tbsp. minced peeled ginger

3 to 10 fresh Thai chiles, thinly sliced

¾ lb. ground or finely chopped beef (scant 1¾ cups)

1½ tbsp. light soy sauce

1½ cups packed mint leaves, roughly chopped

¼ cup roughly chopped cilantro

In a wok, heat the oil over a high flame until very hot. Add the ginger, chiles, and beef, and stir-fry, stirring and flipping frequently and using a wok shovel to break up any large pieces of meat. When the meat begins to brown, add the soy sauce by pouring it across the side of the wok in an arc. Continue to stir-fry the mixture until the meat is fully browned. (If working on a regular stove, press the meat up against the side of the wok and let it sit for 30 seconds at a time to brown.) Add the mint and cilantro and stir-fry for another minute, until the greens have wilted slightly, then remove the mixture from the wok, draining off the oil. Transfer to a serving plate.

SQUASH BLOSSOMS TWO WAYS

Bright, golden squash blossoms rarely find their way onto restaurant menus in Yunnan, but they are popular with home cooks, who buy them by the armful just hours after they're picked, before they begin to wilt. The blossoms are usually prepared very simply to preserve their delicate flavor.

These two ways of cooking the flowers are so simple, they almost don't require recipes. Both come from Safe and Peaceful Restaurant, a family-run spot across the street from the main bus stop in a tiny county seat called Jinping. The county borders the northwestern tip of Vietnam, and the region is populated by the same ethnic groups that make their home in Vietnam's highlands. Miao and Yao villagers dressed in traditional costumes embroidered with colorful designs and elaborate headdresses come here from nearby mountains to buy household supplies. The restaurant does a lively business in the early evening, when shoppers stop to snack on grilled tofu and chat with friends before catching the bus home.

Squash Blossom Soup

南瓜花汤

2 tsp. minced tomato

2 fresh Thai chiles, minced

1½ tsp. minced garlic

2 tsp. finely chopped cilantro

1 tsp. salt

20 squash blossoms, stems and stamens removed

1 tbsp. vegetable oil

Mix the tomato, chile, garlic, and cilantro in a small bowl with ½ tsp. of the salt and set aside.

Bring 3 cups of water to a boil in a wok or medium pot, then add the remaining ½ tsp. salt and the squash blossoms. Boil the blossoms for 30 seconds, then add the oil and boil for another 30 seconds, stirring gently; the squash blossoms should look very wilted and their stem-ends should be tender. Transfer the squash blossoms and broth to a serving bowl; to serve, stir a scoop of the broth into the tomato-chile mixture to turn it into a dipping sauce for the stewed flowers.

Simple Stir-Fried Squash Blossoms

炒南瓜花

¼ cup vegetable oil

3 dried Thai chiles, cut into 1-inch pieces

2 garlic cloves, cut into thick slices

30 squash blossoms, stems and stamens removed

1 tsp. salt

Heat the oil, chiles, and garlic in a wok over a high flame until the garlic is sizzling furiously. Reduce the heat to medium-high and add the squash blossoms and salt. Stir-fry the squash blossoms gently, stirring with the back of a wok shovel and flipping them over just a couple of times, until they are tender and have released a bit of liquid, about 1 to 2 minutes, depending on the size of the blossoms, then transfer to a serving plate.

番茄喃咪

Raw Vegetables with Charred Tomato–Chile Sauce

This zingy sauce, made with grilled tomatoes that have been crushed with chiles and herbs, is a staple on southern Yunnan tables. It can be served as a dip for any number of vegetables, from astringent boiled banana tree hearts or tender bamboo shoots to fragrant herbs to plain old carrot sticks and cucumber slices. Cooks usually arrange a variety of raw vegetables around a small bowl of the sauce for guests to dip into throughout the meal.

Use a wooden chopstick to skewer the tomatoes lengthwise. Grill the tomatoes over hot coals or roast them under a broiler, turning occasionally, until the tomato skin is loose and blackened in spots. Put the grilled tomatoes into a large mortar with the chiles, herbs, and salt and mash them with a pestle until the tomatoes and chile have been smashed into a soupy sauce and the herbs have been ground into small pieces. Serve the sauce in a small bowl with the vegetables and herbs arranged around it.

FOR THE DIPPING SAUCE:

2 Roma (plum) tomatoes

1 to 3 Thai chiles, thinly sliced

1 tbsp. roughly chopped sawtooth herb

1 tbsp. roughly chopped cilantro

1 tsp. salt

VEGETABLES:

An assortment of raw vegetables, such as carrot sticks, sliced cucumber, sliced tomato, lettuce leaves; herbs, such as fresh mint; and/or boiled bamboo shoots (available refrigerated in many Asian markets)

EQUIPMENT:

Wooden chopstick

Charcoal grill (optional)

Beef Noodle Soup

牛肉米线

2 lbs. cross-cut beef shanks including marrow bones

1½ lbs. beef bones, such as knuckle bones

2 black cardamom pods

2 whole star anise

1 tsp. fennel seeds

1 tbsp. salt

4 large handfuls of fresh rice noodles or 12 oz. dried rice noodles, such as Vietnamese rice sticks

12 oz. tender raw beef steak, such as skirt steak or sirloin, sliced very thin (about 1¾ cups)

TOPPING OPTIONS:

Bunch of fresh mint

Handful of garlic chives, blanched, rinsed with cold water, and cut into 1-inch pieces

4 scallions, both white and green parts, very thinly sliced

Light soy sauce

Zhenjiang vinegar

Dried chile flakes

Minced garlic mixed with water to cover by ½ inch

Minced peeled ginger

Dried Chile Oil (page 276)

Sichuan Peppercorn Powder (page 274)

Picked Mustard Greens (page 272)

Pickled Chiles (page 271)

This light, flavorful soup is a potent reminder that foods and cooking methods don't observe international borders. Made from long-simmered beef stock, slices of raw or boiled beef, and wide rice noodles and topped with fresh herbs and chiles, this is exactly the same soup that is called pho just a few miles to the south, in Vietnam. Only the topping options—fresh mint, blanched garlic chives, pickled mustard greens, dried chile oil, Sichuan peppercorn powder, dark vinegar, and other ingredients popular in Yunnan—give it a local twist.

The recipe below comes from Wang Yan Po, the owner and cook at Tuanshan Guolian Beef Noodles restaurant in Ming Jiu Zhen. This Miao minority town—home of the Guanyin Cave Temple, a small, picturesque complex of temples built into the side of a mountain during the Qing Dynasty—is about 45 miles north of the Vietnamese border. Wang offers the soup topped with boiled beef, slices of raw beef that cook in the hot broth, or a combination of the two. When making the soup, she uses a variety of beef bones and tough cuts of meat that will hold up to hours of cooking. If you can't find the cross-cut shanks called for below, substitute another tough cut, such as brisket, and add a couple of extra marrow bones to the pot.

Put the beef shanks and beef bones into a large pot with the black cardamom, star anise, and fennel seeds, and cover with 12 cups of water. Bring to a boil over high heat, skim off any foam and detritus that rises to the surface, and reduce the heat. Simmer, covered, for 3 to 4 hours (the longer the soup cooks, the richer the flavor will be). When the broth is ready, stir in the salt, then remove the cooked meat, bones, and seasonings. Reduce the heat to very low. (To give the soup a very clear broth, strain the broth, then return it to the pot.)

If using the cooked meat in the soup, let it cool, then cut it into very thin slices. Bring a large pot of water to a boil and boil the noodles until just soft and toothsome, then drain and divide them between four bowls. Add a small handful of the sliced meat and/or a quarter of the raw beef, to each bowl, then ladle in 2 cups of broth (if using raw steak, bring the broth to a boil before adding it so that the meat will cook through). Serve with toppings on the side.

Boiled Squash Greens

丝
瓜
尖
汤

In a traditional Chinese kitchen, nothing goes to waste. Anything that can be turned into a tasty dish is eaten, and in the countryside, anything too tough for human consumption is fed to livestock. Thick, hearty squash vines are a popular vegetable in the summer, a way of doubling the usefulness of the seasonal plants. At markets, look for the vines of Chinese bottle gourds (called *hulu*), which have thick leaves and small spiny hairs on their vines. They can be fried with eggs (page 142) or, as in this recipe, boiled until they are just barely tender and served as a simple soup—a healthy, refreshing pairing for fatty meats or spicy, oily stir-fries.

¾ lb. squash leaves and vines, ideally bottle gourd greens

2½ tsp. salt

Pull the leaves and their stems off the thicker vines; discard the vines and curly tendrils. Trim off any remaining stems that are particularly thick and tough-looking. (You will have about 6 cups.) In a large pot, bring 6 cups of water to a boil and add the salt. Add the squash greens to the water. Bring the water back to a boil, then stir and cook until the greens are just tender but not soft, about 2 minutes. Transfer everything to a serving bowl.

傣族味凉粉

Dai-Flavor Pea Curd with Vinegar and Cilantro

Yan Bao Farmhouse Fun restaurant in Man Hui Suo Village, on the outskirts of Jinghong, is a mash-up of old and new Yunnan. On one side is a large wooden building, made in the traditional Dai minority style with wooden pillars and a thatched roof, that originally housed the restaurant. On the other side is a brand-new building with faux-marble pillars, a wide spiral staircase, and elaborate cut-glass chandeliers. The popular spot is owned and staffed by an extended family, most of whom live upstairs in the new building's second and third floors. They first opened the restaurant twenty years ago, and the Dai dishes they make, like this cool pea curd cut into thick slices and topped with herbs, chiles, and a slightly sweet vinegar, are wildly popular with locals and, increasingly, the tourists who drive out from resorts in Jinghong for an authentic taste of Xishuangbanna.

1½ tbsp. very finely minced garlic

½ cup cider vinegar

4 tsp. granulated sugar

2 fresh Thai chiles, finely sliced, then roughly chopped

2 tsp. finely minced peeled ginger

1½ tsp. light soy sauce

1 tsp. Dried Chile Oil (page 276)

1 recipe Pea Curd (page 270)

2 tsp. raw sunflower seeds

1½ tbsp. roughly chopped cilantro leaves and stems

In a small bowl, mix the garlic with 2 tbsp. of cool water; set aside for at least 10 minutes while the garlic mellows and the water becomes flavorful.

In a small bowl or jar, mix the vinegar and sugar until the sugar has dissolved, then stir in ¼ cup of cool water. Add the chile, ginger, soy sauce, and Dried Chile Oil and stir to combine.

Cut the pea curd into ½- to ¾-inch-thick slices and stack them in a shallow bowl. Pour the vinegar sauce and the garlic and garlic water over the curd, scatter the sunflower seeds on top, and sprinkle with the cilantro. Serve immediately.

Eastern Yunnan

THE MOUNTAINS OF HUIZE COUNTY are steep and tightly packed, lined up one behind the other like dominoes ready to tumble. Highways in this region are essentially a series of tunnels and bridges that cut straight through the mountain ranges, and many valleys are so narrow that villagers eke out a living by planting corn on terraces only one and a half yards wide, carved into the bases of the steep slopes. In some small towns, space is at such a premium that the vendors who set up Saturday markets selling fruit, vegetables, jewelry, and housewares simply put their tables and tents along the side of the main two-lane road, creating a gridlock of passing cars and sixteen-wheelers fighting for space with shoppers and pedestrians.

While the region is not blessed with much arable land, it is particularly good for one thing: making ham. The most famous hams in Yunnan come from the area just to the south, in Xuanwei County, which sits on Yunnan's border with Guizhou Province. There, farmland is mainly used to grow corn for pigs, and the hams produced in the area are shipped all over China, where they are prized for their intense flavor and command some of the highest prices in the country.

The largest city in the area, Qujing, is known as the gateway to eastern Yunnan's natural attractions, which include waterfalls and the Colorful Sand Forest, an area of narrow canyons carved from colorful standstone rock. But the city itself is lively, with brand-new glass and steel shopping malls, wide avenues crowded with traffic, and small pedestrian alleys full of old buildings that house shops and snack stalls. Many of Qujing's dishes are relatively mild, and some can be a little bit sweet; cooks here tend to use fewer sauces, chiles, and pickles than those elsewhere in Yunnan, letting the flavor of the main ingredients shine through. A few miles north of Qujing, however, in the district of Zhanyi, you'll find one of Yunnan's

clockwise, from top left: a shopper in Babao; a boat ride on the Xiyang River; kids playing in Bamei; rice paddy and karst mountains; a pagoda in Xihua Park in Wenshan; slicing up some of Xuanwei's famous ham

most famous spicy dishes, *lazi ji*, or "chile chicken," tossed with a searing sauce made of fresh chiles and garlic.

Qujing Prefecture is primarily populated by Han and Yi (see Central Yunnan, page 24), but along the eastern edge of the region are also communities of Shui, a minority who mostly live in Guizhou. The Shui are best known in China for their unique pictographic script, called Shuishu, which has been in use for centuries. Some researchers hold that the writing system was developed using ancient Chinese characters as a base, while others believe it developed separately, possibly growing out of the same original pictographic system from which Chinese characters evolved.

To the north of ham country is Zhaotong Prefecture, the poorest region in Yunnan. The area is mountainous and largely agricultural, with beautiful nature preserves and hot springs that local governments are developing as tourist attractions. But outside Yunnan, Zhaotong is known mostly for its unstable terrain and the earthquakes that regularly strike the area and nearby parts of Sichuan, sometimes leveling local towns and villages.

Most of eastern Yunnan's attractions lie to the south, where the mountains give way to picturesque karst landscapes of distinctive hills with craggy outcroppings, sharp, pointed peaks, sheer cliffs, and undulating ridgelines that lie across the horizon like the scales on a dragon's back. In the wide, fertile basins of Luoping County, this landscape is particularly arresting in spring, when the valley floor is transformed into a carpet of golden rapeseed flowers. Tourists from all over the world come to photograph the blooms, crowding into the handful of hotels in Luoping City.

This area is home to the Buyi (or Bouyi), who live primarily in Guizhou Province but have small communities in Yunnan and northern Vietnam. The Buyi have a long history of relations with the Han majority and have become very Sinocized, adopting Confucian, Daoist, and Buddhist ideas and rituals and combining them with their own polytheistic animist traditions. Before the 1950s they sometimes served as middlemen for trading between the Han and other ethnic groups.

The Buyi are known for their sturdy stone houses, which are strikingly different from the wooden houses built by most of the minorities in the area, and they also take pride in their unique, colorful woven fabrics, which entrepreneurs in Luoping sell in a few tourist shops. Some locals have also started building infrastructure to capture tourist traffic during more of the year, planting fields of purple and pink flowers that bloom after the rapeseed has gone to seed and opening restaurants that specialize in traditional dishes such as multicolored sticky rice and sour-spicy fish hot pot.

A hundred miles south of Luoping, the Puzhehei Scenic Area offers a different but equally stunning karst landscape. This area in a wide, slow-moving section of the Beimen River boasts the kind of scenery found in the loveliest of traditional Chinese paintings, with craggy mountains reflected in still water and balloon-like pink lotus blooms rising in front of quaint arched bridges.

Puzhehei has been built up as a tourist area with an official entry gate (and entry fee), manicured lawns with stone paths, and colorful boats that tourists pile into in hot weather, to splash their friends and use toy water cannons to soak their neighbors. But locals still use the waterways for more traditional pursuits. On quieter days, fishermen set their boats under towering clumps of bamboo while they wait for a bite, and women in small rowboats collect enormous lotus leaves to cook with in the small restaurants and inns that line the riverbanks.

Beyond Puzhehei, the watery landscape continues into the southeast corner of Yunnan, where the karst landscape is threaded with small rivers, and farmers use the waterways to irrigate vast fields of rice paddies.

These valleys are dominated by the Zhuang, a large minority who primarily live in neighboring Guangxi Province. The Zhuang are by far China's largest minority group, with over 17 million people. They are extremely Sinocized, and for a long time many Zhuang, Chinese, and Western scholars considered them a part of the Han majority.

The Zhuang are made up of a number of related groups with different myths. In eastern Yunnan, one popular story tells of a duck maiden who helped a Zhuang youth named Yangang search the world for a magical dragon's egg that could put out the fires that were raging across the earth. Yangang then turned into a mountain with a stream that became the Yangang River and brought the earth back to life.

Zhuang-dominated areas are still relatively unknown to travelers, and even the most modern towns have a very rural feel. In the growing town of Babao, for instance, the four-story brick buildings that house hotels, banks, and shops back up to steep hillsides on one side of town and rice fields on the other.

below: carrying fish from the river

This area is also home to 1.2 million members of the Miao miniority. While the Miao are made up of many groups with similar languages and customs, most in Yunnan are part of the Hmong ethnic group. The Hmong trace their origins to China's Yellow River plain, but they migrated west, fleeing Han expansion, roughly 2,000 years ago and moved into the mountains of western China and Southeast Asia. One of the most important stories in Hmong culture says that they were originally given the Mandate of Heaven by the gods and ruled an ancient kingdom, but they eventually lost the mandate to their younger brother, the Han Chinese, and have had to be a nomadic people without political power ever since. Once pushed into the mountains, the Hmong lived in relative poverty and practiced slash-and-burn agriculture. Hmong food in Yunnan and elsewhere tends to be relatively simple, focused on expertly cooking simple dishes so that the ingredients really sing.

There are also communities of Yao in this part of eastern Yunnan and down into the south of the province. Like the Zhuang, the Yao are made up of many groups with different lifestyles and agricultural practices, and even very different languages. But unlike other groups, the Yao have subscribed for centuries to a common name and a common identity. Official Yao history goes back to the Tang Dynasty (618–907 CE), when Chinese imperial authorities first gave groups of people called the Yao official papers allowing them to roam freely in the mountains without paying taxes. These

documents also record the Yao foundation myth. According to the story, the Yao are descended from the dog king Pan Hu, who fought the enemy of the ancient emperor Gao Xin and won the hand of his daughter. The couple fled to the mountains and had twelve children, each of whom became the head of a Yao clan. During the Southern Song Dynasty (1127–1279 CE), the Yao were converted to Daoism, and today the Yao are still Daoists.

⌁

The foods of all of these groups in eastern Yunnan vary considerably as you travel from the north to the south, and all are influenced by the flavors of the provinces to their east. Around Wenshan, dishes begin to reflect the influence of cooking styles popular in Guangxi province—in fact, many Yunnan locals will tell you that the food of the Zhuang minority is the same as the that of Guangxi. Oyster sauce, which is rarely used in most of the province, is a staple flavoring here, and many dishes feature the kinds of brown sauces common in southern Chinese cuisines. In the most picturesque areas, the region's lakes and slow slow-moving rivers are an important source of food, with fish, ducks, lotus roots, and other edible treats pulled from the waterways and delivered straight to homes and restaurant kitchens.

Lessons from a Master Ham Maker

The wooden aging room is dark and cool. Hams hang from the rafters, strung up in long, crowded rows that reach from the ceiling to just a few inches above the floor. The air is dense with an aroma extraordinarily similar to that of well-aged Parmesan cheese—salt and protein concentrated to their very essence; pure umami.

Peng Qingnan moves carefully among his hams, checking to see how they're aging. He uses a special tool carved from a cow's calf bone, a long, thin needle with a bulbous rounded base. First he uses the base like a xylophonist's mallet, tapping on the hams to see if they sound soft or firm; then he slides the needle into the meat, removes it, and sniffs. The aroma tells him whether the ham is aging well. It should smell the way it will taste: meaty and salty and almost sweet. If the wrong bacteria have crept into the pork, it might smell sour, like pickles or unripe plums.

Peng has been making ham in Fan Jia Village, near the city of Huize, since 1986, when he returned from army service in Henan Province, in central China. Peng and his parents worked as butchers, selling pork at the local market, but in the mid-1980s, as the country's first economic reforms were going into effect, he made the decision to start his own business. Until then, all the hams in the area had been made by community groups and sold through the *gongjia* (the system in which the government bought and sold all local products). Peng knew he could do better on his own and taught himself the art of ham making through trial and error. These days, Peng still butchers whole hogs and sells most of the meat at the morning markets, but in the winter he uses all the rear legs of the animals to make ham.

Two years ago, Peng's twenty-four-year-old son, Peng Zehui, moved back home to learn from his father. The younger Peng and his uncle have since expanded the business, investing in a cold room (a walk-in freezer the size of a shipping container) so that they can make hams year-round. Peng Zehui's wife, Fan Zhucun, also joined the family business, selling the remaining pork at the market each morning.

Peng, however, continues to make his hams the traditional way, starting the process at the winter solstice, when the weather is cold. He has built two aging rooms at his house: a large, concrete room where he ages regular hams, and a smaller wooden room, right next to the family living room, for his highest-quality hams. These are made from larger-than-average pigs raised carefully on small farms, and they age for at least two years before they are sold.

Peng saves some of the best ham for his family, and his wife, Tao Lianfen, prepares it in a wide variety of ways. The meat from the thin part of the ham, near the foot, and from the rounded end are the toughest and are usually boiled or stewed. The meat from the center of the leg is steamed with wedges of potatoes, stir-fried with bright, vegetal green chiles, or simply sliced and served on its own, salty and tender and utterly delicious.

---

top to bottom: Peng inspects the hams in his aging room; tools for cutting up the ham

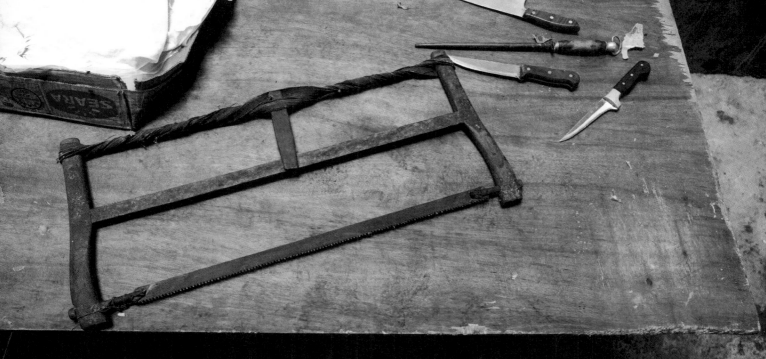

Stir-Fried Ham with Green Chiles

青椒炒火腿

This quick and simple dish, found throughout the province, is a popular way to prepare Yunnan ham. In the east, in places like Xuanwei and Huize, cooks use mild green chiles, such as Korean long peppers, which are particularly flavorful but not very spicy. Cooks in other parts of Yunnan make similar dishes with much hotter local chiles, so if you like heat, feel free to substitute other green peppers.

½ cup vegetable oil or rendered lard

8 oz. Yunnan ham or Spanish Jamón Serrano, rind removed, cut into ⅛-inch-thick slices (about 1½ cups)

2 Korean long chiles, cut crosswise at an angle into long, ¼- to ⅓-inch-thick slices

In a wok, heat the oil or lard over a high flame until very hot. Add the ham and stir-fry, stirring and flipping frequently, until the fat is translucent, about 30 seconds. Remove the meat from the wok with a wok shovel or perforated scoop, leaving the oil. Add the chiles to the oil, and stir-fry until some pieces are beginning to brown a bit, about 30 seconds, then add the ham back in and stir-fry together for 30 seconds so that the ham and chiles flavor each other. Transfer the mixture to a serving plate, draining off the excess oil.

Steamed Ham and Potatoes

火腿蒸洋芋

This dish from Peng Qingnan's wife, Tao Lianfen (page 178), is a genius way to stretch the rich, nuanced flavor of Yunnan's famous hams. Wedges of potato are steamed with thick slices of ham until they soak up the meat's fat and absorb its flavor, and the result is one of the simplest and most delicious dishes in Yunnan.

When Tao makes this dish (pictured on page 181), she steams it in a rice cooker fitted with a special insert that holds the bowl above the boiling water. It can also be made in a deep metal steaming basket; if you don't have a steamer that's deep enough, set a heatproof bowl upside down in the bottom of a pot filled with an inch of water and set the bowl of ham and potatoes on top.

1 lb. red-skinned potatoes or all-purpose, slightly starchy potatoes (about 3 medium-small potatoes)

6 oz. Yunnan ham or Spanish Jamón Serrano, cut into ⅛- to ¼-inch-thick slices (about 1 cup)

EQUIPMENT:

Steamer basket

Peel the potatoes and cut them lengthwise into 1- to 1½-inch-thick wedges. Arrange the slices of ham so that they cover the bottom of a medium-small bowl and come halfway up the sides, overlapping a bit, then fill the rest of the bowl with the potatoes (ideally the bowl will be just barely big enough to contain them).

Fill a pot with 3 inches of water and arrange the bowl in a tightly closed steamer set above it (see note above). Bring the water to a boil, then reduce the heat and steam the ham and potatoes until the potatoes are just tender, about 20 minutes. Remove the bowl from the steamer and invert the mound of potatoes topped with ham onto a serving plate.

Fried Potatoes with Garlic Chives

土豆炒韭菜

Across Yunnan, vendors on street corners set up carts with deep woks in the top and propane tanks attached to the side. These setups are specifically designed for frying sliced potatoes, which customers top with chile flakes and other seasonings and enjoy as a snack. This home-style version of the dish comes from Cui Tonggang, a ham maker who lives in a village just outside Xuanwei, where he has a brand-new aging facility that can hold thousands of high-quality hams at a time.

In this recipe, the potatoes are first fried, then stir-fried briefly with aromatic garlic chives—an ingredient found in many stir-fried dishes served around Xuanwei. The oil used to fry the potatoes is flavored with a bit of pork fat; if you are serving these potatoes with the Stir-Fried Ham with Green Chiles (page 180), you can use the oil left over from frying the ham for that dish as part of the frying oil for the potatoes instead.

3 medium all-purpose potatoes, such as Yukon gold

2 cups vegetable oil

1 oz. fat cut from Yunnan ham or Spanish Jamón Serrano or 1 tsp. rendered bacon fat

½ cup garlic chives cut into 2-inch pieces

1 tsp. dried chile flakes

¾ tsp. salt

Peel the potatoes and cut them at an angle into irregular wedges about 1 inch wide. Heat the oil and the fat in a wok over a high flame until very hot. (To test the temperature of the oil, submerge the tip of a wooden chopstick; it should produce a strong cloud of little bubbles.) If using ham fat, let the pieces of ham brown, then remove them from the wok.

Add the potatoes to the wok and fry them, stirring occasionally, until they are golden brown and the edges have begun to darken, 6 to 8 minutes. Carefully drain all but 1 tbsp. of the oil from the wok into a heatproof container, ideally by pouring everything through a strainer or perforated scoop set over a metal bowl.

Add the garlic chives to the wok and stir-fry gently until they have just begun to wilt, about 30 seconds. Sprinkle in the dried chile flakes and salt, mix well, and transfer to a serving plate, leaving any remaining oil in the wok.

Carrot Greens Salad

曲靖风味凉拌胡萝卜叶

When Yang Lifen decided to open a restaurant, she had no experience with cooking professionally or running her own business, but she did have a mission: to help her parents and the farmers around them in Malong County, near Qujing, find a better way to sell their produce. With that goal in mind, Yang opened a small restaurant called Tusheng Shiguan, or "Native Foods Restaurant," in Kunming that was modeled on the ideals of Community Supported Agriculture. She hired her brother, a restaurant cook, to oversee the food, and bought all her ingredients from her parents and other farmers in her hometown to give them an incentive to grow organic.

This salad is always on the menu in some form or other. In spring, it's made with the tender, flavorful shoots of the Chinese toon tree, but it also works well with other foraged greens and even raw cucumbers. This recipe uses carrot greens as a stand-in for more traditional vegetables. Choose greens that are bright and hearty, and trim off the very bottoms of the stems. You can also make the dish with dark leafy greens such as chrysanthemum greens instead of the carrot tops; just start with a bit less vinegar and soy sauce, then increase the amounts to taste.

6 cups packed carrot greens (1lb.)

5 tsp. Shaanxi vinegar

4 tsp. light soy sauce

1 tbsp. minced garlic

½ tsp. minced fresh Thai chiles

Bring a pot of water to a boil and blanch the greens until the thick parts of the stems are tender and pliable, 1 to 2 minutes. Drain the greens, rinse them with water until cool, then squeeze out all the excess water. Cut the greens into 1½- to 2-inch-long pieces (you will have 1½ to 2 cups of greens).

Transfer the greens to a small mixing bowl. Just before serving, add the remaining ingredients and mix well. Taste and add more vinegar or soy sauce if needed, then transfer to a serving plate.

Gorging on Hot Pot in Yunnan

Walk along the streets of Wenshan looking for dinner, and after a few minutes one thing will become very clear: the residents of this picturesque city love to eat hot pot. Nearly every restaurant in town advertises hot pot of some kind, and in most places it is the restaurant's sole focus. Many of these eateries specialize in two local dishes: Pig's Feet Hot Pot and Golden Clear Broth Beef Hot Pot, the latter a delicious mixture of fatty beef, celery, tomato, julienned carrots, and aromatic herbs cooked in a barely sour broth. Waiters bring out huge pots of steaming soup, set them over gas stoves built into each table, and let them come to a boil. When the broth is hot enough, diners add the meat and vegetables at their leisure, cooking each piece themselves until it is tender and flavorful.

Hot pots are a popular way of preparing food throughout China, but Yunnan boasts an astonishing variety of approaches. Every region and city seems to have its own version. Some are extremely well known, famous specialties that show up in tourist guidebooks and feature prominently on travelers' blogs. In Kunming, for instance, hordes of diners crowd into the city's famous mushroom hot pot restaurants. In Dali, a mild mixture of vegetables and big chunks of firm tofu known as Stone Pot Tofu is simmered gently to preserve the flavors, then served with a dipping sauce of finely ground chile and broth. In Shangri-la, visitors flock to restaurants specializing in yak hot pot, which is traditionally made with short ribs, hand-torn pieces of mushrooms, potatoes, vegetables, and slices of boiled yak meat, all simmered together for a rich, hearty flavor. In some restaurants, these are prepared in the old style, with the ingredients arranged nicely in a special ceramic or metal pot with a large cone in the middle that holds coals to keep the soup hot.

Other hot pots are less famous but equally interesting and delicious. In Qiubei (a small town a couple of hours from Wenshan), locals enjoy a chicken hot pot that includes medicinal herbs foraged from the nearby mountains. In Luoping, Buyi minority cooks make a funky sour hot pot with fish and bamboo shoots. And in Heshun, near Yunnan's western border, you can find the most fascinating hot pot of all, *tou nao*, or "mind." Traditionally made on the second day of Spring Festival, when daughters travel home to visit their mothers, the dish is said to keep the women from feeling any confusion during the rest of the year. It includes taro, sweet potato, mustard greens, bamboo, pieces of fried battered pork, ground pork, thin batons of bacon and pressed tofu, and pork wrapped in chicken skin, and once all of the ingredients have cooked through, it is topped with *nuo mi baba pian*, or "sticky rice cake slices," multicolored chips that puff up when fried like Thai shrimp chips. The dish is as stunning and delicious as it is unusual.

Qujing Stuffed Tofu in Chile Sauce

香豆腐

The façade of Xuanwei Prosperity Farmhouse Foods restaurant in Qujing is covered with rows of aging bamboo, and the sign above the door is painted on flat rice-sorting baskets meant to look rustic and reminiscent of the countryside. Inside, the space is simple but homey, with low wooden tables and stools where families gather to enjoy local foods. This dish, a popular specialty, is made from tofu squares that are stuffed with ground pork, then battered, fried, and smothered in chile sauce. The result is tender and rich, with just enough sauce to impart a spicy, savory flavor that is both surprising and comforting.

2 oz. fatty ground or finely chopped pork (3 to 4 tbsp.)

¼ tsp. salt

24 oz. to 2 lbs. extra-firm tofu (2 grocery-store-style containers), cut into cubes roughly 1 inch by 1½ inches (if working with standard grocery-store-size tofu, cut it into thirds lengthwise and into quarters crosswise)

3½ cups vegetable oil

4 eggs

1 cup cornstarch

½ cup southern-style chile-bean paste (*douban jiang*)

1½ tsp. minced garlic

1 tsp. minced peeled ginger

4 tsp. dried ground chile

In a small bowl, combine the pork and salt and mix well. Arrange the tofu cubes so that the widest sides are face up. Use your index finger to make a small hole in the center of each cube, extending almost through to the bottom of the cube. Insert a bit of the pork mixture into each hole, using a chopstick to press it into place. The meat should be flush with the top of the tofu.

In a wok, heat the oil over a high flame until very hot. (To test the temperature of the oil, submerge the tip of a wooden chopstick; it should produce a strong cloud of little bubbles.) While the oil is heating, beat the eggs in a large bowl until smooth, then add the cornstarch and mix well to make a batter. Add the stuffed tofu to the bowl and use your hands to mix well, so that the tofu cubes are all covered in the batter.

When the oil is hot, carefully put half of the tofu cubes into the oil one by one, making sure that each is covered with batter before adding it. Fry, gently stirring and flipping the tofu with a wok shovel or perforated scoop, for 4 minutes, until the tofu is puffy and has a dark gold color and the edges are beginning to brown. Remove the tofu from the oil with a perforated scoop and set it aside. Repeat with the remaining tofu. Carefully drain all but 3 tbsp. of the oil from the wok into a heatproof container, such as a metal bowl.

(recipe continues)

Heat the oil remaining in the wok until very hot, then add the chile-bean paste, garlic, and ginger and cook, stirring constantly, for 1 minute. Add the ground chile and mix for another 30 seconds. Add 1 cup of water and bring to a boil. Add the fried tofu, toss everything well to coat all the cubes with sauce, and cook, stirring frequently, for 2 minutes. Transfer the tofu and sauce to a serving plate.

炒姜豆

Green Beans Stir-Fried with Garlic and Ginger

This dish of sweet green beans is served at Xuanwei Prosperity Farmhouse Foods in Qujing as a foil for spicy dishes such as Qujing Stuffed Tofu in Chile Sauce (page 188) and Zhanyi Chile Chicken (page 193). The restaurant's cooks prep the beans in the morning so that they are already boiled, sliced, and ready to stir-fry whenever they are ordered.

1 lb. green beans (4 cups)

2 tbsp. vegetable oil

3 dried Thai chiles, cut into 1-inch pieces

1 tbsp. roughly chopped garlic

1 tbsp. roughly chopped peeled ginger

½ tsp. salt

Trim the tips and stem ends of the green beans. Bring a wok or a large pot of water to a boil and boil the beans until tender, 3 to 5 minutes. Rinse the beans with cold water, then cut them in half lengthwise and cut any beans longer than 4 inches in half crosswise.

In a wok, heat the oil over a high flame until very hot. Add the chile, garlic, and ginger and mix just until fragrant, about 10 seconds. Add the green beans and stir-fry, stirring and flipping slowly, until everything is cooked through, about 2 minutes. Add the salt and mix well, then transfer everything to a serving plate.

辣子鸡

Zhanyi Chile Chicken

This dish is exactly what its name says: chicken flavored with a sauce made from masses of searingly spicy chile. Versions of the dish are popular in various parts of China, including in nearby Sichuan, where a particularly famous rendition from the city of Chongqing includes enough dried chiles to completely cover the meat in a thick red blanket. But the dish made in Zhanyi, a small town just outside Qujing, is unique in its simplicity and flavor. It calls for little more than garlic and minced fresh chiles, which combine with the cooking oil to make a sauce that's spicy enough to impress even the most jaded chile enthusiasts. The recipe below lists a range of chiles to be added to this sauce. You can use them all for a truly authentic flavor, but even the smallest amount will still produce a memorably spicy meal.

2 cups vegetable oil

½ chicken, cut across the bone into 1½- to 2-inch pieces (about 2 lbs.)

⅓ cup minced garlic

¼–½ cup minced fresh Thai chiles

2 tsp. oyster sauce

2 tsp. chile sauce (*lajiao jiang*)

1 tsp. salt

½ tsp. Chinese Thirteen Spices Powder (optional)

¼ tsp. Sichuan Peppercorn Powder (page 274)

Heat the oil in a wok over a high flame until very hot. (To test the temperature of the oil, submerge the tip of a wooden chopstick; it should produce a strong cloud of little bubbles.) Add the chicken and cook, gently pushing the meat back and forth with a wok shovel, for 4 minutes. The oil should bubble furiously. Remove the chicken with a spider or a slotted spoon and set it aside. Carefully pour all but about ½ cup of the oil into a heatproof container such as a metal bowl.

Return the wok with the remaining oil to the stove. Add the garlic and chiles and stir-fry, stirring constantly, for 1 minute. Add the oyster sauce, chile sauce, salt, Thirteen Spice Powder (if using), and Sichuan Peppercorn Powder and stir to mix for 10 to 15 seconds. Put the chicken back into the wok and stir-fry for 2 minutes, until the chicken is cooked through. Pour the chicken and sauce into a serving bowl.

茴香酥红豆

Fried Kidney Beans with Fennel

Shelled beans, fresh or dried, are a popular ingredient in eastern Yunnan. You can find them stewed with pigs' feet, cooked in soups with greens, or stir-fried with pickles and chiles. But the most popular (and delightful) way to eat them is coated in a bit of cornstarch and fried until they're crisp on the outside and meltingly soft on the inside. This version of the dish, from Xuanwei Year of the Pig Restaurant in Zhanyi, outside Qujing, pairs crispy red kidney beans with tiny pieces of fennel fronds, which add a hint of their bright, licorice-like flavor to the dish. The original recipe calls for traditional Chinese fennel (see page 18), but the fronds of any style of fennel will work well.

Scant ½ cup dried kidney beans, soaked overnight in water and drained, or 1½ cups cooked kidney beans (approximately a 15-oz. can of prepared beans)

3 tbsp. cornstarch

2½ cups vegetable oil

4 dried Thai chiles, cut into ½-inch pieces

½ cup fennel fronds cut into ½-inch pieces

1 tsp. dried chile flakes

¼ tsp. salt

¼ tsp. Sichuan Peppercorn Powder (page 274)

If using dried beans, put the soaked beans into a medium pot and add enough water to cover by about 4 inches. Bring to a boil, then reduce the heat to medium so that the beans are simmering with just small bubbles rising from the bottom of the pot. Cook until the skins of the beans are tender and the insides are soft but the beans still hold their shape, about 45 minutes to 1½ hours, keeping an eye on the pot to ensure that the water doesn't come to a full boil and adding water if necessary to keep the beans covered. Check the beans frequently toward the end of the cooking to make sure that they don't overcook and become mushy. Drain the beans and set aside to cool.

In a medium bowl, toss the beans and the cornstarch together with your hands, mixing well. Heat the oil in a wok over a high flame until very hot. (To test the temperature of the oil, submerge the tip of a wooden chopstick; it should produce a strong cloud of little bubbles.) Add the beans to the wok and fry them, gently pushing them back and forth in the oil with a wok shovel or a perforated scoop, until crisp, 1 to 1½ minutes. Add the dried chile flakes, then immediately drain the beans and all but 1 tsp. of the oil through a fine-mesh sieve into a heatproof container, such as a metal bowl. Discard the excess oil.

Put the beans back into the wok with the fennel and dried chile flakes and stir for a few seconds, then add the salt and Sichuan Peppercorn Powder. Stir to mix, then transfer to a serving plate.

Bok Choy and Ginger Soup

小白菜汤

Ginger-based soups are popular in the villages and towns around Huize, where locals often eat noodles and pork in a light ginger broth for breakfast—a combination they say warms you up in the winter. This simpler cabbage and ginger soup, made by Tao Lianfen, the wife of local ham maker Peng Qingnan (page 178), is also wonderfully warming, and it is an excellent foil for the salty ham-based dishes she serves, such as Stir-Fried Ham with Green Chiles (page 180). Tao prepares this dish with a large scoop of homemade rendered lard, but a bit of fat from the edge of a well-aged ham or rendered bacon fat gives the soup an equally lovely flavor.

1 tbsp. vegetable oil

1 tsp. flavorful lard or rendered bacon fat or 1 oz. fat cut from Yunnan ham or Spanish Jamón Serrano

3 to 4 small bok choy, leaves separated, with the longer leaves cut in half crosswise (roughly 4 to 5 cups)

2 tbsp. thinly shredded peeled ginger

1½ to 2 tsp. salt

In a wok, heat the oil and fat over a high flame until very hot; if using ham, let the pieces begin to brown. Add 5 cups of water to the wok and bring to a boil. When the water is boiling, add the bok choy and ginger, reduce the heat to medium, and let the vegetables boil, stirring occasionally so that the greens cook evenly, for 10 minutes, until the thick parts of the bok choy are tender and the broth is infused with the ginger flavor. Add 1½ tsp. of the salt, taste the broth, and add more as needed, then transfer to a serving bowl.

炒豆腐皮

Stir-Fried Tofu Skin with Tomato and Bell Pepper

At Native Foods Restaurant, a farm-to-table restaurant that serves Qujing-style foods (page 186), the dishes change with the seasons, but one thing is always on the menu: the famous homemade dried tofu skin. This recipe is about as simple as it gets; the tofu skin is softened in water, then quickly stir-fried with large pieces of bell pepper and tomato until it is tender and almost meaty. For the best results, use the freshest dried tofu skin you can find, and avoid packaged tofu sticks that are so tightly compressed as they are difficult to rehydrate.

6 oz. dried tofu skin

1 tbsp. vegetable oil

3 scallions, white and light green parts only, cut in half lengthwise and then into ½-inch pieces

½ large green bell pepper, thinly cut crosswise into ¼-inch slices

1 firm tomato, cut into ½- to 1-inch cubes

2 garlic cloves, thinly sliced

5 tsp. light soy sauce

Rehydrate the tofu skin by boiling it in a large pot of water until soft but not falling apart (the timing will vary depending on the brand), then drain. When the tofu skin has cooled, cut it into 2-inch-long pieces and set aside (you will have about 3 cups). Trim off and discard any pieces of tofu skin that were so compressed they did not soften in the water.

Heat the oil in a wok over a high flame until very hot, then add the scallions, bell pepper, tomato, garlic, and soy sauce and stir-fry, stirring and flipping frequently, for 30 seconds. Add the tofu skin and stir-fry the mixture, stirring and flipping constantly, for 3 minutes, until the tofu is hot and the vegetables are tender. Transfer to a serving plate.

Carrot Top Soup

川芎汤

This soup of greens seasoned with just a bit of salt and pork fat is traditionally made with *chuan xiong*, or Sichuan lovage (*Ligusticum striatum*), a flowering plant in the carrot family. The roots of the herb are used in Chinese medicine to relieve pain and promote blood circulation, and the greens have a lovely aromatic, vegetal quality similar to carrot greens, which make a fine substitute in this version of the dish.

4 cups carrot greens (leaves and thin stems only, no thick stalks), cut into 3-inch pieces (about 10½ oz.)

2 tsp. salt

2 tsp. rendered pork fat or bacon fat

Bring 5 cups of water to a boil in a wok or medium pot, then add the carrot greens and the salt. Boil the greens for 30 seconds, then add the fat, and boil for another 1 to 2 minutes, stirring gently, until the greens are tender. Transfer to a soup bowl.

Cooking with Flowers

Yunnan is covered in flowers. Azaleas and rhododendrons grow wild in the mountains; sunflowers and morning glories sprout along the sides of country roads. In Luoping, fields of golden rapeseed flowers attract thousands of tourists each year, while in Kunming, China's "Spring City," the parks are planted with tulips, the streets are lined with purple-blossomed jacaranda trees, and nearly every apartment building has a red bougainvillea climbing up its walls. In recent years, the province's climate has made it a center for the commercial flower industry as international companies have established farms here, covering plateaus and hillsides with more bright blooms.

Come summer, flowers begin to show up in home kitchens and restaurants across the province. Squash blossoms and tiny yellow daylilies are cooked with little pieces of ham, jasmine flowers are fried with eggs, and rose petal jam is smeared onto pieces of toasted cheese or baked into sweet cakes that have become such a craze they're sold at specialty stores in nearly every city in the province. In eastern Yunnan, flowers are used to dye grains of rice for the Buyi's most famous dish, "five-color sticky rice." To prepare this dish, the Buyi dye uncooked grains of glutinous rice with flowers, leaves, and herbs to turn them gold, purple, pink, and black, then mix the colored grains with white glutinous rice and steam everything together into a festive dish full of the same colors that brighten the Luoping Valley when flower fields are in bloom.

Babao-Style Duck Stewed in Beer

黄炯鸭

Dragon Spring Restaurant in Babao is a large, two-story affair. It is owned and run by Wei Hanyan, a Zhuang minority woman who grew up in town, and serves dishes such as fried catfish in brown sauce, stewed beans, and this rich duck stew. The sauce the duck is cooked in—a brown sauce made with local beer, oyster sauce, sesame oil, and other flavorings—is full of ingredients rarely seen in other parts of Yunnan. It is a perfect example of how the foods made on the eastern edge of the province resemble those of neighboring Guizhou, with the chiles and pickles popular in Yunnan used alongside flavorings favored in southern China, such as oyster sauce and Chinese cooking wine.

4 cups vegetable oil

5 garlic cloves, smashed with the side of a cleaver

3 slices of unpeeled ginger, each about ½ inch by 1 inch

½ duck (about 2½ lbs.), cut across the bone into 1-inch pieces

1½ tbsp. Chinese Shaoxing cooking wine

10 dried Thai chiles, cut into 1-inch pieces

1 pint weak Chinese lager, such as Snow or Tsingtao

1½ tbsp. oyster sauce

2 tsp. fragrant chile sauce (*xiangla jiang*)

1¼ tsp. sesame oil

¾ tsp. dark soy sauce

2 scallions, both white and green parts, cut into 1½-inch pieces

1 tbsp. cornstarch mixed with 1 tbsp. water

In a wok, heat the oil over a high flame until very hot. (To test the temperature of the oil, submerge the tip of a wooden chopstick; it should produce a strong cloud of little bubbles.) Add the garlic and ginger and cook for about 10 seconds, until fragrant. Add the duck and cook, gently pushing the meat back and forth with a wok shovel, for 1 minute. The oil should bubble furiously. Add the cooking wine and dried chiles and continue cooking, stirring frequently, for 2 minutes.

Carefully pour all but 1 tbsp. of the oil into a heatproof container such as a metal bowl; this is easiest to do if you pour it through a sieve to catch any pieces of meat or aromatics that might fall out with the oil.

Add the beer to the wok, stir the mixture well, and bring it to a vigorous boil. Boil for 2 minutes, stirring occasionally, then scoop out any remaining foam. Add the oyster sauce, fragrant chile sauce, sesame oil, and soy sauce to the mixture and stir well, then continue boiling for 4 minutes as the liquid begins to reduce.

Add the scallions to the mixture and cook until they are soft, about 2 minutes. Add the cornstarch-water mixture, stir everything well for a few seconds to thicken the sauce, and transfer all the ingredients to a serving bowl with just enough sauce to cover.

Crayfish with Chiles and Sichuan Peppercorns

麻辣小龙虾

Boiled, brick-red crayfish fried in aromatic spices are a summertime meal enjoyed in many parts of China. The crayfish are usually eaten in restaurants, where customers set aside chopsticks and don thin plastic gloves before tearing apart the petite crustaceans to get the meat from their tails, heads, and sometimes claws.

This recipe comes from Mrs. Sun, the cook at Green Plum Farmhouse Fun, a small family restaurant in Puzhehei. Mrs. Sun often runs the restaurant by herself, taking orders and then preparing each dish from scratch, sometimes working with a friend's baby strapped to her back, while her own daughter, a charming eight-year-old, helps serve the food. Cooks in some places, such as Chengdu, flavor crayfish with a whole pantry's worth of spices; Mrs. Sun uses a simple combination of chile powder and Sichuan peppercorn with fresh garlic, ginger, and scallions, which lets the flavor of the crayfish shine.

3-inch knob of unpeeled ginger + 2 tsp. thinly sliced peeled ginger

2 whole scallions + 2 scallions, both white and green parts, cut into 2-inch pieces

1 lb. live crayfish

3 tbsp. vegetable oil

2 garlic cloves, thinly sliced

3 fresh Thai chiles, roughly chopped

2 tsp. Sichuan peppercorns

1½ tsp. dried chile flakes

1½ tsp. Sichuan Peppercorn Powder (page 274)

Fill a pot with water, add the knob of ginger and the 2 whole scallions, and bring to a boil, then add the live crayfish. Return the water to a boil and boil the crayfish for 3 minutes. Drain the crayfish and let them cool and dry.

In a wok, heat the oil over a high flame until very hot. Add the crayfish, garlic, and sliced ginger and stir-fry, stirring and flipping constantly, for 30 seconds. Add the cut-up scallions and chopped chiles and stir-fry, stirring and flipping constantly, for 1 minute to cook the chiles. Reduce the heat to low, add the Sichuan peppercorns, chile flakes, and Sichuan Peppercorn Powder, and cook for 1 minute, stirring and flipping until everything is well mixed. Immediately transfer the mixture to a serving platter.

鮮蓮子炒肉

Pork Stir-Fried with Lotus Seeds

Lotus seeds are valued ingredients in Chinese medicine, used to improve heart and brain health and combat fatigue. Also a versatile food, they have a crunchy texture and a mild, nutty flavor that pairs well with a wide variety of ingredients. This simple dish of lotus seeds with stir-fried pork and soft, lightly cooked scallions highlights the seeds' nuttiness with a mild seasoning of garlic and salt.

At Green Plum Farmhouse Fun restaurant in Puzhehei, the cook, Mrs. Sun, makes this stir-fry (pictured on page 202) with fresh lotus seeds plucked from the nearby lake; they come to market in their stunningly beautiful bright green pods, ready to be peeled, blanched, and cooked. Dried lotus seeds, which are readily available in Asian markets, are less crunchy than fresh ones, but soaking them in cool water restores much of their texture and flavor.

⅓ cup dried lotus seeds

8 oz. lean pork, such as boneless pork chop

¼ cup vegetable oil

2 garlic cloves, cut into thick slices

3 scallions, both white and green parts, cut crosswise into 2-inch pieces

1¼ tsp. salt

Put the lotus seeds into a bowl and add water to cover by at least 2 inches. Soak the seeds until they have softened, at least 2 hours. Drain and set aside.

Cut the pork into very thin slices. (The easiest way to do this is by pulling the meat away from the knife slightly with one hand when slicing with the other hand so that there is tension between the knife and the meat. You will have about 1 cup.) If any of the slices are wider than ½ inch, cut them in half lengthwise to make long, thin slices.

Fill a wok with 1½ inches of water and bring it to a boil. Add the lotus seeds, and boil until tender and cooked through, about 5 minutes, then drain the seeds and discard the water.

In a wok, heat the oil over a high flame until very hot. Add the garlic and pork and stir-fry, stirring and flipping constantly, until the pork is just cooked through, about 30 seconds. Add the lotus seeds, scallions, and salt, and stir-fry, pressing the meat up against the side and bottom of the wok so that it browns a bit, for 1 minute. Transfer the mixture to a serving plate, draining away any excess oil.

干腌菜拌饭

Cold Rice Bowl with Stewed Beef and Herbs

½ lb. ground or finely chopped beef (scant 1 cup)

2 tbsp. vegetable oil

2 tbsp. southern-style chile-bean paste (*douban jiang*)

2 tbsp. fragrant chile sauce (*xiangla jiang*)

1¼ cups bean sprouts

1⅓ cups Chinese celery greens (leaves and thin stems)

5 cups cooked rice, at room temperature

½ cup scallions, white and light green parts only, cut in half lengthwise, then crosswise into ½-inch pieces

¼ cup Pickled Mustard Greens (page 272)

6 tsp. minced garlic, covered with 2 tbsp. water

8 tsp. light soy sauce

4 tsp. sesame oil

4 tsp. Dried Chile Oil (page 276)

1 tsp. salt

1 tsp. Sichuan Peppercorn Powder (page 274)

Afternoons are snack time in Wenshan, a sunny city of half a million people and the capital of Wenshan Zhuang and Miao Autonomous Prefecture. Vendors selling freshly grilled tofu, boiled corn on the cob, or pots of steamed rice with sweet sausage, set up carts on the corners of wide, tree-lined streets, and students stop by tiny mom-and-pop shops for bowls of cold sticky rice dumpling soup finished with rose petal jam. Very hungry eaters look for hearty options like this bowl of cooled rice topped with sweet and spicy stewed beef, sour pickled mustard greens, minced garlic and ginger, and chopped herbs—a wonderful combination. When preparing the ingredients for this dish, it's best to cook the rice just a couple of hours before serving; if refrigerated, it will dry out and become a little too firm and mealy. Makes four servings.

Prepare the beef by breaking it up with a fork or chopping it lightly. In a wok, heat the oil over a high flame until very hot. Add the beef and stir-fry, stirring frequently and using a wok shovel to break up any large pieces of meat, until it is just cooked through. Add the chile-bean paste and the fragrant chile sauce and cook, mixing thoroughly, for 2 minutes, then remove from the heat and let it cool to room temperature or chill.

Bring a large pot of water to a boil. Boil the bean sprouts until they begin to wilt, about 3 minutes, then remove them from the pot with a perforated scoop and rinse with cold water to cool. Squeeze them well to remove all the water and set them aside. In the same pot, boil the celery greens until the stems are tender, about 1 minute, then remove them from the pot with a perforated scoop and rinse with cold water to cool. Cut the greens into 1-inch pieces and set aside.

Divide the rice between four bowls (1¼ cups of rice per bowl) and top each with one quarter of the meat sauce (about 3 tbsp.). Add 2 tbsp. each of the celery and scallions, 1 tbsp. each of the bean sprouts and pickled greens, 2 tsp. each of the minced garlic in water and soy sauce, 1 tsp. each of the sesame oil and Dried Chile Oil, and ¼ tsp. each of the salt and Sichuan Peppercorn Powder. Mix well just before eating.

姜
爆
鸭

Stir-Fried Duck with Ginger

Bamei Village is fast becoming one of eastern Yunnan's most popular getaways. The idyllic hamlet of Zhuang minority houses sits in a valley that is accessible only by boat. Villagers grow rice and make extra money hosting visitors in small bed-and-breakfasts. But the real life of the area happens in the small town from which tourists embark on this journey, also called Bamei. Afternoon and early evening are the busiest times on the town's main street. Swarms of kids leaving school crowd around snack vendors selling cold noodles from carts on the side of the road; restaurants set tables and stools out on the sidewalk for early dinner service; farmers make their way home, walking next to carts pulled by plodding water buffalo.

This recipe for duck stir-fried with ginger and garlic comes from Nan Bei Restaurant. The cook, Fu Jin Mai, serves simple dishes at tables set up on a covered area of the sidewalk, and diners enjoy the meal slowly, eating, drinking, and smoking with friends under the light of a few bare bulbs.

½ duck, including one leg, one thigh, and one breast (about 2½ lbs.)

¼ cup vegetable oil or rendered lard

6 dried Thai chiles, cut into 1-inch pieces

2 tbsp. thinly sliced peeled ginger

1 tsp. salt

2 tsp. chopped garlic

Cut the duck across the bone into 1- to 2-inch pieces, then cut any pieces longer than 2½ inches in half. Alternatively, bone the duck, and cut the meat into 1- to 1½-inch-thick strips.

In a wok, heat the oil over a high flame until very hot. Add the duck, chile, ginger, and salt, and stir-fry, stirring and flipping frequently, until the meat no longer looks raw, about 5 minutes. Add 1 cup of water to the wok and bring it to a strong boil. Cook, stirring occasionally, so that the meat cooks evenly, for 3 minutes. Add the garlic and cook for 1 minute to soften, then serve with the broth.

清炒番薯叶

Stir-Fried Sweet Potato Leaves with Garlic

Dishes made with tender sweet potato leaves are enjoyed throughout Asia. Often labeled as "yam leaves," these greens are actually from the vines of sweet potatoes, while true yams are a different vegetable entirely. Here, the greens are cooked simply, stir-fried with a generous scoop of garlic and enough dried chiles to make them a bit spicy. When preparing the greens, pull the leaves and their long stems off the thicker stalks of the vine. Some of the leaves will be up to 5 inches long, but they do not need to be cut up.

¼ cup vegetable oil

5 dried Thai chiles, cut into ½-inch pieces

5 cups sweet potato leaves and stems

3 tbsp. roughly chopped garlic

½ to ¾ tsp. salt

In a wok, heat the oil over a high flame until very hot. Add the chiles and cook for a few seconds, until fragrant, then add the sweet potato leaves and stems, garlic, and salt. Stir-fry, stirring and flipping constantly, until the greens are wilted, about 30 seconds. Add ¼ cup of water and continue to cook, stirring and tossing frequently, until all the water has boiled away and the stems are just tender, about 2 minutes. Taste and add more salt, if necessary. Transfer to a serving bowl.

坝包杂酱米线

Babao-Style Breakfast Noodles

Mornings in Babao revolve around the market. The small city in Yunnan's far southeast has recently counted a population of 70,000, but it is still a very rural place, where most houses stand in little clusters among rice fields. The densest part of the city is only four blocks wide. Across the street from the main market, you'll find a small noodle stall marked simply with a sign that says "breakfast." Instead of spicy chiles or salty pickles, the noodles here are flavored with a variety of mild toppings: a small spoonful of meat stewed in a mild chile-bean paste sits next to poached slices of lean pork and reddish-pink slices of sweet, fatty Chinese sausage (an ingredient far more common in southern China than in Yunnan). Crunchy fried peanuts and a table full of optional sauces and fresh herbs round out the unusual and delightful flavors. Makes four servings.

In a small bowl, cover the dried shiitake with hot water, setting another small bowl on top to keep the mushroom submerged, and soak until it is soft. Drain the soaking water, replace it with cool water, and soak for 5 minutes. Drain the mushroom, squeeze out the excess water, and finely chop.

Prepare the pork by breaking it up with a fork or chopping it lightly. In a wok, heat the oil over a high flame until very hot. Add mushrooms and pork and stir-fry the mixture, stirring and flipping frequently and using a wok shovel to break up any large pieces of meat, until it is just cooked through. Add the chile-bean paste and fragrant chile sauce and cook, mixing thoroughly, for 2 minutes, then transfer the mixture to a heatproof bowl and set aside.

Bring a large pot of water to a boil. Boil the sliced pork until just cooked through, 15 to 30 seconds, then remove it with a slotted spoon. Boil the sausage until just cooked through, 15 to 30 seconds, then remove it with a slotted spoon. (If serving the soup immediately, keep the water boiling to cook the noodles.)

FOR THE PORK WITH BEAN SAUCE:

1 large dried shiitake mushroom

¼ lb. ground or finely chopped pork (scant ½ cup)

2 tbsp. vegetable oil

1 tbsp. southern-style chile-bean paste (*douban jiang*)

1 tbsp. fragrant chile sauce (*xiangla jiang*)

FOR THE SOUP:

5 oz. pork, thinly sliced
(scant ⅔ cup)

1½ oz. Chinese sausage,
thinly sliced (¼ cup)

½ cup vegetable oil

½ cup shelled raw peanuts

4 large handfuls of fresh
rice noodles or 14 oz. dried rice
noodles, such as Vietnamese
rice sticks

8 cups Pork Broth (page 280)

TOPPINGS:

¼ cup Sesame Seeds in Oil
(page 278)

Dried Chile Oil (page 276)

Sichuan Peppercorn Powder
(page 274)

¼ cup finely sliced cilantro leaves

¼ cup finely chopped
Chinese celery

2 tbsp. minced garlic covered with
¼ cup water

2 tbsp. minced peeled ginger

In a clean wok, heat the vegetable oil and peanuts over a high flame until sizzling, then reduce the heat to medium-low. Fry, stirring gently and continuously, for 5 minutes, then remove the peanuts from the wok with a slotted spoon and discard the oil.

Bring a large pot of water to a boil and cook the noodles until just soft and toothsome.

While the water is boiling, bring the Pork Broth to a simmer, then divide it between four large bowls. Drain the noodles, and divide them between the soup bowls. Top each bowl of noodles with one quarter of the pork with bean sauce, one quarter each of the boiled pork and sausage, and one quarter of the fried peanuts. Serve with the toppings on the side.

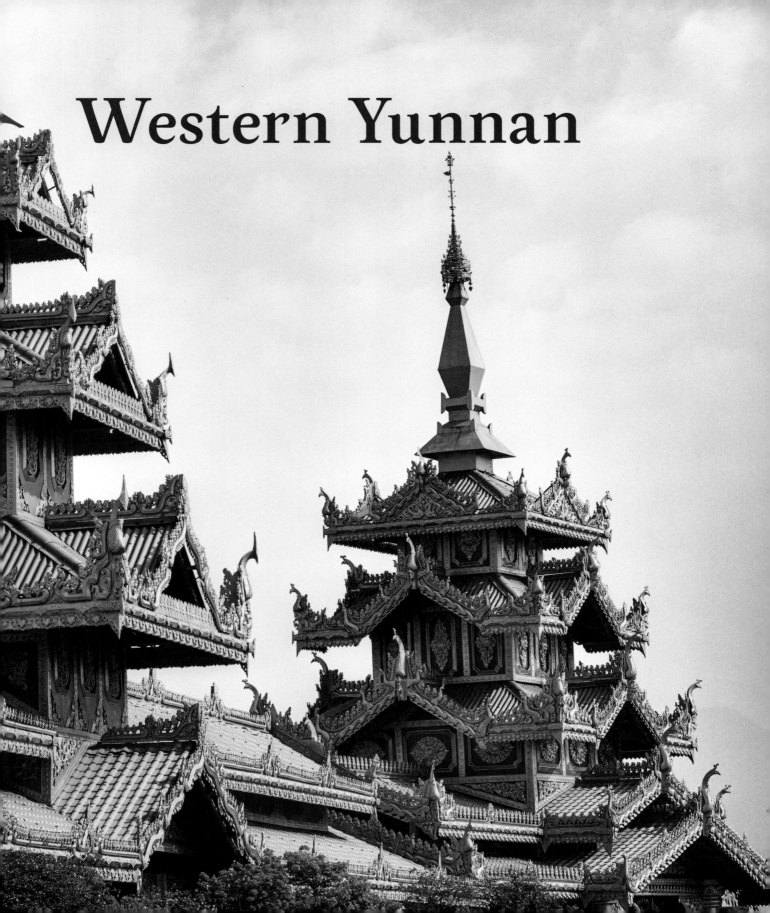

Western Yunnan

THE HISTORY MUSEUM in Heshun Ancient Town is filled with artifacts from the area's heyday—ancient leather saddles and horse bells, golden statues of boddhisattvas imported from Southeast Asia, delicate china plates painted with intricate European patterns and other relics of the British Consulate that operated here in the early 1900s. The items serve as a reminder that this town of Qing Dynasty–era houses and the nearby city of Tengchong were once a major stop on the ancient Tea Horse Road. For hundreds of years, caravans carrying jade from Burma, tea from southern Yunnan, and goods from all across China and South Asia stopped at this now-sleepy border town. In the early 1800s, Tengchong saw more trade than the port city of Guangzhou (the entry-point for the opium then flooding the country).

These days, Heshun's old stone buildings are being refurbished to attract the tourists who come to enjoy the area's tranquil mountain landscape and famous hot springs. Small inns and restaurants have sprung up, and the Chinese and European tourists who make their way up the steep, winding pedestrian streets are delighted to find elderly ladies selling local snacks, and even a couple of third-wave coffee shops specializing in locally grown Yunnan coffee.

Cross-border trade is still evident a few miles away at Tengchong's markets. Vendors in Burmese dress sell a wide variety of tropical fruit and vegetables, as well as salads of lightly pickled Asian pear or spears of jicama and cucumber tossed with fresh herbs, salt, and copious amounts of dried chile. At food stands around town you'll find local specialties that are common in Shan State in Myanmar, such as thin rice noodles mixed with a pudding-like soybean porridge called *xidoufen*, topped with vinegar, chile oil, sesame seeds, peanuts, fresh herbs, and a small scoop of diced tomato.

clockwise, from top left: a new temple in Mangshi, ready to be painted; a Burmese snack vendor in Ruili; breakfast at the market in Baoshan; the Tree-Wrapped Pagoda in Mangshi; a flower vendor at the market in Ruili; an altar in the Bodhi Temple; fabric for sale in Mangshi; statues at the Bodhi Temple; cooks taking a break at Yingjiang Dai Flavor Restaurant

Today, Yunnan's center of trade with Myanmar has moved farther south, to the city of Ruili. At the city's main border crossing, trucks full of goods line up for inspection and groups of young men and women in long Burmese skirts walk to jobs on the Chinese side of the border. Visitors can catch a glimpse of the edge of the Burmese town of Muse on the other side of the border fence, a cluster of brightly painted buildings with signs and billboards of a strikingly different style from what you see on the Chinese side, just a few yards away.

Most visitors to Ruili come for the city's famous jade market, based within a few blocks of low workshops and storefronts in the center of town. The market caters to every kind of buyer; vendors with counters in large, department-store-style markets sell small pendants, simple bracelets, and relatively affordable amulets, while smaller shops manned by businessmen or women in elegant dresses display intricately carved statues and traffic in high-end jewelry. Many of the jade traders are Burmese—including a significant number of Burmese Muslims—and at noon many make their way to a small open-air food court where cooks set up steam tables covered with dozens of Burmese dishes, like pungent fermented tea salads, and Dai minority dishes like a subtly flavored meatball soup.

Of course, Ruili's cross-border trade also has a dark underbelly. The old bridge that linked Ruili and Muse (which was replaced in 2005) was known as the "gun bridge" because of the area's illegal arms trade, and in the past few years, China has erected a series of tall fences along the border to try to stem the flow of illegal drugs. This is the kind of place where you can't drive for more than 45 minutes without being stopped by baby-faced policemen, turned out in full camo and carrying assault rifles, who inspect your papers and open your luggage to check for drugs.

This part of western Yunnan is also one of the richest agricultural areas in the province. The landscape supports tobacco, tea, and coffee production, as well as some mining and logging. Combined with the cross-border trade, these industries have made this corner of Yunnan relatively wealthy. In cities like Ruili and Mangshi, the capital of Dehong Dai and Jingpo Autonomous Prefecture, packed malls sell everything from trendy clothes to international luxury goods, and cars are quickly replacing bikes and motor scooters. Towns in this area don't preserve or rehabilitate their historic buildings as the more touristy spots in Yunnan do, so pressed-earth-brick houses are rapidly being replaced by the kinds of brightly painted three-story homes that are popular throughout Southeast Asia.

The boundary between China and Myanmar was not settled until the 1960s, and the area around Ruili and Mangshi is home to many groups that still have strong ties across the border and whose foods are usually associated with Myanmar rather than China. The largest minority group in the region is the Dai, who are considered members of the same minority group as the Dai in southern Yunnan (page 124) but are more closely connected to Shan communities in Myanmar (who are part of the same ethnic group) and were ruled by Shan princes for centuries. The western Dai are wet rice farmers, like their southern cousins, and their foods are known for their combination of spicy and sour flavors.

The Jingpo also maintain close ties in Myanmar, where members of their ethnic group are classified as part of the Kachin minority. Among Westerners, the Kachin, including the Jingpo, are perhaps best known as guerrillas who fought alongside American troops during World War II. After the war, the Kachin on the Burmese side of the border used their training to fight for independence against the newly established Myanmar government, and that ongoing conflict regularly spills over into Yunnan, with artillery shells and large groups of refugees both occasionally crossing the border.

Western Yunnan is also home to small pockets of Achang and De'ang, two of Yunnan's smaller groups. The De'ang are among the smallest minority groups in China. According to local stories, the De'ang were the first to settle the area around Mangshi, and archaeological remains of ancient roads, towns, and tea plantations are thought to have come from the De'ang's ancestors.

The Achang, like the Dai, live in the valleys and farm rice paddies. Renowned for their skills as knife makers, they have produced sabers, daggers, and swords for more than 600 years, and their "Husa knives" are known across China for their beauty and sharpness. Within Yunnan, the Achang are also known for making a unique and delicious dish, *guoshou mixian*, or "crossing the hand rice noodles." These tender noodles, made with red rice, have a slight reddish hue, but what sets the dish apart is the way it is served: diners take a small handful of noodles in their fingers, top it with a small scoop of a rich sauce made from grilled pork belly, add condiments like raw shredded cabbage and minced chiles, then eat it all together as the sauce runs down their hands.

opposite, top to bottom: tobacco leaves strung up to dry; a vendor at the market in Ruili; dried beans and peas for sale in Tengchong

below: the entrance to Bodhi Temple

top to bottom: stir-frying foraged greens; boiling taro and sour bamboo shoots

East of Ruili, in Fengqing County, are the terraced tea plantations where Yunnan's famous *dianhong* tea grows. This black tea (or "red tea" in Chinese) is a relatively new crop in Yunnan, introduced in the late 1930s when the Japanese occupation of southern China made it impossible to get black tea from China's coast. Tea from Fengqing is considered very high quality, and the best teas—those with inch-long bright golden leaves—are classified as "Special Finest Tippy Golden Flowery Orange Pekoe," the same classification given to the best teas in Darjeeling, India.

Once *dianhong* tea is harvested and processed, it is sold several hours farther south, in Lincang, the county seat. The quiet city has a small-town feel, with relatively little traffic and a slow way of life, but the tea trade is making residents wealthy, and the city center is filled with tall glass office buildings, stores selling Western-style baked goods, and luxury cars.

The mountains around Lincang are home to communities of Lahu and Wa, two groups with histories of resisting Chinese rule. In China, the Lahu (or Luohei) are known primarily for leading rebellions against the Chinese state during the Qing Dynasty. In the late 1700s, Buddhist monks converted the Lahu to a religion that combined Buddhist and Daoist ideas and also incorporated the Lahu creator, E Sha, and they established administrative areas called the Five Buddha Districts. A charismatic monk named Tong Jin and his hereditary successors were considered reincarnations of the E Sha Buddha (a combination of the two deities), and led frequent rebellions against the Qing government and the ruling Dai and Shan. When the Chinese government crushed this movement, the Wa took control of the mountain territories, including important trade routes. The area was hard to farm, so the Wa grew only opium, tea, and cotton and traded them for grain, cattle, and salt. To maintain access to these vital foodstuffs (and keep both the British and the Chinese from taking over their territories), the Wa cultivated a reputation as a culture of fierce warriors; some groups turned to headhunting, a wartime tradition that was also practiced by the Qing army. Today most Chinese still refer to this stereotype about the Wa, and local tourist sites and restaurants play up that history with images of warriors and references to their traditional animal sacrifices—and to the feasts that followed them.

The unifying quality of the foods in western Yunnan is their similarity to foods in nearby areas of Myanmar. In some dishes you can even taste the influence of British imperialism in ingredients like sweetened condensed milk, which is a popular addition to blended fruit drinks and desserts like tapioca with milk and coconut. Cooks make liberal use of chiles, both fresh and dried, and many dishes rely on foraged greens or highlight the astringent flavor of sour pickled bamboo. Many locals still cook over wood fires, and dishes wrapped in banana leaves are staples, as are those made with dried beef that's pounded and mixed with herbs and spices.

The foods of the region's minority groups differ in subtle ways. Cooks will tell you that their foods are distinguished by their use of sour ingredients (the Dai), their reliance on expensive foraged ingredients (the Jingpo), or their skill making rice noodles (the Achang). But if you travel in the region, the first thing anyone will tell you about a particular minority's food is how spicy it is—whether it is more or less spicy than their own food—and whether they think you'll be able to handle the heat.

clockwise; from left: a snack stand in Tengchong; painted glasses; pickled fruit with herbs and dried chiles in the market in Tengchong

Dai Lime Chicken

傣味柠檬拌鸡丝

Meng Mingchun did not set out to become a restaurateur. Now the owner of four busy Dai-style restaurants, Meng originally worked in a department store in Yinjiang, a small city near the Myanmar border. But when her son enrolled in college in Kunming, Meng decided to move with him and opened a restaurant called Yingjiang Dai Flavor Restaurant.

At first Meng cooked everything herself in a small space decorated with painted green bamboo on the façade. She made classic dishes like Vegetables Grilled in Banana Leaves (page 247), Stir-Fried Banana Flower (page 237), and this bright, spicy, herb-laden chicken salad. The flavors proved popular among locals, and soon Meng had the capital to open another branch as well as a noodle shop and a storefront specializing in Dai holiday-style dishes. Meng now oversees a staff of roughly 80 cooks and waitresses, all of whom came from Yingjiang just to work for her.

This popular dish, sometimes called Ghost Chicken on restaurant menus, is served by Dai cooks across western Yunnan, and variations abound. Meng's version uses five different herbs, but in a pinch they can be limited to just cilantro and sawtooth herb. The salad is traditionally made with black-skinned chicken, also called "silky" chicken, which has a lovely, rich flavor and an interesting black and white color, but you can make the dish using regular chicken.

2½ lb. whole black-skinned chicken or 2 lb. whole free-range chicken

3-inch knob of unpeeled ginger, washed and smashed with the side of a cleaver

2 scallions, both white and green parts

5 tsp. salt

1 cup sawtooth herb, cut into 1-inch pieces

1 cup cilantro leaves and stems, cut into 1-inch pieces

½ cup Vietnamese coriander, cut into 1-inch pieces

2 to 5 fresh Thai chiles, thinly sliced

1½ tsp. minced garlic

1 to 2 limes

Put the chicken, ginger, scallions, and 4 tsp. of the salt into a pot and add water to cover by 1 inch. Bring to a boil, skim off any foam and detritus that rises to the surface, and reduce the heat to a gentle boil. Cook the chicken, uncovered, for 1 hour. (If the chicken floats while cooking, rotate it occasionally to ensure all the meat cooks evenly.) Remove the chicken from the broth and let it cool. Discard the broth or reserve it for another use.

When the chicken is cool enough to handle, use your fingers to remove the meat from the bones and tear it into thin strips, discarding the skin, bones, fat, and connective tissue. (You will have about 2½ cups of meat.) Toss the chicken with the herbs, chiles, garlic, and remaining 1 tsp. salt, then squeeze the juice of one lime over the mixture, drizzle on 2 tbsp. of water, and toss the mixture again. Taste the salad and add more lime juice and/or salt as needed; the flavor should be pleasantly piquant.

柠檬春干巴

Dai Dried Beef Salad with Fennel and Chiles

Yunnan's traditional dried beef is often eaten on its own, like jerky, but it also serves as the basis for delicious salads that offset the meat's rich flavor with herbs and chiles. This version, popular at Dai restaurants (where it's called "lemon spring dried beef"), is full of herbs, ginger, and garlic and is dressed with fresh lime juice. Local cooks make this dish with Chinese fennel, a variety that does not grow large bulbs and is prized instead for its flavorful fronds—but the lacy leaves of the bulbous fennel available in Western markets also work well.

1¼ cups shredded Dried Beef (about ½ recipe) (page 266)

2 tbsp. thinly sliced sawtooth herb

1½ tsp. minced garlic

1½ tsp. minced peeled ginger

1½ tbsp. lime juice (from about 1 lime)

Scant ¼ cup fennel fronds cut into 1-inch pieces

1 fresh Thai chile, thinly sliced

Mix the shredded beef with the sawtooth herb, garlic, and ginger, then drizzle over the lime juice and toss until well combined. Add the fennel and chile, toss the salad gently, and transfer to a serving plate.

Serving Up a Taste of Home

Shang Qinzhen came to Mengwen Village for love. A member of the Jingpo minority, Shang grew up in a traditional village near Yunnan's border with Myanmar, but she moved to the city for work and fell in love with a Han man. Shang knew that the elders in her village would never condone an intermarriage, so the couple made their way to her husband's hometown, Mengwen, a small grouping of low brick and cinder-block houses on the side of a hill called Wind Blowing Slope. Once settled, they established a large plantation of *pu'er*-style longleaf tea that climbs the side of the mountain in neatly terraced rows.

At first, Shang cooked only for friends and family, making traditional Jingpo dishes to share a bit of her culture with friends, neighbors, and her Baptist church group. It wasn't until after she was widowed in her forties that she considered opening a restaurant. Her husband's business had left her with substantial debts, and her neighbors and local government officials encouraged her to put her cooking skills to use for the community. With their help, Shang eventually built a simple open-air dining room filled with low, round bamboo tables and a long kitchen in the back, and named it White Flower Rural Foods Restaurant.

Now in her sixties, Shang still does all the cooking at the restaurant herself, with occasional help from her daughter or local friends. Her menu boasts an assortment of traditional Jingpo dishes. Piquant salads are common, such as a mix of four different herbs with shallots and chiles; shredded dried beef flavored with ginger, galangal, and tomatoes; or cold chicken tossed with lime juice and tea leaves that Shang picks directly from her husband's old tea plants. Most cooked foods are prepared on a wood fire, including various dishes that are cooked in freshly cut bamboo: the ingredients (such as thin strips of fish mixed with garlic, chiles, and foraged herbs) are stuffed into wide sections of the bamboo, sealed off with handfuls of banana leaves, then roasted in the fire, where they cook in their own juices until the wood is charred and smoky.

When the food is prepared, Shang covers a table with fresh banana leaves, forms a circle of sticky rice and steamed rice flavored with vegetables and pork in the center, and arranges the dishes around it, the way she would serve food at home on special occasions. Guests are encouraged to eat with their hands, scooping up each bite with a bit of sticky rice while sipping fragrant tea harvested from the surrounding hills.

---

clockwise, from top left: Shang coats pork belly with dried chile and salt before grilling it over wood coals. Many of the traditional Jingpo dishes she serves are made with raw vegetables and served cold, like this salad of Asiatic pennywort and herbs (see recipe, page 229). Shang also adds fish mint root to the dish. Many dishes are roasted over the fire in pieces of fresh green bamboo. The sticky rice Shang serves with Ghost Chicken with Tea Leaves (see recipe, page 228) and other dishes has been dyed gold with dried flowers.

Ghost Chicken with Tea Leaves

The dining room of Shang Qinzhen's restaurant (page 226) looks out over row upon row of the manicured tea plants her late husband cultivated when the couple first moved to his home village. Shang serves the tea with every meal, but she also uses the long leaves to make this wonderful salad, a Jingpo minority take on the region's popular cold chicken and herb salads. Softened in cool water and combined with poached chicken, cilantro, dried chile flakes, and lime juice, the tea leaves have an herbaceous quality that gives the dish a depth and dimension no other ingredient can duplicate.

The tea leaves Shang uses for her salad (pictured page 227) are the three-inch-long leaves used in Yunnan to make *pu'er* tea. This version of the recipe calls for regular green tea leaves in their place, but if you can find long, loose unaged *pu'er* leaves, use them instead.

2½-lb. whole black-skinned chicken or 2-lb. whole free-range chicken

3-inch knob of unpeeled ginger, washed and smashed with the side of a cleaver

2 scallions, both white and green parts

5 tsp. salt

½ cup green tea leaves (ideally long leaves without many stems), soaked overnight in cool water

1 cup roughly chopped cilantro leaves and stems

2 tbsp. sawtooth herb, cut into 1-inch pieces

1 tsp. dried chile flakes

6 tbsp. fresh lime juice

Put the chicken, ginger, scallions, and 4 tsp. of the salt into a pot and add water to cover by 1 inch (about 12 cups). Bring to a boil over high heat, skim off any foam and detritus that rises to the surface, and reduce the heat to a gentle boil. Cook the chicken, uncovered, for 1 hour. (If the chicken floats while cooking, rotate it occasionally to ensure all the meat cooks evenly.) Remove the chicken from the broth and let it cool. Discard the broth or reserve it for another use.

When the chicken is cool enough to handle, use your fingers to remove the meat from the bones and tear it into thin strips, discarding the skin, bones, fat, and connective tissue. (You will have about 2½ cups of meat.) Drain the soaked tea leaves and toss the chicken with the tea, herbs, chile flakes, and remaining 1 tsp. salt, then add the lime juice and toss the mixture again before serving.

Jingpo Herb Salad

Spectacularly aromatic and fresh tasting, this salad of four different herbs with shallots, tomatoes, and chiles is one of most unique and delicious dishes made by Jingpo minority cook Shang Qinzhen (page 226). The main ingredient in the salad is Asiatic pennywort, which tastes like a very mild parsley. It is known locally as *ma ti cai*, or "horse hoof leaf," which is a Chinese translation of the Khmer name, *mying khwar*, but in other parts of China it is called *lei gong gen* ("thunder god's root") or *bang dai wun* ("chipped big bowl"). The green is often available at Thai and Vietnamese markets; if you can't find it, substitute any mild salad green.

In Dehong, this dish (pictured page 227) also includes an herb called *xiang cai*, which Shang says should be eaten when you are missing old friends, and crunchy, fragrant fish mint roots; here, Vietnamese fish mint and chopped cilantro stems take their place. The salad is also traditionally made with a spoonful of *doushi*, dried beans that are crumbled into a grainy powder, which is used across southern and western Yunnan. If you have access to it, add about 1½ tsp. of *doushi* to the salad.

1¾ cups Asiatic pennywort leaves and attached stems

½ cup fish mint leaves

½ cup sawtooth herb, cut into 1-inch-long pieces

2 tbsp. cilantro stems cut into ½-inch pieces

½ cup thinly sliced shallots

4 cherry tomatoes

1 tsp. salt

1 to 4 fresh Thai chiles, very thinly sliced

1 to 2 tsp. light soy sauce

In a medium bowl, mix together all the herbs, shallots, tomatoes, and salt. Massage the ingredients with your hands, crushing and mixing everything well. Add the chiles, drizzle on 1 tsp. of the soy sauce, and use chopsticks to mix well. Taste and add more soy sauce if needed.

Jingpo Dried Beef with Galangal and Tomato

景颇风味凉拌干巴

In Shang Qinzhen's version of Yunnan's popular dried beef salad, the rich, savory meat is combined with the sharp, spicy sweetness of fresh ginger and piny, fragrant galangal, as well as fresh herbs and a handful of bright red cherry tomatoes—an ingredient that distinguishes Jingpo's food from its neighboring cuisines. To give the meat a slightly smoky flavor, Shang toasts it over an open fire before smashing and shredding it. She uses fresh ginger with very thin, tender skin and just washes the skin and mashes it. This dish is also traditionally made with fresh, green cilantro seeds; if you happen to be growing cilantro in your garden and some of it has formed bright green seeds, add about 1 tablespoon.

⅛ cup small knobs of unpeeled ginger or 1-inch cubes of peeled ginger

3 garlic cloves

1¼ cups shredded Dried Beef (about ½ recipe) (page 266)

½ cup peeled galangal cut into very thin shreds

6 red cherry tomatoes

1 to 3 fresh Thai chiles, thinly sliced

1 cup roughly chopped cilantro

¼ tsp. salt

Using a large mortar and pestle, crush the ginger and garlic together until they are broken into small pieces. Put the dried beef and ginger-garlic mixture into a serving bowl and mix. Mash the galangal lightly in the mortar and add it to the meat mixture. Add the tomatoes and massage the mixture, breaking up the tomatoes and mixing everything well. Add the chiles and cilantro and mix well. Taste and add salt if it is needed.

Roasted Eggplant Salad

傣味凉拌茄子

This Dai-style cold salad (pictured page 234), made with grilled eggplant, bell pepper, and tomato mixed with aromatics and herbs, is light, piquant, and spicy—a perfect dish for hot summer days. Surprisingly, the combination of eggplant, tomato, and vinegar is almost reminiscent of Italian antipasti, but the similarity is purely coincidental. This recipe comes from Meng Mingchun and her staff at Yingjiang Dai Flavor Restaurant (page 222).

1 large Asian eggplant
(about 14 inches long)

1 red bell pepper

1 medium tomato

1 tsp. tomato paste

2 tbsp. Chinese white rice vinegar

1 tbsp. roughly chopped cilantro

1 tsp. pickling liquid from Pickled Mustard Greens (page 272) (optional)

1 tsp. light soy sauce

1½ tsp. minced garlic

1 fresh Thai chile, thinly sliced

Pinch of salt

Using a grill or a broiler, cook the eggplant, bell pepper, and tomato, turning as needed, until the skin is blackened on all sides and the vegetables are soft and beginning to collapse in on themselves. Set them aside to cool.

When the vegetables are cool enough to handle, peel the eggplant and bell pepper, remove the stems, and remove the bell pepper's seeds. Cut the eggplant crosswise into 2- to 3-inch pieces, then roughly chop both the eggplant and pepper lengthwise to create rough strips about ¼ to ½ inch thick. Peel the tomato, remove any fibrous parts near the stem, and finely chop. In a small bowl, mix the chopped tomato with the tomato paste. Mix the chopped vegetables and tomato with all the remaining ingredients. Taste the salad and adjust the vinegar, soy sauce, and salt as needed.

风味芭蕉花

Stir-Fried Banana Flower

Purple banana flowers are eaten all across Asia. While the colorful outer petals (or bracts) are relatively tough, the golden petals inside are tender and toothsome, with a texture reminiscent of strips of slow-cooked leeks. In this recipe, from Yinjiang Dai Flavor Restaurant (page 222), the petals are sliced thinly and then cooked with bell peppers, chile-bean paste, and slices of tomato, which combine to give the dish (pictured page 234) a spicy, piquant, sour, and even slightly sweet flavor.

½ lemon

1 medium-size banana flower (about 25 oz.)

3 tbsp. vegetable oil

6 dried Thai chiles

½ medium tomato, cut into wedges ⅓ inch thick

⅛ red bell pepper, thinly sliced crosswise about ¼ inch thick

⅛ green bell pepper, thinly sliced crosswise about ¼ inch thick

2 garlic cloves, thinly sliced

1 scallion, thinly sliced, white and light green parts separated from dark green parts

1 tbsp. southern-style chile-bean paste (*douban jiang*)

1½ tsp. chile sauce (*lajiao jiang*)

1 tsp. salt

Fill a medium bowl halfway with water and squeeze the lemon into the water. Peel away the outer purple petals of the banana flower and the thin florets inside them until you reach the tender, golden center of the banana flower—only the tops and edges of the petals should have a purple tinge. Slice the inner part of the banana flower crosswise into ½- to ¾-inch-thick pieces, and separate the pieces, dropping them into the lemon water to keep them from oxidizing. (You will have about 2 cups of slices and sliced florets.)

In a wok, heat the oil over a high flame until very hot. Add the dried chiles and cook for 10 seconds. Add the drained banana flower, tomato, bell peppers, garlic, and the white and light green parts of the scallion; stir and flip everything a couple of times to mix. Add the chile-bean paste, chile sauce, and salt and stir-fry, stirring and flipping constantly, until everything is well mixed and the banana flower is very tender, 2 minutes. (The banana flower may darken and even blacken a bit as it cooks.) Add the dark green parts of the scallion and continue to cook until they are wilted, 30 seconds; then transfer to a serving plate.

Minced Pork Grilled in Banana Leaf

Dinner at Xian Yutian's home in the small De'ang minority village of Meng Wen is a communal affair. Xian and her daughter-in-law work together in a large, airy kitchen that is open on one side, with only a low wall separating it from the family's courtyard. Other members of the family pitch in, and the men often take on the job of preparing a dish of raw minced pork flavored with fresh herbs.

Everyone cooks over a wood fire built in a large iron basin on the kitchen floor. This setup is used for everything from boiling soup to stir-frying vegetables, and it is especially useful for grilling foods wrapped in banana leaves, like this pork mixed with fresh herbs and chiles.

The dish can also be made in a cast-iron skillet, but it tastes best cooked over a fire because as the banana leaf begins to burn, it browns the meat inside the packet. If using a skillet, remove the dense loaf of meat once it is cooked and let it brown directly in the pan for a couple of minutes to replicate the flavor (see instructions below).

¾ lb. finely minced pork belly (about 1⅓ cups)

2½ tsp. minced peeled ginger

3 tbsp. finely chopped sawtooth herb

2 tbsp. finely chopped Vietnamese coriander

1½ tsp. minced garlic

2 to 4 fresh Thai chiles, finely chopped

1 tsp. salt

¼ tsp. Sichuan Peppercorn Powder (page 274)

12- to 14-inch square piece of banana leaf

EQUIPMENT:

Gas or charcoal grill (optional)

Put the pork, ginger, herbs, garlic, and chiles into a medium bowl and use chopsticks to mix well. Add 1 tbsp. of water and mix, then add the salt and Sichuan Peppercorn Powder and mix very well. Spread the mixture out on the banana leaf, shaping it into a 7-inch square. Fold the top and bottom edges of the banana leaf over to completely enclose the mixture like an envelope, and secure the leaf with toothpicks, then fold the sides over and secure them with toothpicks, so that you have a square package around the filling.

Grill the packet on a gas or charcoal grill over direct heat, turning occasionally, until the banana leaf is browned on both sides and the filling is cooked through, 20 to 30 minutes (the time will vary depending on how close the grate is to the flame). Alternatively, heat a lightly oiled cast-iron skillet over high heat until it is very hot, then reduce the heat to low and sear the packet, covered, until the outside of the banana leaf is browned on both sides and the filling is cooked through, about 15 minutes for each side. Remove the meat from the banana leaf and sear it directly in the skillet until lightly browned, about 2 minutes per side.

Stir-Fried Rice Cakes with Pork Belly, Tomatoes, and Spinach

大
救
驾

Dishes made with *er kuai* rice cakes are popular throughout Yunnan, but this is the most famous preparation. It comes from the city of Tengchong, a busy trading center on Yunnan's border with Myanmar, and dates from the end of the Southern Ming Dynasty in the 1660s. According to local lore, the Yongli Emperor, Zhu Youlang, took refuge in the city in 1661, having fled from the Manchus (the founders of the Ming Dynasty). He arrived in Tengchong tired and starving and called for food, and a cook rushed to prepare something for the emperor to eat. At the time, locals prepared *er kuai* by cutting it into thin, noodle-like strips and boiling them in soup, but with no time to waste, the cook decided to stir-fry thin slices of the rice cake instead. The emperor ate the dish gratefully, then asked the cook what it was called. When he learned that the recipe had no name, he decreed it would be called *dajiujia*, or "saving the life of the emperor." Unfortunately for Zhu Youlang, the dish couldn't save him from his ultimate fate—he was captured and executed by the Manchus a few months later. But the dish he named lived on and is now served in restaurants across Yunnan.

This is the rare stir-fry that is perfect to eat on its own—a combination of meat, egg, and vegetables all on one plate. This version comes from Beside the Lotus Kitchen Secrets, a large restaurant built in the countryside a few minutes outside of Heshun, where it is served with a mild soup on the side to help diners digest the meat and starch. Other versions of the dish substitute sweet pea greens or sliced cabbage for the spinach, use different cuts of pork, or swap garlic chives for the scallions. All are utterly delicious.

Cut the pork belly into strips ⅛ inch thick (cutting through the layers of meat and fat so that each piece is striated, like bacon), then cut the strips into 1-inch-long pieces (you will have about ¾ cup). Lightly beat the egg and mix it with the pork belly.

6 oz. pork belly with the skin removed

1 egg

3 tbsp. vegetable oil

⅓ cup thinly sliced brown button mushrooms

¾ lb. Yunnan Rice Cakes (er kuai), cut into triangular slices ⅛ inch thick (2½ cups), or the same amount of sliced Korean rice cakes, sometimes labeled "ovalettes" (page 268)

1½ cups spinach leaves, cut in half crosswise (3 oz.)

1 large, firm tomato, or 2 Roma (plum) tomatoes, cut into slices ¼ inch thick

5 scallions, white and light green parts only, cut into ½-inch pieces

1 tbsp. light soy sauce

¼ tsp. salt

In a wok, heat the oil over a high flame until very hot. Add the meat and egg mixture, let the egg puff up, without stirring, for 30 seconds, then flip it and break up the egg, separating the pieces of meat from one another. Add the mushrooms and cook for 1 minute, pressing them up against the sides of the wok for a few seconds at a time to brown. Add the rice cakes, spinach, and tomato and stir-fry, stirring and flipping constantly, for 1 minute. Add the scallions and stir-fry for 1 more minute. Add the soy sauce and salt and stir-fry until the rice cake slices are tender, about 3 to 4 minutes.

椿牛干巴

Wa-Style Pounded Gan Ba

Dried beef salads are popular throughout western Yunnan, but the Wa minority version is much heavier on the meat and lighter on the herbs than similar Dai and Jingpo salads. It is also much spicier, because the dried and fresh chiles added to the meat are so finely minced that they permeate every bite. The result is less of a salad and more of a flavored jerky, with the rich, savory flavor of the meat just offset by a bit of freshness from the sawtooth herb and the searing spiciness of the fresh chiles.

1¼ cups shredded Dried Beef (about ½ recipe) (page 266)

1½ tsp. dried chile flakes

¼ tsp. salt

¾ cup thinly sliced sawtooth herb

½ to 1 tbsp. minced fresh Thai chiles

Using a mortar and pestle, mash the shredded beef to break it up, turning the pile over a few times, until it resembles dried hay. Add the chile flakes and salt, and mash the mixture again, turning the pile a couple of times, until thoroughly mixed. Put the meat mixture into a medium bowl; add the sawtooth herb and minced chile, and mix well before serving.

生拌茼蒿

Chrysanthemum Greens Salad

Dishes of raw vegetables are extremely rare in China. In fact, the Han used to say that only foreigners, or "barbarians," ate raw foods. Even now, in most of the country salad-like dishes of cold vegetables are usually made with blanched greens. But as Yunnan is home to many of those non-Han "foreigners," a number of raw foods can be found throughout the region, especially near the border with Myanmar. Simple salads of lightly dressed, lacy chrysanthemum greens, whose flavor is similar to chrysanthemum tea, can be found at Dai restaurants near Menghai; this recipe comes from Lao Fangzi (Old House) restaurant in Kunming, which showcases dishes from all over the province.

Cut the greens crosswise into thirds (3 to 4 inches long). Discard the bottom third of the greens, which will mostly be thick stems, and sift through the remaining greens to eliminate any other thick stem pieces. Wash and dry the remaining greens, and pile them onto a small serving plate. Sprinkle them with the soy sauce, vinegar, and sesame oil and top with the fresh chile.

4 cups lightly packed chrysanthemum greens (also called *tong ho* or *shungiku*) (8oz.)

1 tsp. light soy sauce

1 tsp. Zhenjiang vinegar

½ tsp. sesame oil

1 fresh Thai chile, thinly sliced

Vegetables Grilled in Banana Leaves

包烧蔬菜

For cooks in Yunnan's tropical southern and western border regions, no plant is more useful than the banana tree. The fruit can be sold at market, the flowers can be stir-fried, the core of young trees can be cut out and eaten (much like a bamboo shoot), and the leaves can be wrapped around everything from meat to vegetables to form packets for grilling over a fire.

Like many of the best cooking techniques, the practice of grilling foods in banana leaves probably began as a utilitarian trick that allowed farmers to prepare a hot meal without a wok or other cooking tools. But the banana leaves also add some of their own essence to foods, infusing them with a distinctive flavor. This recipe lends itself to a variety of vegetables but is usually made with mushrooms or dark leafy greens like spinach and Chinese watercress. If you want to use another type of greens, remove any thick stems.

½ lb. dark leafy greens, such as spinach or Chinese watercress (about 7 cups) or 5 oz. enoki mushrooms, root ends trimmed (about 2½ cups)

2½ tsp. minced garlic

1 fresh Thai chile, thinly sliced

1 tsp. salt

12-inch square piece of banana leaf

EQUIPMENT:

Gas or charcoal grill (optional)

If using leafy greens, blanch them in boiling water until they're just wilted, 15 to 45 seconds, then rinse with cold water. Squeeze the greens to thoroughly remove any excess water and cut them into 2- to 3-inch pieces.

If using enoki mushrooms, separate the clumps of mushrooms so that no more than 3 or 4 mushrooms are clinging together.

Toss the greens or mushrooms with the garlic, chile, and salt and pile them in the center of the banana leaf. Fold the top and bottom edges of the banana leaf over to completely enclose the vegetables like an envelope, then fold the sides over so that you have a package about 5 by 7 inches. If cooking in a cast-iron skillet, secure the packet with toothpicks; if grilling, wrap the packet in foil.

Grill on a gas or charcoal grill over direct heat, turning occasionally, until the packet is soft, 10 to 15 minutes (the time will vary depending on the heat of the coals or flame). Alternatively, heat a lightly oiled cast-iron skillet over high heat until it is very hot, then reduce the heat to low and sear the packet until the outside of the banana leaf is browned on both sides and the vegetables are cooked through, about 5 minutes on each side. Unwrap, and leave the vegetables in the banana leaf to serve.

Breakfast Noodles with Pork and Sweet-Spicy Sauce

杂酱米线

These breakfast noodles with *zajiang* ("mixed sauce") from Yingjiang County, a semitropical area along the Burmese border, are perhaps the most flavorful and delicious in Yunnan. The sweet, spicy, and savory meat sauce imbues the soup's broth with rich flavor and marries wonderfully with the brightness of the cilantro and celery, and the nutty sweetness of the homemade sesame oil that are served, along with other toppings, at local noodle shops. Traditionally, the *zajiang* is made with a couple of different chile-bean sauces that are so local, even restaurants that serve the dish in Kunming truck them in from Yingjiang. In this recipe, the combination of chile-bean paste and sweet-salty soybean sauce produces a very similar result. If you can't find *pixian* chile-bean paste (page 16), substitute more of the southern-style chile-bean paste in its place. Makes four servings.

FOR THE PORK AND BEAN SAUCE:

½ lb. ground or finely chopped pork (scant 1 cup)

2 tbsp. vegetable oil

2 tbsp. minced peeled ginger

¼ cup southern-style chile-bean paste (*douban jiang*)

2 tbsp. Sichuan-style chile-bean paste (*pixian doubanjiang*)

5 tsp. ground bean sauce (page 15)

1 tsp. Dried Chile Oil (page 276)

MAKE THE PORK AND BEAN SAUCE: Prepare the pork by breaking it up with a fork or chopping it lightly. In a wok, heat the oil over a high flame until very hot. Add the ginger and pork and stir-fry the mixture, stirring and flipping frequently and using a wok shovel to break up any large pieces of meat, until it is just cooked through. Add both chile-bean pastes and the ground bean sauce and cook, mixing thoroughly, for 2 minutes. Add the Dried Chile Oil, mix until well incorporated, and remove the mixture from the heat.

ASSEMBLE THE SOUP: Bring a large pot of water to a boil and boil the noodles until just soft and toothsome. While the water is boiling, bring the pork broth to a simmer, then divide it between four large bowls. Drain the noodles and divide them between the soup bowls. Top each bowl of noodles with one quarter of the prepared pork (about ⅓ cup) and serve with toppings on the side.

FOR THE SOUP:

4 large handfuls of fresh rice noodles or 14 oz. dried rice noodles, such as Vietnamese rice sticks

8 cups Pork Broth (page 280)

TOPPINGS:

½ cup vegetable oil

¼ cup raw sesame seeds

Dried Chile Oil (page 276)

Sichuan Peppercorn Powder (page 274)

¼ cup finely sliced cilantro leaves

¼ cup finely chopped Chinese celery

2 tbsp. minced garlic covered with ¼ cup water

2 tbsp. Sesame Seeds in Oil (page 278)

2 tbsp. minced peeled ginger

1 tsp. Pickled Chiles (page 271) (optional)

Western Yunnan–Style Pineapple Sticky Rice

紫米菠萝饭

Sticky rice cooked in a pineapple is popular in both southern and western Yunnan, but the version of the dish found in the west is significantly more complex than the one served to the south (page 136). Here, in addition to fresh pineapple, the rice is mixed with sweetened condensed milk, a common ingredient in the area (thanks to the region's proximity to Myanmar), as well as sugar and sesame seeds. The result is sweet, sticky, and decadent enough to substitute for dessert, though Chinese cooks generally serve sweet and savory dishes together.

¾ cup sticky rice, soaked overnight

¼ cup Thai purple rice, soaked overnight

2½-lb. whole pineapple (about 7 inches tall and 13 inches in circumference)

⅓ cup granulated sugar

1 tbsp. sweetened condensed milk

2½ tsp. white sesame seeds

2½ tsp. black sesame seeds

Mix the sticky rice and purple rice together and prepare them according to the instructions on page 281. Set aside to cool.

Cut one side off the pineapple, removing about 1 inch from top to bottom and leaving the leaves at the top of the fruit intact. Hollow out the pineapple by cutting into the flesh about ½ inch from the skin, then angling the knife to cut the flesh out in chunks. Cut out and discard the firm core, and cut the rest of the flesh into pieces ½ inch wide or smaller. Set the hollowed-out pineapple aside.

When the rice is cool enough to handle, transfer it to a mixing bowl. Add ¾ cup of the pineapple pieces to the rice along with the sugar, condensed milk, and sesame seeds and mix by hand, squeezing the fruit to break it up into small pieces and release its juices into the rice. Pack the rice mixture into the hollowed-out pineapple, shaping it into a mound if necessary to accommodate all the rice.

In a wide pot fitted with a wire rack or a steamer basket, steam the stuffed pineapple for 10 minutes, until the rice is nice and sticky and the flavors have blended. Let it cool slightly and serve warm or at room temperature, in the pineapple. (If you don't have a pot wide enough to fit the pineapple, a Thai sticky rice steamer covered with a stockpot or wok lid will work well, as will a wide skillet; set the pineapple on an overturned heatproof bowl in the center of the pan, add enough water to steam, keeping it below the bottom of the fruit, and tent the whole thing in foil to form a lid.)

Stir-Fried Okra with Pressed Tofu

秋葵炒豆腐干

Okra is surprisingly popular in the western regions of Yunnan. It is often steamed, chilled, and served whole with tomato and chile dipping sauce (similar to the one on page 165), but in this dish, it is cut crosswise into pieces that look like delicate stars, then stir-fried with cubes of pressed tofu. With this method, the okra cooks so quickly that it doesn't develop much of its characteristic slimy texture, and the vegetable's crispness and bright flavor pair beautifully with the dense texture and slightly smoky flavor of the pressed tofu.

¼ cup vegetable oil

8 oz. spiced pressed tofu, cut into squares about ½ inch by ¼ inch (1½ cups)

4 garlic cloves, thinly sliced

2 dried Thai chiles

6 oz. okra, cut crosswise into ¼- to ⅓-inch-thick slices (about 2½ cups)

½ tsp. salt

In a wok, heat the oil over a high flame until very hot. Add the tofu, garlic, and chiles and stir-fry, stirring and flipping constantly, for 1 minute. Add the okra and continue to cook, stirring and flipping frequently, until the okra is just cooked through, but still very firm, 2 minutes. Sprinkle in the salt and stir to mix well, then transfer everything to a serving plate.

Yunnan's Coffee Boom

As coffee culture has taken hold in China over the past decade or two, local coffee production has also grown, especially in Yunnan. Every year, more of the mountains in western and southern Yunnan where tea or tobacco were once grown are given over to brand-new coffee plantations. Coffee first came to Yunnan with the French in the 1890s, but commercial plantations weren't established until after 2000. At first, growers focused on inexpensive beans to sell to international conglomerates, but in recent years, some farmers have begun to focus on higher-quality coffee, and international companies have opened offices in Yunnan to help farmers grow and process their beans. These days, high-end coffee shops in tourist-friendly areas like Heshun and Shangri-la offer a chance to taste some of Yunnan's highest-quality, most expensive coffees, carefully brewing cups of pour-over that rival any in the world.

Beef with Pickled Bamboo

酸笋炒牛肉

Sour pickled bamboo shoots are a staple ingredient for Dai cooks in western Yunnan. In this popular dish, their distinctive sour, slightly astringent flavor provides a bright, funky contrast to the richness of fatty beef and the spice of fresh red chiles. This recipe comes from Qianzuo Dai Flavor Restaurant, a small family-run eatery on a quiet street in the city of Mangshi. It has been adapted to work with Thai sour bamboo, which has the same flavor but is much softer than the Yunnan ingredient. If you have access to the kind of freshly made shredded sour bamboo used in Yunnan (which has a very firm, wiry texture), use 1 cup (rather than amount indicated), and skip the slicing and drying steps below.

1½ cups Thai sour bamboo, cut into very thin strips

¾ lb. ground or finely chopped beef (scant 1⅓ cups)

½ cup vegetable oil

4 garlic cloves, thinly sliced

2 red Fresno chiles, cut at an angle into long, thin slices

2 fresh Thai chiles, minced

½ tsp. salt

2 tbsp. finely chopped cilantro

Preheat the oven to 200°F and spread the sour bamboo on a rimmed baking sheet. Bake for 45 to 60 minutes, stirring about halfway through, until the bamboo has shrunk by about half and the thinnest pieces are beginning to brown. Let the bamboo cool to room temperature.

Prepare the beef by breaking it up with a fork or chopping it lightly. In a wok, heat the oil over a high flame until very hot. Add the beef and garlic and stir-fry, stirring and flipping frequently and using a wok shovel to break up any large pieces of meat. When the meat is cooked through, use the wok shovel or a perforated scoop to transfer the meat and garlic to a bowl, leaving the oil in the wok.

Add the bamboo and both kinds of chiles to the wok with the leftover oil, and stir-fry, stirring and flipping occasionally, for 1 minute. Add the beef back into the wok, add the salt, and cook, stirring and flipping occasionally, until everything is well cooked and some of the meat has browned, about 5 minutes. (If working on a regular stove, press the meat up against the sides of the wok and let it sit for 30 seconds at a time to brown.) Transfer the meat and vegetables to a serving plate, draining off any excess oil, and top with the cilantro.

Steamed Butterfish

小米辣蒸鱼

This delicate butterfish, steamed with ginger, garlic, and chiles and topped with fresh herbs, is a refined, restaurant-style take on traditional Wa food. It comes from Jiangshan Buluo Restaurant in Lincang, a Wa-themed restaurant (located next to a golf course) built to look like a village with thatched-roof buildings and buffalo skulls mounted on posts at the entrance. The waiters and waitresses perform Wa-style dances in a dinner theater set up in the largest dining room; at the end of the show, guests join in for games.

While much of what's presented in these shows is only questionably authentic, this kind of restaurant is one of the few places where visitors can see Yunnan's minority cultures. That is particularly true of Wa culture, since Wa communities are in extremely remote, mountainous areas. The staff at Jiangshan Buluo Restaurant are all from areas near Lincang and have been trained in traditional dances and customs specifically so that they can find work sharing their culture. The waiters and waitresses are teenagers—most around sixteen years old—and live in a dorm next to the restaurant. In the afternoon, while the staff is waiting for dinner customers, the restaurant's courtyard can resemble a high-school parking lot as the young men and women relax, gossip, flirt, and tease one another, enjoying their first experience of living away from home.

½ cup sesame oil

⅓ cup minced fresh Thai or Anaheim chiles (or a combination of the two)

2 tbsp. minced garlic

1 tbsp. minced peeled ginger

¼ tsp. salt

2 lb. whole butterfish (two large fish or four small), cleaned and butterflied so that the fish can lie flat

½ cup thinly sliced sawtooth herb

3 scallions, white and light green parts only, thinly sliced

½ cup vegetable oil

EQUIPMENT:

Bamboo steamer with two layers and a lid, or similar steaming setup

Put the sesame oil and chiles into a cold wok and heat over a high flame until all the chile pieces are bubbling and fizzling, then immediately reduce the heat to low. Continue to cook, stirring with a wok shovel to keep the pieces on the edges and bottom from burning, for 5 minutes. Add the garlic and ginger and cook, stirring frequently, until the garlic begins to brown, about 10 minutes. Turn off the heat, and continue stirring for 2 minutes while the mixture cools, then stir in the salt and transfer the sauce to a small bowl.

Divide the fish between two rimmed plates that will fit inside a bamboo steamer with a clearance of at least ½ inch (to let the steam through); the fish should be skin side up. Spoon the sauce onto the fish. Place the plates in the steamer, lid on, and set aside.

Bring a large pot of water that will fit under the bamboo steamer to a rolling boil. Place the steamer on the pot and steam the fish for 20 minutes, until they are just cooked through, swapping the two layers of the steamer halfway through so that the fish steam evenly.

When the fish are cooked through, slide them skin side up onto a platter large enough to keep the fish from overlapping, and pour the sauce over them. Scatter the herbs on top of the cooked fish. Just before serving, heat the vegetable oil in a wok until very hot, then use a wok ladle to spoon the hot oil onto the top of the fish to quickly cook the herbs and crisp the fishes' skin.

Sour Stewed Vegetables

Tomatoes, green beans, eggplant, mushrooms, and seasonal greens all take on the distinctive sour flavor of pickled bamboo in this hearty, bright, and slightly spicy stew. The dish is made throughout western Yunnan, and cooks vary the ingredients depending on the season and the local palate. This version of the stew is adapted from the recipe used at Taste of Dehong restaurant in Mangshi. The large restaurant showcases local Dai, Jingpo, and Wa foods, and the teenage waitresses wear bright, shimmering gold dresses and go from table to table singing drinking songs to the guests. The restaurant is particularly popular with large groups of Chinese tourists, local businessmen, and families celebrating birthdays, most of whom come to enjoy special set meals of dishes arranged on the table to look like enormous peacocks with the food laid out in the shape of colorful feathers.

1 cup Yunnan or Thai sour bamboo, drained and cut into thin strips

¼ cup vegetable oil

1 medium tomato, cut in half and thinly sliced crosswise

½ medium waxy or all-purpose potato, such as Yukon gold, peeled and very thinly sliced

½ Asian eggplant (about 5 inches long), cut in half crosswise, then cut at an angle into thin, long slices about ¼ inch thick

4 fresh Thai chiles

½ small zucchini (about 3 inches long), cut at an angle into long, thin slices

⅛ cup fresh wood ear mushrooms

¾ cup tender squash greens or other green vegetable cut into 3-inch-long pieces

1½ tsp. salt

1 tsp. Sichuan Peppercorn Oil (page 277)

½ tsp. light soy sauce

Rinse the bamboo and set it aside. In a wok, heat the oil over a high flame until very hot. Add the bamboo, tomato, potato, eggplant, and chiles to the wok and stir-fry, stirring and flipping frequently and using a wok shovel to separate any pieces of potato and eggplant that stick together, for 3 minutes.

Add 4 cups of water to the wok and stir in the zucchini and mushrooms. Bring the water to a boil, then let the vegetables cook, stirring ccasionally, for 4 minutes. Add the greens and cook until all the vegetables are ender, about 2 more minutes. Add the salt, Sichuan Peppercorn Oil, and soy sauce and mix everything together, then transfer the stew to a serving bowl.

Bubble Ruda

Part snack, part dessert, this chilled dish combines tapioca, agar agar jelly, purple sticky rice, Melba toast, whole milk, shredded coconut, and sweetened condensed milk. Popular throughout western Yunnan, it is made by stand-alone vendors at markets who will customize the dish for you, adding just the ingredients you like (and turning some combinations into a thick drink to sip with a wide straw), and by restaurants that will sometimes experiment with new versions that include fresh fruits.

This treat is similar to desserts found in other Southeast Asian countries, but the dish may have its roots in ancient Persia. According to historians, it and its cousins are descendants of *faloodeh* (or *falooda*), a dish that traveled with traders to India, where it is usually made with rose water, vermicelli, and basil seeds, and then to Burma, where it likely picked up the British touches (the condensed milk and Melba toast) found in Yunnan today—a delicious reminder of the trade routes that once crisscrossed this region.

To make the dish, you can use both agar agar and sticky rice, or just the one you like better. When making the jelly, be sure to use the brand indicated or follow the instructions on the package you buy, as agar agar powders are not consistent across brands. The tapioca pearls should be the kind packaged in clear bags that are used for making bubble tea and Asian desserts; those packaged in cardboard boxes for quick puddings are uneven and won't hold their shape when boiled. Makes six servings.

½ cup purple sticky rice, soaked overnight in water

1½ tbsp. Golden Coins brand unflavored agar agar powder

½ cup dried small tapioca pearls

½ cup granulated sugar

12 pieces of 2-inch square Melba toast

1½ cups whole milk

1½ cups crushed ice

6 tbsp. dried, unsweetened shredded coconut

6 tbsp. sweetened condensed milk

COOK THE RICE: drain the soaked rice and rinse well. Put the rice into a small pot with 1 cup of water. Bring the water to a boil, then cover the pot and reduce the heat to very low. Simmer the rice, covered, for 40 minutes, then turn off the heat and let the rice stand for 10 minutes before removing the lid.

COOK THE AGAR AGAR: in a small pot, bring 1½ cups of water to a boil. Sprinkle in the agar agar powder and boil, stirring constantly, for 30 seconds. Pour the mixture into a heatproof bowl and let cool to room temperature, then refrigerate until set, about 1 hour.

COOK THE TAPIOCA: put the tapioca pearls into a small bowl, add cool water to cover by at least 1 inch, and let soak for 30 minutes, then drain. In a pot, bring 6 cups of water to a boil. Add the tapioca and boil, uncovered, until translucent, 5 to 10 minutes, stirring frequently to keep the pearls from sticking to the bottom of the pot. Drain the cooked tapioca in a fine-mesh sieve and rinse well with cold water. Store in cold water (to keep the pearls from sticking to one another) until ready to use.

Put the sugar and ½ cup of water into a small pot. Cook the mixture over high heat, stirring occasionally, until the sugar has dissolved. Set the syrup aside to cool to room temperature.

When the ingredients are ready, divide them among 6 dessert bowls: put 2 pieces of Melba toast into each bowl, then add 2 tbsp. purple sticky rice and/or 2½ tbsp. agar agar and 3 tbsp. drained tapioca pearls, along with ¼ cup milk, 2 tbsp. sugar syrup, 1 tbsp. of water, and ¼ cup crushed ice. Top each dessert with 1 tbsp. dried coconut and drizzle 1 tbsp. sweetened condensed milk on top. Serve with spoons.

Feeding a Sweet Tooth in Western Yunnan

Bodhi Temple sits high above the city of Mangshi, gleaming with gold paint and surrounded by statues of Buddhist gods and mythical creatures. Inside, tourists and local worshipers light incense and pray to statues of the Buddha, but the busiest part of the complex is outside, in the shops and juice stalls that line the main walkway. Find a table, choose from a colorful array of mangoes, dragon fruit, passion fruit, oranges, papaya, pineapple, and avocados, and with a whir of a blender you'll have a fresh, icy juice or a milk-shake-like mix of fruit, sugar syrup, and sweetened condensed milk. Or opt for a bowl of "bubble *ruda*," a concoction of tapioca, sticky rice, coconut, Melba toast, and milk that clearly owes its character to ingredients introduced to Burma by British colonialists.

Pea Porridge with Rice Noodles

稀豆粉拌饵丝

2½ cups whole round yellow dried peas, soaked overnight in water to cover by at least 3 inches (about 6 cups after soaking)

¾ tsp. salt

2 large handfuls of very thin fresh rice noodles or prepared dried rice noodles, such as thin Vietnamese rice sticks (from about 4½ oz. of dried noodles)

4 tsp. minced tomato

4 tsp. Peanuts in Oil (page 279)

1 tsp. thinly sliced cilantro leaves

1 tsp. thinly sliced scallions, white and light green parts only

1 tsp. Dried Chile Oil (page 276)

1½ tsp. Garlic in Oil (page 279)

1 tsp. Sesame Seeds in Oil (page 278)

½ tsp. Fragrant Oil Infused with Spices (page 278)

¼ tsp. Sichuan Peppercorn Powder (page 274)

EQUIPMENT:

Blender

Fine mesh sieve

Cheesecloth, about 3-foot length

Creamy pea porridge, made with large, round dried yellow field peas and called *xidoufen,* or "diluted bean flour," is a popular snack in western Yunnan. It is sometimes served on its own, with crackers made from a dried version of the porridge to dip into it, but the most common way of eating it is to mix it with very thin *er si*—Yunnan-style rice cakes cut into thin noodle-like strips—where it takes on the texture of a creamy sauce. This recipe substitutes thin rice noodles for the traditional *er si* (which is available only in Yunnan) and uses toppings popular in the city of Tengchong, including a fragrant oil made with cardamom, star anise, and Sichuan peppercorns; crunchy peanuts fried in oil; fresh cilantro and scallions; and flavorful chopped tomatoes. **Makes two servings.**

Put the drained peas into a blender with 2 cups of water. Blend the peas on high, stopping to stir a couple of times as needed, until the mixture is very smooth, about 3 minutes.

Line a fine-mesh sieve with a 3-foot length of cheesecloth; make sure to unfold the cheesecloth and refold it so that there are no overlaps or gaps in the cloth, and leave a generous overhang on the edges of the sieve. Set the sieve over a medium pot and pour half of the pea mixture into it. Let as much of the liquid as possible drain into the bowl, gently stirring and pressing the mixture in the sieve. When the mixture has stopped dripping, gather up the edges of the cheesecloth and gently squeeze out as much of the liquid as possible, until the lees in the cheesecloth are dry and crumbly. Repeat with the remaining pea mixture, using an extra ¼ to ½ cup of water to rinse out the blender and adding that extra water and mixture to the sieve. Discard the pea solids.

Add another 1 cup of water and ½ tsp. salt to the pot, and cook the pea mixture over medium heat, whisking frequently, until it begins to steam. Reduce the heat to low and continue to cook, whisking slowly and scraping the bottom and corners of the pot with a whisk, until the mixture is almost a paste and the whisk leaves stiff ridges, 45 to 60 minutes, depending on the heat of the stove and the speed of the whisk. (Don't increase the heat to speed the cooking; the mixture needs to cook for at least 30 minutes so that the pea sediment cooks through and loses its raw flavor.)

Divide the rice noodles between two bowls and top each with half of the pea porridge (ideally you will have a little more than 1 cup in each bowl, enough to just cover the noodles). Top each bowl with 2 tsp. minced tomato, 2 tsp. Peanuts in Oil, ½ tsp. each cilantro and scallions, ½ tsp. Dried Chile Oil, ¼ tsp. Garlic in Oil, ½ tsp. Sesame Seeds in Oil, ¼ tsp. Fragrant Oil Infused with Spices, and a pinch each of Sichuan Peppercorn Powder and salt. Mix well just before eating, and adjust seasonings to taste.

凉粉

Mangshi-Style
Cold Pea Curd Salad

Liang fen (cold pea curd) makers line up in front of the entrances to markets throughout western Yunnan, their carts packed with big bowls of golden curd and toppings that range from fried peanuts to fragrant oil made from star anise, black cardamom, and Sichuan peppercorns. Outside the market in Mangshi, an hour east of the Burmese border, Dai women in bright skirts and Jingpo women with yellow *thanaka* paste smeared on their cheeks (in a style more common across the border) stop to snack on small bowls of *liang fen* before doing their daily shopping. *Liang fen* is usually served in small portions, as a snack, but this recipe makes enough to share as part of a meal. If you'd like a more traditional portion, divide the ingredients into two smaller servings.

¼ cup lightly packed bean sprouts

¼ cup garlic chives, cut into 2-inch pieces

1 recipe Pea Curd (page 270)

1 tsp. Dried Chile Oil (page 276)

1 tsp. Sesame Seeds in Oil (page 278)

1 tsp. Garlic in Oil (page 279)

½ tsp Fragrant Oil Infused with Spices (page 278) or Sichuan Peppercorn Oil (page 277)

¼ tsp. salt

⅛ tsp. Sichuan Peppercorn Powder (page 274)

4 tsp. Peanuts in Oil (page 279)

Bring a medium pot of water to a boil. Boil the bean sprouts until tender, 1 to 2 minutes, then remove them from the pot with tongs or a perforated scoop, rinse them with cold water, and squeeze out as much moisture as possible. Set them aside. Use the same pot to boil the garlic chives for 30 seconds, then rinse them with cold water, and squeeze out as much moisture as possible. Set them aside.

Cut the pea curd into long slices and pile them up in a serving bowl. Top the pile with the blanched bean sprouts and garlic chives, then add the Dried Chile Oil, Sesame Seeds in Oil, Garlic in Oil, and Fragrant Oil Infused with Spices, and sprinkle on the salt and the Sichuan Peppercorn Powder, distributing them as evenly as possible. Top the pile with the Peanuts in Oil. Mix well just before eating.

Base Recipes
and Sauces

Dried Beef

牛干巴

Dried beef, or *gan ba*, is a staple food all across Yunnan. It was originally a means of preserving meat, but it has become prized for its rich flavor and is often eaten plain, like jerky (sometimes heated a bit over a wood fire), or mixed with herbs and spices in dishes like Wa-Style Pounded Gan Ba (page 243), Dai Dried Beef Salad with Fennel and Chiles (page 225), and Jingpo Dried Beef with Galangal and Tomato (page 233).

Gan ba is usually made by hanging strips of beef over a wood fire or a *shao kao* grill for a few days to cure in the smoke and heat while the fire is used to cook other dishes, but here it is dried over the course of a day in a very low oven. The key to picking meat for *gan ba* is to find a cut from a long muscle, so that once it's cooked you can tear it into long pieces along the grain of the meat. One batch of this dried beef will make enough for two of the above-mentioned dishes.

1 lb. beef fillet from a long, lean muscle, like bottom round, eye round, or flank steak

2 tbsp. salt

1 tsp. chile flakes

Preheat the oven to 250°F. Line a baking tray with aluminum foil, then set a wire rack on top of the tray.

Cut the meat into 8 pieces—each about 2 inches wide, 3 to 4 inches long, and ½ to ¾ inch thick—keeping the pieces as uniform as possible. (The thickness is the most important; the length and width may vary depending on the cut of meat.) Mix the salt and chile flakes in a small bowl, and use the mixture to coat the meat, then set the meat on top of the rack.

Dry the meat in the oven, turning the pieces every hour or two, until they have lost all of their moisture, approximately 10 hours. Let them cool, then store in an airtight container and refrigerate for a couple of weeks.

Once cooled, the *gan ba* can be cooked briefly over a wood-fire grill to add a bit of smoky flavor if you like. To use in a recipe, mash the dried beef in a large mortar and pestle to break it up, then use your fingers to tear it along the grain of the meat into very thin strips, each about as thick as a piece of grass. You should have about 2½ cups of torn meat.

BUYING OPTION: If you don't have the time to make your own, you can use store-bought beef jerky that has been flavored with just salt and

pepper or a little chile. Look for a brand that has chewy intact strips of beef (rather than meat that has been ground and pressed into a tube) and avoid anything with sugar or strong flavorings. When preparing the jerky for use in a recipe, you might have to slice the meat into very thin strips instead of shredding it with your hands because most store-bought jerky is too dense to tear. About 3 oz. of jerky will provide enough for one of the recipes listed in the recipe introduction.

餌块

Er Kuai—Yunnan Rice Cakes

Er kuai—dense, chewy rice cakes made from steamed white rice that has been ground, pounded, and pressed until it is uniform and firm—forms the base for some of the most popular dishes in Yunnan. It is cooked in homes and restaurants throughout the province and served for breakfast, lunch, or dinner. *Er kuai* lends itself to an amazing array of shapes. It can be sliced into thin triangles and stir-fried, shredded into long, thin noodles that are delightfully springy in soup, or even made into thin pancakes to be grilled over coals.

In Yunnan, *er kuai* is made with rice varietals that soften without becoming sticky, so that when they are ground up they have a clay-like consistency. These kinds of rice are not available in the West, but Nishiki rice, which is often used in Japanese cooking abroad, makes a reasonable substitute if cooked long enough. One batch will produce enough *er kuai* to make two of the recipes in this book.

3 cups Nishiki rice

EQUIPMENT:

Meat grinder with small grind plate (the size meant for grinding raw meat); a grinder attached to a food processor will work

Chinese steamer or any kind of steamer with a wide bottom that will fit on top of a very large pot of boiling water

Cheesecloth

Rinse the rice well, until the water runs clear. Put it in a large bowl, cover it with at least 2 inches of water, and let it soak overnight. Drain well.

Fill a large pot roughly three-quarters full of water and bring to a boil; the water should not reach the top of pot when it's at a rolling boil. Line a steamer with two layers of cheesecloth, letting it hang over the edges of the steamer, and fill the steamer with the drained rice, spreading it out evenly. Fold the edges of the cheesecloth over the rice.

Steam the rice, covered, for 1 hour; when finished, it should feel partially cooked, and still very firm. Turn off the heat under the pot and let the rice cool to room temperature, about 20 minutes. Refill the pot, bring the water in the pot back to a boil, and steam the rice again for another hour, until it is cooked through but still a little firm.

As soon as the rice is finished cooking, use a meat grinder to grind the rice into a sticky paste, then re-grind the paste two more times so that it becomes a relatively smooth dough, keeping the paste covered when it is not in the grinder so that it stays warm. Transfer the dough to a clean counter, and knead it by hand for a minute, then shape it into 2 loaves, each about 5 inches long and 3 inches wide. (The loaves may still have ridges from the grinder.) Cover the loaves with a clean dish towel and let them sit on the counter overnight to firm up. After 6 to 8 hours, store in the refrigerator for up to a week.

To use the *er kuai*, cut a loaf into slices about ¼ inch thick and 2 inches wide. The easiest way to do this is to is to cut the loaves in half lengthwise, then turn them cut side down and slice them into semicircles. Alternatively, you can start cutting at one corner of the loaf and cut slices until they begin to be more than 2 inches wide, then rotate the loaf and start cutting at another corner.

If you cut the *er kuai* the day after it is made, it may still be very pliable in the center; if so, let the slices sit to dry out for a few hours before cooking.

BUYING OPTION: If you don't have the time to make your own *er kuai*, sliced Korean rice cakes, often labeled "rice ovalettes," make a good substitute. They are made with sticky rice, rather than regular rice, so the final texture will be chewier than traditional *er kuai*, but the results are still delicious.

Pea Curd

鷹嘴豆凉粉

Cool, slick slices of pea curd, or *liang fen*, topped with spices, vinegars, and herbs are a popular snack all across Yunnan. The base can be made from a variety of legumes, from mung beans to tiny lentil-like "chicken peas," and each produces a different color and flavor. Pea curd has a firmness like tofu, but making it doesn't require the addition of a coagulant. The legumes are ground with water, strained, cooked down until they thicken to a texture like smooth pudding, and then left to firm up into dense blocks that can be cut into smooth, noodle-like strips.

Home cooks make *liang fen* using preground powders instead of starting with whole peas. This version, which is similar to a version also common in the Shan areas of Myanmar, is made with chickpea flour (sometimes labeled "garbanzo flour"), which is readily available in the West. It produces a dense, off-white curd that is similar to one also common in the Shan areas of Myanmar. It is not as slick and noodle-like as some of the other curds found in Yunnan, but it is an excellent base for making Dai-Flavor Pea Curd with Vinegar and Cilantro (page 169) or Mangshi-Style Cold Pea Curd Salad (page 263). One batch will produce enough pea curd for one of the recipes listed above.

1 cup chickpea (garbanzo) flour

½ tsp. salt

In a medium pot, mix the chickpea flour with ½ cup of water to make a slurry, then mix in another ½ cup water and let the mixture sit for 5 minutes. Whisk in 2 more cups of water and the salt, and cook over low heat, whisking slowly, scraping the bottom and corners of the pot, then more quickly as it begins to thicken and look like pudding. Continue to cook, whisking, until the mixture is so thick that it is almost a paste and the whisk leaves stiff ridges, 30 to 45 minutes, depending on the heat of the stove and the speed of your whisking.

Pour the finished mixture into a bowl, smooth the surface with the back of a spoon, and let it sit until cooled to room temperature, about an hour. Use as soon as it sets or refrigerate for up to one day. To use the pea curd, slice it while it's still in the bowl, then transfer it to a serving plate or bowl.

Quick Pickled Cabbage

This simple quick pickle is used in some parts of central Yunnan in place of the darker, richer mustard green pickles. The leaves are left in long strips that mimic the shape of wide noodles, and they add a bright, mild flavor and a bit of crunch to many soups. For the best texture, use green cabbage with smooth leaves.

12 oz. green cabbage, core removed and leaves separated and cut into 1-inch thick strips

1½ tbsp. salt

½ tsp. dried chile flakes (or 1 fresh Thai chile, thinly sliced)

Massage the cabbage and salt together in a large mixing bowl for 1 minute until the salt is evenly distributed and the cabbage begins to soften a little. Mix in the chile, then set the mixture aside to pickle for 2 to 4 hours, mixing occasionally.

Pickled Chiles

Pickled chiles, whole and chopped, are a common ingredient in many parts of China where spicy food is popular. They are simple to make— just mix fresh chiles and salt and leave them to soften and ferment slightly—and they keep indefinitely once refrigerated. The trickiest part is simply chopping this many fresh, spicy Thai chiles; avoid touching the chiles any more than absolutely necessary (hold them by the stems whenever possible). Afterwards, wash all of your cooking tools and hands very thoroughly with lots of hot soapy water.

8 large fresh red Thai chiles, stems removed

1 tbsp. salt

Finely chop the chiles along with their seeds. Mix the chiles and the salt in a small jar, place a lid on top, and set the jar aside in a cool place for a week. When the chiles are ready, store them in the refrigerator.

Pickled Mustard Greens

Fall is pickling season in Central Yunnan, where this simple pickle is the key ingredient in many dishes. Chefs and home cooks all buy huge armloads of thick mustard greens, known locally as *kucai* or "bitter vegetable," and lay them out in the sun to dry until they're thoroughly wilted. Then they chop them up and mix them with crushed dried chile, Sichuan peppercorns, and copious amounts of salt, kneading the mixture in huge plastic tubs until the vegetables have started to give up their remaining juices. The pickles are then sealed up and left to ferment like sauerkraut. They are ready to use in just about a week, but many cooks keep them much longer, for up to a year, letting the flavors deepen with time.

In the West, the greens used for these pickles are also known as *gai choy* or Indian mustard greens. They have wide green leaves and thick stems that curve in toward the vegetable's core with faint ridges that give them a seashell-like shape. To make these pickles at home, you can skip the step of drying the greens and just use them fresh. Traditionally, these pickles are made in special Chinese pickle jars that have a well along the lip of the jar to form a water seal (see page 22), but you can also use a Western-style pickle crock, a regular jar, or a plastic container as long as you add a weighted plate or cup at the top to make sure the greens stay submerged in the liquid. Makes about 8 cups of pickles.

4 lbs. mature Chinese mustard greens (*gai choy*)

¼ cup salt, plus extra for the jar

3 tbsp. dried chile flakes

2 tsp. Sichuan peppercorns

1 tbsp. cooked rice

EQUIPMENT:

Chinese pickle jar or a nonreactive pickling container with a weight to keep ingredients submerged in liquid (page 22)

Cut each head of mustard greens in half lengthwise, and remove its cores. Cut the leaves crosswise into strips ½ inch wide, and then cut the strips into quarters, so that each is about 1½ inches long (you will have 14 to 16 packed cups).

Put the mustard greens and all the rest of the ingredients into a large bowl and knead the mixture forcefully for 3 to 4 minutes, until the volume has reduced by at least half and the greens have given up much of their moisture.

Sterilize your pickling container by rinsing it with boiling water, and put the pickle mixture into the jar with all of its juices, pressing down with a sterilized spoon so that all of the vegetables are covered with liquid. (If the vegetables are not covered with liquid, you can add a bit

of water.) Sprinkle a little bit of salt on top of the mixture. If working with a Chinese pickle jar, pour water into the well around the lip of the jar and cover with the lid. If using a different type of container, top the vegetables with a pickling weight or a plate just smaller than the container's opening and place cans or clean rocks on the plate to keep everything weighed down.

Leave the pickles to ferment, away from direct sunlight and at cool room temperature, for about a week, then taste them with a sterilized spoon. The chiles in the mixture will turn the pickling liquid a reddish brown color, and the greens will darken. Once the greens have taken on a pleasantly sour flavor, transfer them to airtight jars or containers and store them in the refrigerator, where they may be stored indefinitely if well sealed.

BUYING OPTION: Sichuan Gao Fu Ji Food Co. makes a "Preserved Pickled Mustard" that has a similar base ingredient but is much sweeter and spicier than Yunnan pickles. This can be used as a substitute, but the pickles should be rinsed thoroughly first and will give dishes a slightly different flavor. Large pieces of pickled mustard greens that have not been sliced can also be found in the refrigerated section of some Asian markets. They are usually not as sour as the Yunnan version, and are made without chile, so to use them, chop them into rough pieces, and mix with dried chiles.

Sichuan Peppercorn Powder

花椒粉

Ground Sichuan peppercorns are readily available in Asian markets and online, but grinding your own will give you a much fresher ingredient with a stronger, more nuanced flavor. You can grind the peppercorns in a mortar and pestle, but it is significantly easier to do it in a spice grinder—and you'll get a much finer powder.

¼ cup whole red
Sichuan peppercorns

Toast the peppercorns in a dry wok over medium heat for about a minute, stirring constantly to keep them from burning. When they are toasted, remove them from the heat, and crush them into a fine powder using a mortar and pestle or a spice grinder. (If using a mortar and pestle, sift the powder to remove any large pieces.) Store in an airtight container.

Ground Black Cardamom Seeds

草果粉

Smokey, piny black cardamom is used both whole and ground in central and northern Yunnan. Black cardamom does not need to be toasted before it is ground, but it does need to be opened up so that you can discard the tough, fibrous outer shell.

3 to 5 whole black cardamom pods

Break open the pods (or use a knife to cut them open), and remove the hard, black seeds, which may be sticking together or held together by a fibrous membrane. Discard the pod and any membranes and use an electric spice grinder to grind just the seeds to a fine powder. Once ground, the spice loses its flavor quickly, so it should be used right away. If necessary, you can store it in an airtight container for 3 to 4 days.

Shao Kao Spice Mix

烧烤料

5 tsp. dried ground chile

2½ tsp. Sichuan Peppercorn Powder (opposite)

1 tbsp. ground white pepper

4 tsp. Ground Black Cardamom Seeds (opposite)

4 tsp. salt

1 tbsp. Chinese Thirteen Spices Powder

2 tsp. ground cumin

2 tsp. MSG (optional) (Accent spice or Chinese *wei jin*)

Barbecue (*shao kao*) cooks all across China use piquant and fragrant spice mixes to flavor skewers of grilled meat and vegetables, turning everyday ingredients into a treat with the shake of a jar. Cooks usually make their own blends, using whatever flavors are popular locally. This version comes from vendors in Kunming, and it is redolent with the region's favorite spices, including dried chiles, Sichuan Peppercorn Powder, and the piny, fragrant black cardamom powder that is so important in central Yunnan cooking. It also includes Chinese Thirteen Spices Powder (十三香, *shisanxiang*), which is a spice mix that included cinnamon, clove, sand ginger, angelica root, fennel, and other spices and is available in Chinese groceries or online.

Combine all of the ingredients and mix well.

All-Purpose Tibetan Dough

藏式面团

2 cups all-purpose flour

¾ cup water

This two-ingredient dough is used in Shangri-la, in northern Yunnan, to make everything from momos to fried bread to noodles. One batch of dough will produce enough wrappers for 24 momos, 2 meat-filled flatbreads, or 4 to 6 servings of noodle soup.

Put the flour into a large mixing bowl, then drizzle in the water slowly, stirring with chopsticks. Once all the water has been added, knead the mixture together with your hands until it comes together. If the dough won't come together, add a tiny bit more water, and if it is very sticky, add a tiny bit more flour so that the dough is soft and pliable.

Turn the dough out onto a clean surface and knead it vigorously for 10 minutes, until it is smooth and silky. Form the dough into a ball, set it back in the bowl, and cover it with plastic wrap, without letting the plastic touch the dough. Let it sit for at least 15 minutes and up to 2 hours before using. Knead it a couple of times just before using.

辣
椒
油

Dried Chile Oil

This mixture of dried chiles and oil is one of the most useful and popular condiments in Yunnan. You'll find crocks of it on tables at most restaurants, and it's always available at noodles stalls so that patrons can customize the spiciness of their soups. This mixture is made with different kinds of dried chiles in different parts of Yunnan, but the most common is dried Thai chile flakes.

⅓ cup vegetable oil

⅓ cup dried chile flakes

⅛ tsp. Sichuan Peppercorn Powder (page 274) (optional)

⅛ tsp. salt

Place the oil, chile, and Sichuan Peppercorn Powder in a cold wok and heat on high until the chile is bubbling and fizzling, then immediately reduce the heat to low so that the chiles don't burn. Continue to cook, stirring with a wok shovel to keep the flakes on the edges and bottom from burning, for 2 minutes, until the oil has turned red and the chiles have browned. Remove from the heat and continue stirring for two minutes while the mixture cools, then stir in the salt and transfer the oil and chiles to a glass or metal jar. You can store the oil at room temperature for a few days or in the refrigerator indefinitely.

BUYING OPTION: Lao Gan Ma makes a good chile sauce called "Chili in Oil" that has a similar flavor. However, it has whole peanuts mixed with the usual ingredients; they should be removed if you are using the sauce to make Yunnan food.

Sichuan Peppercorn Oil

花椒油

This wonderful oil has the same distinctive citrus flavor and spicy-numbing feel as whole or ground Sichuan peppercorns but is milder and more subtle. Once the oil is made, it is stored with the peppercorns still in it, and they can also be added to dishes if you like.

1 cup vegetable oil

½ cup red Sichuan peppercorns

Place the oil and peppercorns in a cold wok and heat on medium-high until all of the peppercorns are bubbling and fizzling rapidly, and many have risen to the surface of the oil, then immediately reduce the heat to medium-low so that they continue to cook without burning. Simmer the mixture, stirring occasionally with a chopstick, for 10 to 15 minutes, until the oil takes on the characteristic citrus flavor and numbing mouth-feel of the peppercorns; the peppercorns will darken and lose their color but shouldn't be allowed to turn dark brown. (To test the oil, dip a chopstick or spoon into it, let it cool for a minute, then taste. The oil should leave a numbing aftertaste on the tongue.) Turn off the heat, allow the mixture to cool, and transfer the oil and the peppercorns to a glass or metal jar. You can store the oil at room temperature for up to a month, but the oil will gradually lose flavor as it sits.

BUYING OPTION: Sichuan peppercorn oil is available at Chinese markets (where it is sometimes labeled as "prickly ash oil") but the flavor is not quite as fresh and strong as the homemade version, and it does not have the whole peppercorns in it.

香油

Fragrant Oil Infused with Spices

This oil made from ginger, black cardamom, star anise, and Sichuan peppercorns is the key to the flavors of some of Western Yunnan's most famous dishes. Make sure to use green Sichuan peppercorns. While red peppercorns are more common and can be added whole to all kinds of dishes, they don't have as much punch as the green variety, which are so strong that they are used only for flavoring oil.

1 cup vegetable oil

2-inch piece of ginger (about 1 inch wide) peeled and smashed with the side of a cleaver

3 whole black cardamom pods

2 whole star anise

2 tsp. green Sichuan peppercorns

Place the oil in the wok over high heat until very hot. (To check the temperature of the oil, stick the tip of a wooden chopstick in; it should produce a strong cloud of little bubbles.) Turn off the heat, add the ginger to the oil, and cook, stirring a bit with chopsticks, until the ginger is dark brown in many places, about 1½ minutes, then remove the ginger from the oil. Add the cardamom pods, star anise, and Sichuan peppercorns to the oil and let the mixture sit until it has cooled to room temperature. You can store the oil at room temperature for up to a month, but the oil will gradually lose flavor as it sits.

芝麻油

Sesame Seeds in Oil

This mellow oil made from whole sesame seeds is used as a topping for noodle soups and other snacks. The sesame seeds (which are left in the oil after they're cooked) also add a bit of crunch.

½ cup vegetable oil

¼ cup white sesame seeds

Put the oil and sesame seeds in a small pot over medium-low heat until the sesame just begins to cause small bubbles. Turn the heat very low and cook the sesame seeds, stirring slowly, until they are just starting to turn golden, about 2½ minutes. Turn off the heat, continue stirring until the seeds have stopped sizzling, then transfer the mixture to a heatproof container, and let it sit until it has cooled to room temperature. You can store the oil at room temperature for a few days.

花生油

Peanuts in Oil

Crunchy peanuts cooked in oil are a flavorful topping for western Yunnan's noodle dishes and pea curd–based snacks. While some cooks use whole fried peanuts, many chop them first, then cook them just enough so that they become toasty and crunchy and imbue the cooking oil with their distinctive savory flavor.

½ cup finely chopped peanuts

¾ cup vegetable oil

Put the peanuts and oil in a small pot, and heat slowly over medium-high heat until the peanuts just begin to release small bubbles. Turn the heat to medium and cook the peanuts, stirring frequently, until they are golden brown and crunchy, 4 to 6 minutes. Turn off the heat, and continue stirring until the peanuts have stopped sizzling (they will continue to brown), then transfer the oil and nuts to a heatproof container, and let them sit until they've cooled to room temperature. You can store the oil at room temperature for a few days, but the oil and nuts will gradually change flavor as they sit.

大蒜油

Garlic in Oil

The key to making flavorful garlic oil is to cook the garlic so slowly that it can infuse the oil with a heady fragrance before it begins to brown. When cooking, be sure to turn off the heat long before the garlic darkens, because if it burns, the acrid flavor will ruin the oil.

6 tbsp. vegetable oil

2 tbsp. minced garlic

Put the oil and garlic in a small pot and heat slowly over medium-low heat until the garlic just begins to release small bubbles. Turn the heat very low and cook the garlic, stirring slowly, until it is tender but hasn't started turning golden, about 2½ minutes. Turn off the heat, continue stirring until the garlic has stopped sizzling, then transfer the oil and garlic to a heatproof container. Let it sit until cooled to room temperature. You can store the oil in the refrigerator for a few days. Let it come to room temperature before using.

猪骨湯底

Pork Broth

Light pork broth is the workhorse of the Chinese kitchen. It forms the base of a wide variety of soups and can be added by the ladleful to stir-fries to gently poach or steam vegetables. This version has a hint of the bright, piny flavor of black cardamom that is popular in central Yunnan; for soups from other regions, see the variation below. Makes approximately 8 cups.

2 lbs. bone-in pork ribs or a mix of pork meat and rib bones

4 scallions, white and light green parts only

1 black cardamom pod

3-inch knob of unpeeled ginger, washing and smashed with the side of a cleaver

1 tbsp. light soy sauce

2 tsp. salt

Thoroughly rinse the pork (and bones, if using) and put it in a pot with 10 cups water and the scallions, cardamom, and ginger. Bring the water to a boil over high heat, skim off any foam and detritus that has risen to the top, then reduce the heat to low. Simmer, covered for 2 to 3 hours. Stir in the soy sauce and salt. Let the broth cool, and strain it to remove the solids.

VARIATION: In Eastern Yunnan this broth is often flavored with ½ tbsp. of whole Sichuan peppercorns instead of black cardamom.

牛肉汤

Beef Broth

Peek into the kitchen of any Hui minority restaurant in Yunnan and you'll see on the stove a large pot of beef broth with big pods of black cardamom bobbing along as it simmers. This forms the flavorful base of many Hui dishes, and restaurants cook it all day, adding water as necessary. You can make this with any cheap, long-cooking cut of meat; cuts with the bone included, like beef shank, work especially well. Makes approximately 8 cups.

2 lbs bone-in beef shank

1 black cardamom pod

½-inch knob of unpeeled ginger, washed and smashed with the side of a cleaver

1 tbsp. salt

Put all of the ingredients into a stockpot with 12 cups of water. Bring to a boil, then reduce the heat, skimming any foam that has accumulated on the surface of the broth. Simmer, covered, for 3 hours. Strain the broth, reserving some of the meat to use in soup if making Tibetan Noodle Soup (page 114).

Sticky Rice

Many cooks in Yunnan's south and west serve sticky rice, rather than regular rice, with every meal. This glutinous rice is traditionally made in a specially designed sticky rice cooker—a conical basket woven from bamboo or reeds set over a round pot—but you can also make it using a regular stockpot and a fine-mesh sieve (though you may need to cook the rice in two smaller batches). Either way, you'll want to line the cooking vessel with a clean dish towel to keep the rice from sticking to it. The finished rice is usually served wrapped in plastic bags that are placed in small bamboo baskets with lids to keep it warm. Makes four servings.

2 cups Thai sticky rice (sometimes labeled "sweet rice" or "glutinous rice")

EQUIPMENT:

Thai Sicky Rice Steamer (page 23) or a pot and a fine-mesh steamer and cheesecloth, about 3-foot length

Put the sticky rice in a bowl with enough water to cover by 2 inches, and leave it to soak for 10 hours or overnight.

Drain away the soaking water, then add more water to the bowl and mix the rice well to rinse off the starch on the outside of the grains. Drain the rice, and repeat with more water until the liquid draining from the bowl runs clear.

Fill the pot of a traditional sticky rice cooker with 2 to 3 inches of water. Wet the basket and line it with a damp dish towel. (Alternatively, fill a medium stockpot with 2 to 3 inches of water and line a fine-mesh strainer with a damp cheesecloth.) Bring the water to a boil over high heat, then put the drained rice into the lined basket and use a spoon to spread it out as much as possible to form a thin layer. (You can fold the edges of the cloth over the rice to keep it from falling into the pot if necessary.)

Place the basket over the boiling water and cover it with a lid that fits into the basket but is large enough to cover all of the rice; the lid for a stockpot should work well. Cook the rice for 10 minutes, then use a wooden spoon to stir the rice and flip it over, so that it cooks evenly. Cover and continue to cook the rice for 5 more minutes, until it is tender but not mushy. Transfer the rice to a bowl, cover, and let sit for 15 minutes before serving.

Index

Acknowledgments

I would like to thank the many people who helped me research and produce this book over the course of the past decade. First and foremost, I would like to thank my teachers in Yunnan who shared their expertise with me and encouraged me to learn about the region's specialties, including Zhu Bo, Li Yan, Ma Chunye, Li Bing Zhi, Duan Janpin, Lanrong Zhancang, Jashi Yangzong, Najie Zhuowu, He Ayi, Xi He, Gaozuo Zhima, Zhu Wenqing, Mi Zhuang, Wang Qiu, Wang Lizhu, Wang Yan Po, Peng Qingnan, Peng Zehui, Fan Zhucun, Tao Lianfen, Cui Tonggang, Yang Lifen, Wei Hanyan, Lin Guowu, Sun Taitai, Fu Jin Mai, Meng Mingchun, Xiaojun "Vivian" Yang, Shang Qinzhen, Xian Yutian, Guo Zhen, John Xie, Yi Zhuangfang, Yuan Xi, Hannah Noy, Wu Hai, Wu Haowei, Tsebho Ritsang, and Luxi Yuan.

I am also extremely indebted to many anthropologists and other scholars who have worked in Yunnan and the surrounding regions, who shared their expertise with me and helped me understand the area's history and the cultural and historical contexts of the many people and ethnic groups who live in Yunnan: Dr. Tami Blumenfield, Dr. David Brenner, Dr. Katia Buffetrille, Dr. Siu-woo Cheung, Dr Jane Ferguson, Dr. Brendan A. Galipeau, Dr. Stéphane Gros, Dr. Stevan Harrell, Dr. Jacob Hickman, Dr. Ben Hillman, Dr. Ma Jianxiong, Dr. Lai Jingru, Dr. Hjorleifur Jonsson, Dr. Katherine Palmer Kaup, Lau Ting Hui, Yu Luo, Dr. Susan K. McCarthy, Dr. Charles F. McKhann, Dr. Gary Sigley, Dr. Koenraad Wellens, and Ling Zhao.

I would like to thank Julia Norton, Tracie McMillan, Ariana Lindquist, Joseph Orkin, and Isa-Delphine Seydon Raiter for joining me on research trips and helping me explore Yunnan, and I would particularly like to thank Lea Redmond and Sita Raiter, who not traveled with me but also contributed beautiful illustrations and photographs to this book. Once I translated these recipes for the Western kitchen, I relied on a small army of volunteer recipe testers, including Anna Ansari, Helen Baldus, Caroline Buehring, Mei Chin, Nicole Civita, Anita Crofts, Robyn Eckhardt, Matt Gross, Mary Hirsch, Susan Hwang, Chikara Kakizawa, Sarah Karnasiewicz, Hal Klein, Dan Luna, Manon Koopman, David Proudman, Karen Shimizu, and David Trimmer, whose notes and feedback were all invaluable.

This book would not have been possible without the amazing work and support of my editors, Christopher Steighner, whose enthusiasm for the project turned my dream of making a Yunnan cookbook into a reality, and Hannah Coughlin, whose vision saw the book over the finish line. I am eternally indebted to the book's designer, Toni Tajima, who took our ideas and photographs turned them into something even more beautiful than I could have envisioned. And I would like to sincerely thank our copy editor Dorothy Irwin, who helped me go over the recipes with a fine-tooth comb, Karen Shinto, who styled the impeccable noodles on the cover and the few other dishes that weren't photographed on location, and Emily Wolman, who provided extremely thoughtful proofreading.

My deepest thanks to my family, including Jerry Freedman and Christine Bell, Matthew and Lauren Freedman, Susannah Freedman, and Maeve Bell-Thornton, who have all been incredibly supportive, as well as Rendy Freedman, Jennifer Freed, Barbara and Mitchell Wand, and Anne Millikin, who all traveled to Yunnan with us on some of our research trips. I am also thrilled and grateful to have been able to do the last few years of my research with my young daughter, Nora, who has gamely been traveling with me to Yunnan every few months ever since she was an infant. And I would like to thank the mentors who encouraged me throughout the course of the project, including Marianne Partridge, Grace Young, Dana Bowen, Hiroko Shimbo, Beth Kracklauer, James Oseland, Carolyn Phillips, Kian Lam Kho, Naomi Duguid, and Andrea Nguyen.

Lastly, I could not have undertaken this massive project without my collaborator and husband, Josh Wand, who gamely packed up his whole life and moved to Yunnan with me, whose enthusiasm for that province and its foods kept me going through nearly a decade of travel and research, and whose gorgeous photos make this book whole. I would not have been able to (or wanted to) bring this book to life without him.